ECON

CW01502269

MISERY &
CRIME WAVES

The second great depression and the coming crime wave,

and what we can do about it

Severin L. Sorensen, CPP

Sikyur

Sikyur Publications
Sikyur LLC

Advisors to Chief Security Officers (CSOs), C-level executives,
and boards of directors
www.sikyur.com

Washington, DC
March 2009

Sikyur Publications
Sikyur LLC
PO Box 3310
Gaithersburg, MD 20885
202-386-6790
240-597-8877 fax
publications@sikyur.com

Library of Congress Control Number: 2009904009
Library of Congress Cataloging-In-Publication Data
Sorensen, Severin L.
Economic Misery and Crime Waves: The Second Great Depression and the coming Crime Wave, and what we can do about it.

Includes bibliographical references and index.
ISBN 1-936072-00-9 978-1-936072-00-2 (hardback)
ISBN 1-936072-01-7 978-1-936072-01-9 (paperback)

Sikyur Publications
Sikyur LLC
PO Box 3310
Gaithersburg, MD 20885

Visit the Sikyur Publications Site: www.sikyur.com
Visit the Book Site: www.crimewaves.com

Abstract

Economic Misery and Crime Waves:
The Second Great Depression and the coming Crime Wave, and what we can
do about it

The theory behind this book is that every sharp negative economic shock since 1954 has resulted in a crime wave. Sharp economic contractions such as our current global deep economic recession can create conditions of heightened economic misery (i.e. unemployment, loss of purchasing power through inflation, home equity loss, or asset deflation) which, if left unabated, can create conditions of increased crime opportunity and crime waves, where some people will choose crime as a 'rational' means of support to augment, or replace, their prior legal income. The author posits that the present economic downturn is comparable to the most severe economic shocks from the past 100 years, and this includes events such as the 1929 stock market crash and Great Depression. In the book, the author reviews the past to discern clues about the types of events that occurred, including past trials of crime waves and the crime control policies designed to arrest crime waves. The author is also aware that our past criminal justice policies are limited, and we must include modern technology and crime problems with no 100-year history to follow, and determine how to combat these new challenges as well. As the coming crime wave is foreseeable, it is imperative that government officials, businesses, communities, and families prepare themselves for this imminent threat. Governments can be proactive and get in front of this crime wave, preparing institutions, revising laws, targeting serious habitual offenders and known crime hotspots, and reducing the number of the most likely new offenders through diversion programs such as employment relocation. Individuals and families can change their locations, secure their places of residence and business, and repel much of the crime opportunity through situational crime prevention. The book concludes with chapters and appendices that focus on solutions and suggestions for what individuals, families, communities, businesses, and governments can do to shield themselves from the crime wave.

Periodic updates on signs of economic misery and crime waves as well as subsections of content from my research are posted on the author's economic misery and crime wave website (**www.crimewaves.com**) and periodic blogs posted at (**http://d2crimewave.blogspot.com**).

For my children,

and children everywhere

who will suffer the consequences of the Second Great Depression

and the crime wave that follows,

as an unintended consequence of

a generation of unbridled greed, avarice, risk-taking,

and the moral hazard of taking the waiting out of wanting

through excessive debt-based finance.

"The parents have eaten sour grapes,

but it is the children's teeth that are set on edge,

to the third and fourth generation." - Moses, quoting Euripides[1]

"Too much change in too short a period of time"

- Alvin Toffler *Future Shock* (1970)

two pictures

Two pictures hung on the dingy wall of a
grand old Florentine hall-

One was a child of beauty rare
With a cherub face and golden hair;
The lovely look whose radiant eyes
Filled the soul with thoughts
of Paradise.

The other was a visage vile
Marked with the lines of lust and guile,
A loathsome being, whose features fell
Brought to the soul weird thoughts
of hell.

Side by side in their frames of gold,
Dingy and dusty and cracked and old
This is the solemn tale they told:

A youthful painter found one day,
In the streets of Rome, a child at play,
And moved by the beauty it bore,
The heavenly look that its features wore,
On canvas, radiant and grand,
He painted its face with a master hand.

Year after year on his wall it hung;
'Twas ever joyful and always young-
Driving away all thoughts of gloom
While the painter toiled in his
dingy room.

Like an angel of light it met his gaze,
Bringing him dreams of his
boyhood days,
Filling his soul with a sense of praise.

His raven ringlets grew thin and gray

His young ambition all passed away;
Yet he looked for years in many a place,
To find a contrast to that sweet face.

Through haunts of vice in the night
he stayed
To find some ruin that crime had made.
At last in a prison cell he caught
A glimpse of the hideous fiend
he sought.

On a canvas weird and wild but grand,
He painted the face with a master hand.

His task was done; 'twas a work sublime-
An angel of joy and a fiend of crime-
A lesson of life from the wrecks of time.
O Crime: with ruin thy road is strewn
The brightest beauty the world
has known
Thy power has wasted, till in the mind
No trace of its presence is left behind.

The loathsome wretch in the
dungeon low,
With a face of a fiend and a look of woe,
Ruined by revels of crime and sin,
A pitiful wreck of what might
have been,
Hated and shunned, and without
a home,
Was the CHILD that played in the streets
of Rome.

- Anonymous

Contents

Acknowledgements

There is an old adage, "success has many fathers, and failure is a bastard." If this book is a success, it is because of the prior efforts of many others who have participated in conducting research on economic crises and crime problems of the past and the present. It is also the indirect outcome of the influence of my mentors, teachers, coaches, and peers who have led, taught, and inspired me to learn more about international political economy and the impact of crime on the general economy and the criminal justice system. If this book is a failure, the blame rests squarely on me. Indeed, in this writing, I sincerely hope that my critics are correct and that I am wrong, and that we will not have a second Great Depression, and with it an ensuing crime wave the likes of which has not been seen on this planet in 100 years. Time shall prove this work to be fact or fiction; I will be pleased if this work encourages people to be on their guard, to take action, and to soften what will surely be a hard landing for the unprepared if my fears are realized.

I wish to publicly thank the operators and employees of the U.S. Department of Justice, National Criminal Justice Reference Service (NCJRS), including Kreg V. Purcell and his colleagues, for their timely assistance in locating and tracking down dozens of hard-to-find publications and source materials for this book. NCJRS was most instrumental in identifying and recovering titles, some rare and obscure, that have been in archive storage for decades waiting for such a time as now to come alive and be instructive in our day. The reader will also note that many of the appendix recommendations for 'things to do to prevent crime opportunity' are NCJRS suggestions and may be found on their website at **www .ncjrs.gov**. In the preparation of the data collected for review prior to writing this book, it was truly beneficial for me to have access to the U.S. Government Library, and the publications and some five members of the staff who made themselves available to conduct follow-up research, extract titles, and suggest additional articles for inclusion in the literature review have been of immense help.

I am grateful for the academic contributions and works of the many scholars whose works are cited in the text and bibliography, with particular appreciation given to John Kenneth Galbraith (1954) and his seminal work on the Great Depression, entitled *The 1929 Crash*; Dixon Wector, *The Age of Great Depression, 1929-1941*; Richard J. Lundeen (2009), "1929 vs 2007-2009 Bear Market Race To The Bottom"; Richard Freeman (1999), "The Economics of Crime"; John A. Pandiani (1978), "The Crime Control Corps: An Invisible New Deal Program," paper presented at the meeting of the Society for Social Problems, September 1978; Andrew Sinclair (1962), *Prohibition: The Era of Excess*; Steven Box (1987), Recession, Crime and Punishment; Jonathan A. Conley (1971), *The New Deal's Response to Crime: The Politics of Law and Order*; Paul and Patricia Brantingham (1981), Environmental Criminology; Brandon C. Welsh and David P. Farrington (2002), "What works, what doesn't, what's promising, and future directions:" John Eck, (2002) "Preventing crime at places"; and Ronald V. Clarke, Situational Crime Prevention.

I am particularly grateful for the tutoring and professional relationship shown me through the past fifteen years by Professor Ronald V. Clarke, who agreed to work with me first in 1994 on adopting methods of Situational Crime Prevention to help resolve crime problems in our nation's low-income housing communities. Since our early collaboration, Ron has been an insightful mentor and an encouraging agent helping me understand more fully the nuances of criminal justice theory and situational crime prevention, and I am indebted to him for his kindness and clever thinking on crime. Some fifteen years ago Ron invited me to participate with his circle of colleagues in annual international seminars on environmental criminology and situational crime prevention where I was first introduced to other influential thinkers on crime such as Martin Gill, John Eck, Paul and Patricia Brantingham, Marcus Felson, and many others.

I am grateful further to some of my graduate economics tutors from Cambridge University that include Professor Geoffrey Harcourt teaching post-Keynesian economics, Professor John Eatwell teaching Keynesian macro economics in public policy context, and my several economic philosophy instructors who challenged me throughout my graduate research programme. I am grateful for the experience and for the foundation it gave me for my future career. I am also grateful to several of my over achieving peers at King's College and Cambridge

University for the many dialogs on economics and world politics, and for their lasting friendship. I am particularly thankful for getting to know Robert Borghese, (King's '85), a fellow Kingsmen and now faculty member at The Wharton School, for his confidence, encouragement, and lasting friendship. Thanks also for my undergraduate training in economics by Professor E.K. Hunt, a critical thinker who encouraged me to challenge the norm and view economics with a more critical eye; and to Dr. John Francis, who persuaded me to think broadly about politics, theory, public policy, and international political economy.

In terms of the preparation of this book for publication, I wish to thank publicly Dr. P.J. George, who supported me as technical editor throughout this project; Sidney L. Jones, a senior economist who has served in five presidential administrations in various roles including Assistant Secretary for Economic Affairs, Department of Treasury 1974-75 during the last deep recession; Robert Simmons, who provided contextual editing and economic sounding boards for periodic discussions of the general thesis, including his deep familiarity with the mortgage situation; Ronald V. Clarke, who I consulted at the project formulation and who provided some valuable comments and criticism of the book that were instrumental in its improvement; Eugene F. Ferraro, CPP, CFE, PCI from Business Controls, who provided valuable insights in the preparation and background production of this book; and to Lisa Peterson for her custom book cover art and book layout in preparation for printing and publication by Sikyur LLC. Lastly I am grateful to Sikyur LLC (**www.sikyur.com**) for publishing this book and sponsoring the author's time in preparation of this opus, and making it accessible to more people and policy makers.

Lastly, and not least importantly, I want to thank my family, from my late grandmother June Johnson who lived through the Great Depression and whose stories provided color analysis for static data narrated on pages of history, to my mother, who has been an inspiration to me throughout my life and who beat me to the doctoral podium, to my wife for faithfully nurturing our young children in their early years while I was frequently away working long hours to support my family, and thanks to my children and their great promise of life, their energy, inquisitiveness, and generosity of time enabling me to write this book.

Now, there is a saying that "good is enemy of the best," and at the risk of being too late with this publication, I decide that it is good enough, and hopefully in some future revision of this book I can improve it to make a good book great. However, there is a certain urgency and timeliness of the message that motivates me to move it to a point of conclusion now, convinced that the message and conclusions herein might have value to others as we as individuals and society face the surge wave of crime that will surely follow this second Great Depression.

Foreword

This book will be controversial in many ways on account of its title and subject matter. The author takes the position that this current deep recession will become the second Great Depression, ushering in a massive crime wave and that we must act now to prepare for, forestall, or at least minimize its consequences. The author argues that the speed of the destructive financial consequence of lost capital, lost personal wealth, lost jobs, and contracted credit in a global economy of electronic markets is too great to pull back on the flight stick soon enough for world leaders to create an effective soft landing. We must bear in mind the fact that the force of water from a broken dam is too great for several follow-up dams to hold back. This is not to say that world leaders should not try to lessen the velocity of the consequences of the global economic collapse, but rather that "all the king's horses, and all the king's men," with all their central bank efforts and treasury actions cannot put Humpty-dumpty back together again. We are constrained to think proactively about the next dams to break in the raging waters of the financial crises and their likely consequences.

To many living through the economic misery of the second coming of the Great Depression (the deep recession we have entered now will likely to be relabeled so by historians at some future date), this time will be remembered as a decade of severe financial hardship, unemployment, loss of purchasing power, and loss of wealth. Those who have prepared for the hardships through their diversity of income and employment, and preparations for food and self-protection, should navigate the choppy waters better than most. Employment once humorously picked on by Dilbert and *The Office* will become valued treasure. Employment implies being able to keep your dignity, keep food on the table, keep the heat on your home – it means life. Those with jobs should do everything within their power to be excellent employees to keep their positions in an environment of increasing economic hardship. Household bread winners and employees should be nimble; being prepared to move their ground when their "cheese" is moved is very important. They must go where the work is, or create their own effective work opportunities, and for some, unfortunately, this will mean crime – this book is meant to bring awareness about it, discuss it, and suggest immediate actions to be taken to minimize the consequences and curb the coming crime wave.

This book will be political dynamite to those politicians who wish to ignore the economic trends and state, like President Bush, that the "fundamentals of the economy are sound," when they clearly are not. Politicians, particularly in an American presidential election cycle, focus on optimism. Yet their actions, inactions, and attitudes may have led some to believe that conditions are actually better than what they really are, only to find, at long last, that the conditions are far worse and we are at greater risk. Sadly, many state and local governments are shedding their payrolls of law enforcement and support services just at a time when the data suggest that preparation for a crime wave is needed.

There will be many critics of this book and thesis, and they will likely fall along the following lines.

This book will be criticized by some in the public who will say, "Why write the book at all – the relationship between economic misery and crime is so obvious." While this book was being written, my wife had a brief conversation with a convenience store shop clerk who formerly operated a few liquor stores, and she discussed the topic of this book with him, and he thought the relationship of unemployment and crime was so obvious that he wondered why write a book about it at all – everybody knows this, he said. Well, the real fact is, not everybody understands the relationship between economic misery and crime. Tightly constricted econometric models can safely assess the validity of the hypotheses of scientific experiments in controlled environments; however, these same tools are frequently poor instruments for examining our living workshop of the community. How many mayors, governors, or presidents dare roll out public policy in the face of crises and say, now you're the control group, you just fend for yourselves, and you other lucky ones, you get the funding because we want to measure the effectiveness of the policy measure? During significant negative economic shocks, policy makers frequently flip through the cookbook of recovery recipes hoping that something found there will work. While it may be intuitive at the "gut" level to most people, what we are experiencing, or about to experience, is not obvious to all.

This book will also be chided by some mainstream criminologists and criminal justice scholars who will say that "bad economic times like the Great Depression do not create crime waves."[2] As a chorus they will argue that "overall unemployment seems to bear little or no relationship to crime… there's no basis for a prediction that a deepening or contination of the recession will lead to increases in crime."[3] This seems to fly in the face of facts that are so conspicuous even to the layman. These empiricists will exclaim that there is "no significant statistical relationship, or minimal statistical relationship" between unemployment and crime over time using long-term serial data, as they examine the movement of these variables over time not at the individual level, but across a broader population using long-term serial data. On the other hand, some of these same academicians might say that crime and unemployment variables do move together, but one does not cause the other; otherwise they would say, the inverse side of the recession equals (=) crime relationship must hold, and it does not-- in boom times we still have crime, though at disproportionate rates that are not as great as during hard times. The literature shows that criminal behavior can be habit-forming, particularly if the behavior becomes an entrenched lifestyle and if criminal behavior is not abandoned when better economic times return. Just as the bootleggers and organized criminals did not return to legitimate employment once Prohibition was repealed, but instead moved to other crimes such as kidnapping and extortion, the entrenched patterns of crime may become too "sticky", or too tempting, for some to abandon their crime behavior when good times return.

There is another misconception about the incidence of crime during the Great Depression that needs to be debunked. Many scholars will say, "There was no crime wave during the Great Depression: indeed, the data show a decrease in crime since 1934." Unfortunately, when these scholars look at historical crime data, they sometimes fail to understand the underlying circumstances that impacted the collection of the data, and by examining incomplete data sets, incorrectly perceive relationships that do not exist. Consider the following: it is widely held by criminologists that crime went down during the Great Depression, and they cite statistics from 1934 onwards that demonstrate that the crime rate decreased throughout the remainder of the Depression. However, these scholars merely cite statistical data that show that crime reports diminished from 1934 through the end of the Great Depression in our nation's cities, without taking into account the significant measures that were taken by President Roosevelt to impact crime, the reporting of crime, and the public fear of crime itself.

From an empirical standpoint, the dramatic reduction in crime figures during the latter half of the Great Depression can be explained by any one or combinations of the following measures that have nothing to do with the real level of crime:

1. Decriminalizing acts that were formerly illegal, as in repealing Prohibition and the attendant crimes that accompanied bootlegging and rum-running operations, would have the natural effect of reducing the number of reported crimes, although without changing the behavior of organized crime or causing them to turn from their vicious practices.

2. Re-focusing law enforcement efforts tightly on the objective of incapacitating the most serious habitual offenders such as desperados, and de-emphasizing and underreporting crimes of opportunity would cause a reduction in reported crimes. Merely by stopping to count petty crimes and civil disobedience, such as breaking into railroad box cars, stealing food, etc., we can reduce the level of reported crime without impacting the underlying conditions with the exception that an incapacitated habitual offender would be one less habitual offender.

3. President Roosevelt implemented, within three weeks of taking office, a massive crime-opportunity reduction program that actually served to extract 25% of the likely offender population of the unemployed, at-risk males from the high-density city centers, and to relocate them to rural military managed work camps called the Civilian Conservation Corps (CCC). On March 23, 1933, Roosevelt created the CCC, an organization that at its peak (in 1935) extracted 500,000 unemployed young men at risk for crime involvement living in the inner cities and took them to the isolated rural areas of our national forests and parks to live and work in camps, effectively getting them out of the cities, thereby reducing the number of potential offenders. Over 2.2 million young men worked in the CCC during the Great Depression, reflecting the incapacitation of between 25%-33% of our nation's poor men. The locations of the encampments were so rural and transportation so inadequate that few workers ventured away from the camps on weekends, nor were the workers close enough in proximity to reach the cities from which they had been extracted. Whether by court-ordered placement in the CCC as a diversionary program, or by volunteer sign-up, so many likely offenders from the at-risk young male population had been enlisted that it served to reduce crime in specific places.

What was it that was happening so significantly in the country between 1929 and 1933 that caused President Roosevelt to start the CCC within three weeks of his inauguration? It was in fact an economic misery-based crime wave that is largely ignored by criminologists and criminal justice scholars today who site only the statistics of cities to show that crime went down during the latter half of the great depression. This author is, therefore, not surprised that since the largest cohort of potential criminal offenders were extracted from our city streets and sent to the rural areas, reported crime in the cities decreased.

The crime wave that started in the early 1920s with Prohibition became much worse when economic depression hit rural regions following the fallout of the 1929 stock market crash. The sharp economic contraction and subsequent failures of banks, insurance companies, and many employers caused massive unemployment waves and increasing economic hardship. The hard economic times worsened living conditions significantly and the crime wave that originated in the early 1920s increased dramatically in gravity and frequency. The economic misery weighed heavily on families and separation, abandonment, and runaways increased, as did homelessness. Large bands of males were observed walking from city to city, along the railroads, not welcome in many places since they were viewed as a risk. In view of these conditions, it would not be unreasonable to expect that some of those individuals resorted to crime to eat food or to secure a place to sleep, and such petty crimes, if not abated, can soon turn into more serious crime behaviors. The mere frequency, creativity, violence, and self-justification of crime increased when early Robin Hoods transitioned into other hoods with less honorable intents, and later became entrenched in crime patterns not easily broken.

Still other criminologists will say that the current deep economic recession, even if it turns into an economic depression, will not produce a crime wave, as the security and protective measures implemented in the past 15 years will serve to inoculate society from the open exposure to a crime wave. These criminologists will argue that the decrease in reported crime over the past decade is the result of carefully applied situational crime prevention techniques designed to make crimes harder to commit; therefore, there is less crime opportunity, and as a result there will be less crime. It is true that, for example targeted prevention efforts have made packaging, delivery mechanisms, access control, and key systems more difficult for vehicle thieves to steal cars on the street. Similar techniques are used to make crimes more difficult to commit at certain places such as banks and convenience stores. However, what must not be ignored is that the criminal response to situational crime prevention measures is frequently the selection of a softer entry location for the same target.

For instance, in the case of auto theft, some criminal offenders merely adjust their method of auto theft and steal cars by other means. For example, in Seattle, the Russian mafia has been noted stealing the doors and seats out of Honda Accords. These cars are subsequently 'totaled' by insurance agencies and the cars auctioned off for parts, only to have these same cars purchased at auction and reconfigured with the original equipment put back into the vehicles and sold in retail markets. In this example, crime was displaced, not eliminated, and to the credit of the criminal organization, it may be said that they lowered their risk profile by stealing lower-value seats and doors, rather than the whole car, enabling them to run under the radar of law enforcement trolling for larger cases. So in this instance, is there truly a reduction in car theft? Or have criminal organizations adjusted their business practices to lower their risks and costs even as they work through the rubric of law enforcement prioritization of focus to minimize their own risks?

Thinking further about the security-protective measures preventing crime opportunity, one may realize that far too much weight is given to the value of the installation of equipment only; without capable trained operators, maintenance, and supervision, these systems lose crime prevention value quickly. The sad reality is that the life cycle of physical security interventions is limited, systems age, and state and local governments are rolling back spending on law enforcement. Corporations are cutting back security staff and personnel, and the 'capable guardians' that were so important in reducing crime have been placed on holiday through pink slips and redundancy notices, or evicted through foreclosures on their homes. Further, in the background of the budget cuts that have reduced public and private sector control resources, research shows that sharp economic contractions can create imbalances or peak demand for social control services not able to handle the surge wave of demand arising from the asymmetric sharp economic event. Indeed, research of past economic contractions shows that the dislocation of resources, swamping of social control systems, and overwhelming force of the surge wave of demand for services can overrun preparations for a normal time. We must remember that these are not normal times. We are experiencing a 100-year event.

Criminal justice research shows a positive correlation between negative economic shocks and crime; the implication is that when market crashes occur, crime goes up. Research also shows that "rapid consumption growth tends to depress property crime growth, and vice versa" meaning that when you have plenty of access to money, for instance, through the proverbial ATM of your home through a home equity loan, people don't commit as many crimes, as their economic necessity is being met. All of these seem too simple, yet it is a complex issue for criminologists and policy makers alike.

Let me now turn to negative economic shocks. When I started writing this book in September 2008, Lehman Brothers had just collapsed, along with a number of other sizable financial institutions, and there were just three economic shocks comparable to our times: the 1987 stock market crash, the 1974 deep recession, and the 1929 stock market crash and deep depression. By mid-October 2008, the lows of the 1987 stock market crash were breached and there remained only two economic events greater than our current economic collapse: the 1974 deep recession and the 1929 stock market collapse and Great Depression. By mid-November 2008, the stock market collapse dropped down below the 1974 low levels, yet unemployment levels still remain lower than that during the 1974 deep recession. This will not last.

A friend and respected economist, Sidney L. Jones[5], a senior official who has served in five presidential administrations in various roles including Assistant Secretary for Economic Affairs, Department of Treasury during the last deep recession in the mid-1970s, has been monitoring current economic events and has postulated in early October 2008 that if national U.S. unemployment holds at 8.4 percent, then, our recession will be difficult, but not as deep as the 1974 deep recession. However, if unemployment breaks the 8.4% threshold and rises to the teens, then our only comparable remaining experience is the Great Depression of the 1930s. In February 2009, the national data revealed that unemployment continued to rise through massive job losses, and the unemployment rate rose to 8.1%[6] for metropolitan non-farm employees (U-3); if one adds to the U.S. unemployment figures those individuals who are unemployed, underemployed, and who have stopped looking for work, the aggregated unemployment figure rises above 14.8% (U-6).

In many localities the (U-3) unemployment rate has surpassed 10%, and the trend of massive unemployment layoffs shows no signs of peaking as of this writing. At the current pace, by mid-summer we should be well above the 8.4% unemployment tipping point, and breach 9% by 2009; Jones described our current economic conditions as "a once-in-a-lifetime series of severe shocks and systemic changes… The cumulative effects of economic events and politics will have a major long-term impact that will not be fully recognized for many years."[7]

Ronald Clarke, arguably one of the most respected criminologists of our time, and one not accused of looking through the glass darkly, has found numerous crime prevention studies which argue that "crime is not spread evenly across all places, people or times and, to be effective, preventative measures must be directed to where crime is most concentrated." Focusing on 'hot spots' – those places with a high rate of reported crimes or calls for assistance – has proved useful in directing police patrols and crime reduction measures.[8] The concept of Situational Crime Prevention is an important part of the solution. The author outlines a strategy and method for reducing crime opportunity at specific places, along with providing advice on how to prepare now for the coming crime wave. But before adopting the solution, we must revisit our past, examine the lessons learned, and determine how best to navigate the troubled waters of our current condition.

Summing up, we can say that there is an express linkage drawn in this book that unemployment is correlated with crime generally, but the relationship is particularly more important during sharp negative economic contractions such as we are experiencing now. As this deep economic recession moves toward depression, we can expect more crime, not less, until the economy recovers and we as a nation implement broad measures to combat crime in its modern context. Simply repeating our past steps and programs of the first Great Depression, while potentially helpful, will be insufficient to combat the modern crime opportunity. This book concludes with a prescriptive set of strategies and recommendations that should be considered sooner, as opposed to later, to reduce the consequences of the coming crime wave.

CHAPTER 1 Past as Prologue

"What's past is prologue."

– Shakespeare, *The Tempest* Act 2, scene 1, 245–254

"Those who cannot learn from history are doomed to repeat it."

– George Santayana, *The Life of Reason*, Vol. I, "Reason in Common Sense"

Shakespeare frequently used prologues to set the scene and stage of the play that was to unfold. His often repeated phrase, "What's past is prologue," can be a double entendre meaning the past will repeat itself if you don't watch out, or implying that the past has set the stage for the truly significant events to come. Either way, to forget the past can be costly and portentous and lead to worse outcomes. We shall be destined to repeat history unless we are imaginative enough to learn valuable lessons from it. And lessons there are, in plenty, if at all we pause and reflect.

We are living through a 100-year event, to be sure. The financial markets collapse that started in November 2007 has had many steps down, and at each step there has been some catastrophic event that has led to further financial losses and economic contraction. From a quiet beginning when the phrase "sub-prime" was added to the American lexicon in early 2007, through the fall of Bear Stearns in March 2008, to the bankruptcy of Lehman Brothers on September 15, 2008, and the litany of other economic problems with AIG, Fannie Mae, Freddie Mac, Merrill Lynch, Countrywide and others to follow, there has been a seismic destruction of wealth in a shorter space of time than has been seen in modern history. Wall Street exists now as just a shadow of its former self. Match up a chart of the peak to trough collapse of the stock markets in the last 100 years and you will see that we today have fallen faster, harder, and swifter than any other economic downturn event in history including the Great Depression. Indeed, it took from 1929 to 1932 for the Great Depression to hit its bottom.

Taking up this challenge, Mark J. Lundeen, a frequent financial news blogger providing commentary on the economy, observed and charted this historical pattern and tracked it in an informative chart that shows the "1929 vs 2007 Bear Market Race To The Bottom." Lundeen's chart shows the rapid parallel descent of the equity markets in terms of months and stock valuation losses in percentages. What is most interesting to this author is that outside of the Great Depression and Second Great Depression that is developing now, no other recession, not even the 1974 deep economic recession ever broke the -40% stock market devaluation threshold without recovering. The -40% Stock Market Equity valuation floor was pierced rapidly in October 2008 within weeks of the Lehman Brothers collapse and the stock market has further deteriorated in early 2009. That we may enjoy volatile, periodic rebounds or 'Bear Market Rallies' is well understood, and is to be expected. However, none should take comfort that the 'real' bottom has been hit, or that we shall not retest the lows at some future date on further deterioration of the underlying conditions of the financial markets and the broader economy.

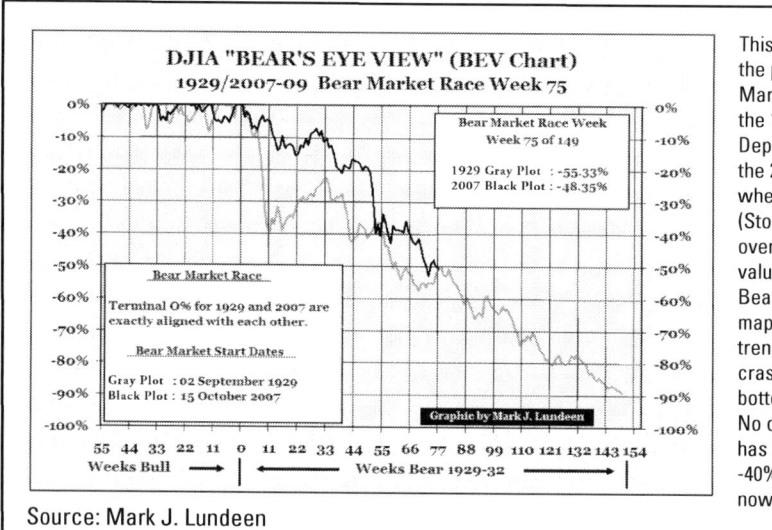

This chart shows the parallel Bear Market tracks of the 1929 Great Depression and the 2007 crash, wherein Equities (Stocks) have lost over 50% of their value in the current Bear market, and maps our current trend to the 1929 crash that when bottomed lost -89%. No other recession has broken the -40% barrier until now.

Source: Mark J. Lundeen

Massive unemployment and job loss waves occurred in various geographic locations, industries, and companies starting in late September 2008, accelerated in October 2008, and the trend continued into November 2008. By November 22, 2008, the stock market had come down to the proportional lows of the Great

Depression (by week 55), seen in the chart above, yet our descent was much quicker, and we have yet to see the massive job losses portended by such a rapid loss of capital. Massive unemployment waves continued to mount in December 2008 and January-March 2009, with 600,000+ new job losses per month, and there is no sign of the bottom in sight at this moment.

Individuals, corporations, and state and local governments have significantly cut back spending on capital projects, services, and jobs. Demand for luxury goods and non-essentials has dropped off, and in some markets fallen off severely, yet we have not yet experienced the catastrophic fall in economic demand caused by these massive unemployment layoffs. The Bureau of Labor Statistics of the U.S. Department of Labor reported in January 2009 that both the number of unemployed persons (11.6 million) and the unemployment rate (7.6 percent) rose in January. Within 13 months, the number of unemployed persons increased by 4.1 million and the unemployment rate has risen by 2.7 percentage points.[9] This number is expected to increase in real terms and percentage throughout 2009 to 9% or greater. On March 20, 2009, the U.S. Bureau of Labor Statistics reported that "employers took 2,769 mass layoff actions" in February 2009 that resulted in the separation of 295,477 workers, seasonally adjusted, as measured by new unemployment insurance benefits filings. Layoff events for all industries and for the manufacturing sector rose to their highest levels on record, with data available back to 1995. As a result, the national unemployment rate rose to 8.1 percent in February 2009, seasonally adjusted, up from 7.6 percent from January, and up from 4.8 percent a year earlier. Total non-farm payroll employment decreased by 651,000 over the month and by 4,168,000 from a year earlier. If one examines a broader index of unemployment (U-6), those unemployed and underemployed, the index rises to 14.8% in February 2009.

There is a massive contraction of capital spending of consumers and businesses, and with it, a contraction of employment that will lead to great economic misery, and—if unchecked—to crime waves. Large firms and many small businesses are just now sending out pink slips, the proverbial check on employee redundancy. At some point, the severance, buy-outs, and unemployment benefits end, and then, if employment is not replaced, or when personal savings, 401k plans, and equity are tapped out, life automatically becomes much harder for individuals and companies, and collectively we experience a hard landing for the economy, or search for a bottom.

"Human beings are not made to resist lightning bolts," and the sharp economic contraction experienced by many in this hard economy will lay heavily on individuals, families, businesses, and governments. Most people will choose law abiding behaviors when given the opportunity to commit crimes, as their personal character, integrity, moral code, and laws help them resist crime opportunity when presented. Unfortunately, in times of increasing economic misery, an increasing number of individuals will make what to them are "rational choices" to commit crimes of opportunity as they strive to cling to their standards of living, or just to eat and pay their bills, as these same individuals have put off what proper planning, savings, and reduction in household spending could have prevented. Ancient Egypt was benefited by Joseph's interpretation of the Pharaoh's dream of seven fat cows, and then seven thin cows. A voice of warning was given to the Pharaoh and he heeded the warning, putting wheat and provisions away in times of plenty for the hard times to follow.

Unfortunately, in our day, our past decade of plenty was not stored in a lasting commodity of value to prepare for hard times as done in Ancient Egypt. We have no seven years of wheat or plenty stored to distribute to the poor and needy. We do have a social network and services that are better prepared now than what was available during the Great Depression. But these social cushions have limits. Outside of incurring more debt, for most people there is no savings plan or store of lasting value that may be distributed measurably, thoughtfully, and charitably, during this current sharp economic contraction. We individually and collectively have consumed the plenty during this past decade through conspicuous consumption, increasing self-proclaimed needs, and additional claims on the earth's scarce resources. Now in our hour of need, we find ourselves ill-prepared for what next shall befall us.

This book is about the consequences of the economic collapse and the resurrection of the Great Depression and the crime wave that followed, and what to do about it. This grievous tale does have a beginning, but no ending is in sight at the time of this writing. The ending, when it comes, will require the combined effort of the collective genius of our generation, ultimately finding a way amidst the problems to overcome the unenviable present situation. Through greed, avarice ("that reprehensible acquisitiveness; an insatiable desire for wealth personified as one of the deadly sins)"[10] and impatience taking the 'waiting out of wanting,' and a public policy enabling and encouraging extreme leverage, our markets have collapsed, and we are in a free fall. With the collapse of Bear Stearns in March 2008, we hoped in vain for a soft landing, but public confidence failed with the collapse of Lehman Brothers in September 2008 and the concomitant collapse of markets, credit contraction, and contagion of lost market confidence.

We are now motivated temporarily by the hope that the new Obama Administration will lead our nation out of its economic misery, to guide us to safer waters and those Elysian fields of economic prosperity once again. However, Obama will need all his youth, his intellect, his charisma, and his hope to help the nation weather this next period of economic misery. After all he can do—and let us hope he will do many things—we will be told to do more with less, be kinder to each other, to share with one another, and not to lose our civility in these difficult times, as a return to better days is far off. Unfortunately, the hopes and colorful dreams of this generation have been completely wrecked through unbridled greed, avarice, risk-taking, and leveraged use of credit. The most devastating piece of information is that the sharp economic crises and capital contagion has spoiled several generations of wealth and economic well-being for years to come, and we have not even approached the subject of the demographic train wreck ahead with burgeoning Social Security obligations. However, resolving future Social Security funding issues is beyond the scope of emergency room triage examined for our current economy in this book.

Moses quoted the ancient playwrights who made this striking remark: "The parents have eaten the sour grapes, but it is the children's teeth that are set on edge, this to the third and fourth generation." How profound this statement is in light of the market meltdown and the market depression which will come in its wake. Those millenialists looking for the Second Coming surely did not consider that it would be the Second Great Depression and the coming crime wave that would be revisited on this earth in global consequence so great as to bring great nations and peoples to their knees. If there were ever a time for spiritual guidance and a savior it is now, or will soon be. However, this is neither a religious treatise nor a call waiting for Jesus Christ, Moses, Mohammad, Buddha or any other prophet to return posthumously in wisdom to guide us through our current dilemma.

This is rather a polemical treatise designed to call attention to *Economic Misery and Crime Waves: the Second Great Depression and the coming Crime Wave, and what we can do about it*. I will leave to others the onerous responsibility of documenting the reasons for the recent market collapse and the parallels between this and the depression in general terms. My focus is prescriptive and, therefore, targeted at creating a softer landing to protect our children, and our children's children, by moving swiftly and deliberately to safeguard these generations from the coming crime wave that the present severe economic crisis will definitely usher in, most probably within one year of the stock market crash of September 2008. Indeed, there are some who believe that the crime wave has already started. It is my earnest hope that by becoming acutely aware of the past and taking stock of our present situation, we can navigate a pathway of considered and thoughtful strategic actions to stem the tide and, hopefully, escape from the consequences of the coming crime wave.

My last human link to the Great Depression died on October 22, 2008, and that day closed the eyes of yet another soul that suffered unfathomable deprivation and hardships following the 1929 stock market crash and the Great Depression, and the hard times that ensued. The Stock Market Crash of 1929, when finally hitting bottom in 1932, decreased the value of the market by -89% and left most banks ruined and most people's fortunes depleted. The events that followed the great crash resulted in financial ruin for most including lost savings, unemployment, and personal debt without means of repayment, leaving them in a state of economic misery. Having gone through prolonged, indescribable suffering, be it lost fortunes, unemployment, food lines, or doing whatever it took to put food on the table, the generation that lived through the first Great Depression collectively vowed never to relive it. Consider Isaac Asimov's observation on the impact of the first Great Depression: "No one can possibly have lived through the Great Depression without being scarred by it. No amount of experience since the depression can convince someone who has lived through it that the world is safe economically."[11]

Ironically, even on the eve the Stock Market Crash of 1929 and the Great Depression that followed, politicians and captains of industry were continually trying to assure the public that the "fundamentals of the economy were sound." This seems strangely familiar, as it is almost exactly what we heard repeatedly from President George Bush and his chorus of Cabinet leaders.

Now let us quickly review a few statements made as part of the Great Depression dialog. In September 1929, U.S. Treasury Secretary Andrew Mellon said: "There is no cause to worry. The high tide of prosperity will continue." Or look at the response made on October 14, 1929, by U.S. Commerce Secretary Samuel Lamont, hoping to prop up market hopes with the Administration's denial of "rumors that a severe depression in business and industrial activity was impending," which, he stated, "was based on a mistaken interpretation of a review of industrial and credit conditions issued earlier in the day by the Federal Reserve Board."[12] Or here is another comment from January 1930, where President Hoover reported seeing "definite signs that business and industry have turned the corner from the temporary period of emergency that followed deflation of the speculative market;" wherein the President and his Cabinet remarked "the tide of employment had changed in the right direction."[13] This unbridled public display and declaration of falsehoods continued for many months. Consider this pronouncement made on September 12, 1930, by James J. Davis, U.S. Secretary of Labor: "We have hit bottom and are on the upswing." Here is one more premature announcement made on June 9, 1931, by Dr. Julius Klein, Assistant U.S. Secretary of Commerce: "The depression has ended." The reality is that despite the public optimism shown by our leaders, the economic depression did not hit bottom for four years from the date of the crash, and it would take 12 long years for the stock market to return to its pre-crash levels.

For a time, people were overjoyed that the worst was over. They were also convinced that it would never happen again, that the men who were in control would never allow it to happen again. And for a time people had been cautious, even overly cautious.

So how did it happen that we find ourselves today heading down quite unexpectedly into the mire of untold economic misery once again? In retrospect, we realize that it is nothing but the unintended consequences of a generation of unbridled greed, avarice, excessive risk-taking, and the moral hazard of taking the waiting out of wanting through excessive debt-based finance. And now, we, as a people, are called upon to pay a great price for the sins of our past – overleveraging of real estate, the unfettered use of opaque financial derivatives (those "nuclear financial weapons of mass destruction"), and the massive tax-subsidized recovery plan(s) and wealth destruction. We have seen nothing yet; we are only into the opening act of a grand and tragic play.

My grandmother, June Howe Johnson, an old sage with a mischievously keen wit, spoke to me many times about the era of the Great Depression. June Johnson was born in 1917 and was a teenager when she lived through the Great Depression. She used to say that those times were so difficult that families pulled together to make ends meet. She recalled many times how her parents had all the children, teenagers and all, find work wherever they could find it, doing whatever, to collect the nickels and dimes daily that would be collected nightly and put toward the household care and feeding of the family. June vividly remembered the hard lessons she and her family learned in those days that were instrumental in transforming the lives of her generation so completely. Never again would June consider owning a single share of common stock or equity listed on an exchange, but rather she favored cash, interest bearing notes, treasury certificates, and mortgage interest. Many of those who held or carried equity paper through the Great Depression suffered catastrophic loss of wealth and confidence in the market. Ironically, others who thought they were insured found themselves wanting when the insurers themselves were undercapitalized and failed. Is it any wonder that the U.S. government is willing to lose so many billions of dollars keeping mega-insurer AIG afloat? Letting AIG fail without unwinding and reassigning the underlying insurance instruments would cause a crash far greater than the fall of the house of Lehman Brothers.

My grandmother's story, like so many others stories from this era, reminds us that the Great Depression was a most difficult and trying time for families and children. Consider the recent reflection of 91-year-old Walter Stoiber[14] commenting on his memory of the Great Depression.

My family was "an average blue-collar family" from Altoona, PA. "My father worked at the silk mill, as a shipping clerk, and later as a supervisor. As businesses in Altoona cut back and then closed entirely, the silk mill did too. My father had a backup career, giving piano lessons and playing a five-piece band for weddings... As the Depression got worse, those things were no longer affordable. He took a job as an insurance agent. But people didn't have the money to buy more insurance. I was in the sixth grade in 1929. I got a job at our grocery store, stocking shelves for 25 to 50 cents per day, plus a bag of penny candy... We patched holes in our shoes by lining the insides of the soles with cardboard separators from old Shredded Wheat boxes..."

You get the picture. Times were tough.

Remembered by this generation are old slogans such as "Better belly burst, than good food waste," or the old Mormon pioneer slogan of "Eat it up. Wear it out. Make do, or do without."[15] These heartfelt stories of the hardships overcome by families during the Great Depression are frequently repeated by many families remembering those difficult times. Making an honest living in this era took great character, integrity, and hard work for the whole family.

Demand destruction and lack of confidence in banking, insurance, and common stock was another phenomenon that occurred along with such great change and hardship. Anyone relying on the stock market bouncing back and stabilizing at pre-November 2007 highs should consider the experience of the past. The generation that lived through the Great Depression was forever changed by the grist mill experience. Indeed, the events that occurred with the 1929 stock market collapse were a springboard of trouble, leading to a situation where people in every walk of life were severely affected. The confidence lost proved difficult to be regained and the economy took many years to overcome the terrific fall. If you had purchased the stock index equivalent on the day before the market crash in October 1929, it would be 1952 before a buy-and-hold strategy would return it to its original value, but by that time, it would be robbed of interest, and beggared by inflation through that period.

It was under such conditions of hardship and untold suffering that persons of lesser moral stature increased their crime involvement with a thoroughly altered attitude to crime opportunity. Hard times do not make one a criminal – there is always agency and choice. But crime opportunity put too often in front of the needy will most probably be accepted gladly and crime may also be chosen when no other alternatives present themselves.

The deprivation and indignities of the Great Depression experienced by many included bankruptcy, home losses, unemployment or underemployment, bread-lines for bagholders, and make-work projects to find work to provide some purpose in everyday living. What passed for a blind eye towards civil disobedience of Prohibition gangsters and bootleggers in the 1920s now took greater blurriness of moral code in the 1930s as outlaws, rational Robin Hoods, and other hoods committed more serious crimes. In terms of the Depression Desperados—the "public enemies"—the public looked on with some cruel sense of justice as these criminals were stealing from the banks and insurance companies during this era, as though they had it coming to them because they were the proximate cause of the public's economic misery.

In the early 1920s there was great technological change in transportation, commu-nications, employment expectations, and entertainment, and with it came great societal change. The rapid changes in technology, culture, and politics created chal-lenges for government institutions that proved to be ill-prepared for these changes. A public perception of national moral decay, lawlessness, and crime motivated the United States to adopt Prohibition in an attempt to return to forgotten values of "clear thinking and clean living." The unintended consequence of intoxicants prohibition was to increase political and police corruption and create a climate for widespread civil disobedience, and in this environment, organized crime flour-ished. Indeed, Helmer (1998) wrote of this period: "if bootlegging was respect-able in the twenties, Americans in the Depression found something to admire in the bold and desperate men who only 'stole from the banks that stole from the people.'"[16]

During the Great Depression, regional gangs branched out and linked with other organized crime organizations in large cities and rural areas to be more intercon-nected, and their gangster crimes became more daring. The petty corruptions of the 1920s became an all-out gangster street-war on ethics and the moral code in the 1930s. Criminals who mocked the rule of law and Prohibition through bribery, flaunting of their wealth and connections, became much more ruthless in the 1930s, committing violent crimes and exploiting new technologies to thwart the process of law and to ensure that less advanced law enforcement agencies never caught them. The level of crime in the early 1930s shot up considerably with increasing economic misery, including unemployment, underemployment, and despair of the Great Depression. In these conditions, in many parts of the country, there was tolerance for crime rooted in individual civil disobedience, self-rational abandonment of the rule of law, and dishonoring property rights, or worse, mob bullying, looting, thievery, oppression, and violent crime including murder.

By 1932, the crime problem had become so widespread that President Hoover increased the gravitas and authority of federal law enforcement through the renamed United States Bureau of Investigations that was directed to fight an unrelenting campaign against organized crime and serious habitual offenders. This same law enforcement bureau was renamed in 1935 the Federal Bureau of Investigations, or FBI. In one violent incident, depicting the depravity and desperation of the times, mob action against an Indian tribe resulted in the slaughter of many innocent people by the mob that wanted to usurp their land and oil rights. This story is highlighted on the FBI website documenting the historical origins of the FBI. The systematic build-up of the federal response to organized crime and other violent crimes like property crimes led Congress to abandon the enforcement of certain provisions against crimes that were deemed either too difficult to enforce, or too labor-intensive to enforce. Congress also moved to legalize some crimes that were too economically beneficial to organized crime to allow such illegal markets to be maintained by organized crime (e.g., the repeal of Prohibition).

Crime that grew during the early years of the Great Depression would recede halfway through the Depression only after significant broad sweeping crime control and employment creation actions occurred, including the remote relocation of approximately 25% of the nation's unemployed young males in encampments operated by the Civilian Conservation Corps (CCC).

Since the 1950s, crime waves have almost always followed significantly sharp economic crises. In each of these instances, there has been shown to be a positive correlation between economic misery, unemployment, and crime – meaning that if unemployment rises, so also does crime.

When we scan the available literature, we find that there is some consensus among criminal justice professionals and public policy specialists about how and why crime receded and that is extrapolated to the following factors: 1) regime change – laws were changed, structure of response, new criminal justice institutions formed (e.g., the FBI was created, Prohibition ended, etc); 2) serious habitual offenders causing the greatest crime impact were targeted and incapacitated; 3) crime demand reduction programs were instituted to reduce the pool of likely offenders, particularly those most vulnerable to crime opportunity; 4) broad scale employment programs were designed, investing in the economy, providing meaningful contributions to household incomes, eventually leading to a decrease in need and an increase in the opportunity cost of illegally produced income. We can expect that some of these very solutions will be taken up to address the current crime situation in our day. However, we will need to look with new eyes as conditions have changed. Our population size is greater. We are more interconnected than ever before with the rest of world.

Communication technologies have become far more rapid, global, and boundless. In 1929, communications were not as swift as they are today. Newspapers and radio were leading vessels of news. Though television technology was invented in 1928 by Philo Farnsworth, only limited programming transmitted over primitive television sets were available in the U.S. through 1938. By 1942, there were only 5000 television sets operational in the U.S., and it was not until 1953 that some rural parts of the U.S. (such as Idaho) were served by licensed television stations. It took days for updates from radio, newspaper and television news to reach all parts of the country. Though news travelled throughout the country, it did not appear as though the Great Depression was impacting all areas. For instance, some parts of Idaho seemed unimpacted for nearly one year before the consequence of the market crash and depression hit them. However, in the age of the Internet, it takes only micro-seconds to communicate with automated text mail, SMS messaging, Internet sites of many kinds, and 24-hour news channels such as CNBC, CNN, Fox News and the other major networks that push the news out nearly non-stop on a daily basis. Beyond the Internet and the plethora of computing technologies, Internet access to personal information and commerce, Global Positioning System (GPS) radios, transportation modernization, roads, railways, ports, and skyways have accelerated the free flowing exchange of ideas and commerce, and with these comes an increase in criminal fraud opportunity that our current criminal justice and social control institutions are not adequately prepared to handle when surge waves of crime hit specific individuals, communities, businesses, governments, and our planet as a whole.

Our age of high speed computing technology has made it much easier for criminals to conduct identity theft, organized retail crime schemes, fraudulent eBay or Craigslist sales ploys, and many more sophisticated financial frauds by bogus financial institutions. With modern technology, criminals thrive; it seems that only stupid criminals get caught. Commit a number of frauds of low-dollar amount in numerous jurisdictions changing tradecraft frequently and a fraudster is unlikely to get caught. The government must get smarter in dealing with fraud and criminal enterprise. Indeed, a lesson of Bernard Lawrence "Bernie" Madoff, a name that will go down in infamy, is that the smarter criminals may operate for years, only to become exposed when some asymmetric event dislocates their scheme.

Bernie Madoff, the former chairman of the NASDAQ stock exchange, admitted to operating the largest investor fraud ever committed by a single person. On March 12, 2009, Madoff pled guilty to an 11-count criminal complaint, admitting to defrauding many thousands of investors through a massive Ponzi scheme. Federal prosecutors estimate that Madoff's client losses total $65 billion. Great frauds like those perpetrated by Bernard Madoff are exposed in times of economic crises, yet there will doubtless be new frauds perpetrated to capture the stimulus funds sent to aid the distressed in their hour of need. Whether it is the criminals who ambush a cargo truck of UN aid to small villages, or organized crime that commits fraud to redirect funds for the U.S. stimulus sent to the cities – fraud and corruption flourish in environments of chaos. Criminals follow the money, and where stimulus needs to be spent rapidly to have near-term impact, the opportunity for fraud is immense. Look for heightened demand for Certified Fraud Examiners, forensic accountants, and attorneys with financial background experience in the coming years.

As has happened throughout history, criminals have exploited technology to further their criminal exploits. Our time is no different, as criminals in our era have taken the leading edge in Internet technologies, complex financial transactions, business intelligence, and supply chain management, and use these tools to exploit the unfocused and under-funded aims of law enforcement. Modern technologies have added increased capability for criminals to exploit crime opportunity. For instance, in 1979, sophisticated narco-traffickers reported to have used CNN Space Shuttle launch coverage to determine when the virtual gates to America would open, in order to send their planes and illegal narcotics cargo into the US when the limited assets of the US government deployed for narcotics trafficking were temporarily redeployed to support NASA Space Shuttle operations and vehicle re-entry missions. Imagine today how much more freely, quickly, and boundlessly our technology, transportation, and communications enable near-real time coordination and feedback of the global supply chain of illegal commerce.

Organized crime is much more organized, and it has gone global and corporate. The corporation now legitimizes organized crime and provides cover for trafficking illegal goods, laundering money, and banking operations. One lesson of the 1920s-1930s was that the initially disorganized crime groups became more organized in time. Territorial turf battles were violent between rival gangs at first and then solidified along treaty lines, and in time the inward battle turned outward as some collective reasoning of self-survival seemed to turn their focus outward to the world. It appears the same is happening now in the current economic downturn as rival drug gangs turn each other in, battle it out for market share, and mafia-type organizations prey on each other for expanded turf seemingly trying to hold on to their own prior standards of living.

Nowhere has this been more evident than in Mexico and along the US-Mexico border where criminal gang violence has been raised to new extremes as the economy has worsened. In 2008, over 5,500 people were murdered by Mexican criminal gangs along the US-Mexico border; this means that twenty percent more people have died along the border in slayings than all of the U.S. soldiers who have died in the US-Iraq War since May 2003. Add to this number a reported 1,028 kidnapping cases in Mexico, 65 of whom were killed, and an untold number of unreported cases, and you have real mayhem across the Mexican border.[17] The Mexican criminal gangs are masters in executing domestic terror in the forms of violent kidnappings, beheadings, multi-gunshot wounds, killings, and gang-style massacres of families. They have not been stopped at the border and are now exercising their violent trade in border states like Arizona and Texas, and deep into the United States following the migratory patterns of Latin American immigration and transportation thruways.

Terrorism remains a real and prevailing threat. Terrorism did not start with the World Trade Center bombing on September 11, 2001, nor did it end with the U.S. invasion of Afghanistan and Iraq shortly thereafter. Terrorism may be fought by the U.S. in the sandbox of the Middle East, but the face of terrorism has a reach that is global, and the proposed retreat of the U.S. from combating terror on the ground nearest its roots in radical Islam may create an unintended vacuum where the terror follows our troops home to U.S. soil. Speaking now as a U.S. citizen, I have to confess that our enemies still hate us, and increasingly more people worldwide think that the current economic misery cocktail served up to the world in this deep recession is the result of U.S. largesse, overconsumption, greed, toxic paper and debt, leverage, speculation, and corruption. Consequently, we Americans should expect more, not fewer threats from our adversaries.

The developed world should remember that the World Trade Center (WTC) bombing took place on September 11, 2001, some 18 months after the NASDAQ stock market crash, when it appeared that economic recovery for America was just around the corner; suddenly, America was struck by our enemies at the heart of Western capitalism and commerce seized up almost immediately. The attacks killed 2,974 innocent people and created widespread confusion among news organizations and air traffic controllers across the United States. International civilian air traffic was banned from landing on U.S. soil for three days. It seemed that everyone's focus was fixed firmly on the 9/11 WTC terrorism events and time stood still. This same building complex was targeted by radical Islamic terrorists in the WTC bombing on February 23, 1993, that killed six and injured 1,042.

Commerce contracted sharply, few paid their bills on time in September 2001, and our economy headed downward fast. Alan Greenspan, the Chairman of the U.S. Federal Reserve Bank, wisely observed the situation and moved rapidly to lower interest rates to get the economy moving again. The trouble was that when Greenspan attempted to haul back the economic stimulus by raising interest rates, mortgage rates did not rise in tandem. Indeed, low mortgage rate loans existed for many creating what some observe to be the lynch pin of our current overextended housing bubble, only to burst, and now rapid home value deflation began to add fuel to our current economic misery cocktail.

As with the schoolyard bully, there is a theory within terrorism that you must kick a man when he is down, and it would not be unrealistic to assume that before the stool legs of our fragile economy are put back upright, radical Islamic terrorists, or other purveyors of terrorism may strike the developed world again, and more particularly within the United States. We must remember that there is no singular face of terrorism; our enemy is a hydra, and with every head that is lopped off, several others take their place. Unfortunately the economic misery experienced the world over will create the possibility for greater terrorism, not less.

Make no mistake, this deep economic recession is impacting us all, the good and the bad, the law abiders and law breakers. This deep, sharp economic crisis is causing untold readjustments to operations, spending, and political stability worldwide. When the dust settles and we exit from this extended economic contraction, the world's wealth will undoubtedly be less; what remains will be redistributed in ways yet to unfold, and the political map will most probably look different.

In a race against time to find solutions, people and politicians must be on their guard to be appropriate, timely, and temporary in their alleged Keynesian stimulus spending priorities. Spending is either investment or consumption – planting apple orchards or burning them for fire wood. Too many politicians confuse Keynesian stimulus with consumption. Keynes' idea of 'social insurance' was job and employment creation, building valuable infrastructure that left the country better and more prepared to compete in the marketplace. Keynes was not a vocal proponent of demeaning handouts or unproductive assistance in lieu of labor. For Keynes, the role of government was to get the train back onto the economic tracks. It is, therefore, the role of government to provide investment in infrastructure and other lasting things of value, until such time as the economy got back on the train tracks of progress, and the government supports would withdraw.

Increasing numbers of people are in real pain; jobs are being lost in massive waves. Home values are plummeting and many homes are being forfeited, further reducing the purchasing power of the populace. Bankruptcy is becoming a common and accepted practice. We must be careful not to surrender the ideal of self-reliance for ease of socialist aims of too greatly entrenched government interventions. Limited, timely, and targeted stimulus, yes. Long-term, entrenched, growing social program networks without a tax base to fund them, no.

It would be well for all to remember that the economic climate of the first Great Depression created a breeding ground for the Hitlers and other fascist extremists that came to prominence in eras of great economic misery not unlike our own.[18] Make no mistake, President Obama stands for little that Hitler stood for, yet the parallels of the calls for change and the massive crowds that President Obama attracted during his election remind us easily of the public rallies for change in the 1930s. Therefore, it is imperative that President Obama and the Democratic leaders use their political currency wisely, taking care not to overextend their aims of government intervention into old socialist traps, or we may soon find less harmony on our own soil.

While the 2008 U.S. Presidential election was an Electoral College landslide for President Obama, the popular vote was less lopsided. The call for change, in a climate of pain, may cause otherwise reasonable people to act unreasonably, or to exceed reason. The tenuous balance of conventional wisdom and order may be thrown out if change is too radical. Indeed, though the probabilities are low in the U.S. at the time of this writing, it is not out of the question that localized insurrection and calls for dis-union within the U.S. could occur as the economic condition worsens. This sort of social unrest is already occurring in other nations that are experiencing worse conditions as a result of this economic depression.

This is why the leaders of both the World Bank and the International Monetary Fund have each called attention to the great weakness of the global economy, and the great mischief that can occur in times of heightened economic misery and wealth destruction. Recently, Joby Warrick wrote, "some analysts warn that a prolonged economic crisis could trigger a period of widespread unrest that could strengthen the hand of extremists and threaten Pakistan's democratically elected government – with potentially grave consequences for the region and perhaps the planet."

So the past is a prologue indeed, but our future steps are what we make them. We must, as a people, take into account our history, our present, and our future to be effective.

In the remaining sections of this book, the author examines the economic relationship between economic misery and crime, the lessons learned from the first Great Depression, a review of our current situation that started with the collapse of Lehman Brothers in September 2008, some review of lessons learned from combating crime waves, a chapter on the limits of past experience, and a final chapter on what governments, businesses, communities, and families can do to stem the tide of the coming crime wave, and make a softer landing for what otherwise will be a cruel hard landing indeed.

2 Economic Misery and Crime Waves

"An economist is a surgeon with an excellent scalpel
and a rough-edged lancet, who operates beautifully
on the dead and tortures the living."

– Nicholas Chamfort (1741 - 1794)

I have been trained in the art and science of economics and international political economy at King's College, Cambridge University, where economics was valued for its explanatory ability to make sense of economic events in an age of imperfect markets and periodic economic shocks requiring policy actions to get the invisible hand working again. John Maynard Keynes, that illustrious King's College, Cambridge University scholar who gained notoriety for his macroeconomic theory and public policy leadership during Great Depression, called Malthus the "first of the Cambridge economists," praising his philosophical, moral, historical, theoretical, and observational approach to economic problems, and his ability to "penetrate these events [with understanding] by a mixture of intuitive selection and formal principle and thus... interpret the problem and propose the remedy."[19] This approach characterizes the Cambridge economics approach and the author of this book has used it to "stylize facts" in order to tell an economic story, in the manner of Lord Kahn, also a King's economist, who used stylized facts to describe economic events in a meaningful way to inform public policy.

By definition, "Economics is the social science that studies the production, distribution, and consumption of goods and services."[20] Put simply, economics is a means of explaining the behavior of wants and needs in an environment of scarcity. In this book, we examine the economics of individual decision-making under extreme duress when such individuals are impacted by economic misery (prolonged unemployment, inflation, loss of income and wealth destruction), and its attendant crime opportunity consequences. Essentially, when individuals lose their jobs, provided the job loss is prolonged and income is not sustained by any other legal means, these same individuals are more prone to consider augmenting their income through illegal means. This is not to say that all unemployed persons become criminals; quite the contrary, it only implies that individuals with prolonged unemployment and without other means of support are more likely to exploit criminal opportunities than employed persons.

Although this chapter, and indeed the whole book itself, focuses on economic misery and the consequences of the increased crime opportunity that results from diminished income, purchasing power, employment, etc., it is to be remembered that there are other forms of deviance that occur in times of economic misery and they include increased alcoholism, suicide, depressive-type disorders, and mental health disturbances. Besides these individual disruptions, there are family disruptions that may occur in difficult economic crises such as severing family ties, petty crime, delinquency, or violence. Some of these consequences are direct and conspicuous outcomes whereas the others have already been there in dormancy waiting to be triggered by a life-impacting stress or event, which need not concern economic problems at all. What is important, however, is to remember that, though simple economic models may show strong relationships, life is complex. Nonetheless, it is worthwhile to examine more closely the interrelationship between economics and crime primarily because it can help explain or predict future events.

ECONOMICS AND CRIME

Both poverty (including unemployment) and affluence (where there are relatively great disparities of wealth between the rich and the poor) can be independently correlated with high crime rates.[21] Economic shocks, particularly unexpected, sharp, negative economic shocks, can result in conditions of severely heightened economic misery that can foster crime waves if they are unabated or prolonged. These crime waves, a consequence of sharp negative economic shocks, will take about a year to start making their publicly recognizable appearance.

This book focuses specifically on the impact of economic misery—that toxic cocktail of unemployment, inflation, and, more poignantly today, the rapid loss of household wealth and purchasing power (whether by home equity loss, asset deflation, or slippery wealth lost in the burst bubble markets)—and increasing crime opportunity and crime waves, and what to do about them all.

In the late 1960s, Arthur Okun[22] coined the term, "economic misery" that has been used ever since to describe a "misery index"[23] that equals the sum of the rate of inflation plus the rate of unemployment. There is simplicity and ease of measurement in the economic misery index, though it fails to capture the realities of true economic misery in our day, as deflation also results in reductions in purchasing power but the index does not reflect this. Further, the inflation value used in the index (U-3) does not reflect the true nature of unemployment or underemployment (U-6) that figures into the crime opportunity milieu. Seasonally adjusted national unemployment in February 2008 was 8.1%, whereas the figure for the total Unemployed and Underemployed was 14.8%, and is not characterized in the traditional Economic Misery Index shown below.

Month	Index	Unemployment + Inflation	Discussion
2007-12	9.08		The economic misery index is a simple function where economic misery index equals unemployment and inflation, where Misery Index = Unemployment and Inflation. However, in our current economic contraction, the misery index fails to capture the true misery in the economy. In the original index, inflation represented a 'loss of purchasing power.' Today loss of purchasing power includes deflation, such as extreme asset devaluation of commodities, falling housing prices, and lost savings that all reduce a household's ability to purchase. A new definition is needed. Further, unemployment does not capture under-employment or unemployment of persons not actively searching for legal employment.
2008-01	9.18		
2008-02	8.83		
2008-03	9.08		
2008-04	8.94		
2008-05	9.68		
2008-06	10.52		
2008-07	11.30		
2008-08	11.47		
2008-09	11.04		
2008-10	10.16		
2008-11	7.77		
2008-12	7.29		
2009-01	7.63		

Therefore, in this book, economic misery is a term that describes a much broader condition than the Misery Index (of simply unemployment and inflation) in that economic misery includes additional forms of unemployment and loss of purchasing power negatively impacting individual economic condition. In this book, economic misery is that **economic misery cocktail** of unemployment and underemployment that includes unemployment, under-employment, and those unemployed not actively seeking employment; additionally the measure includes a broader measure of the loss of purchasing power through inflation, contraction of credit (e.g. bank credit tightening), loss of retirement savings (e.g. 401k plan assets losses), and deflation of individual assets (e.g., home price deflation reducing homeowner equity), or worse, deflation creating negative homeowner equity. This broader definition of economic misery will be troubling for academics that like narrow definitions, since this sharp economic contraction has produced new means of unemployment and loss of purchasing power that impact individual economic conditions are not accurately reflected in unemployment and inflation rate.

Economic Misery Cocktail =

Unemployment (i.e Total unemployed, plus all marginally attached workers, plus total employed part-time for economic reasons, as a percent of the civilian labor force plus all marginally attached workers), being those persons characterized by the US Bureau of Labor Statistics as U-6.

Plus (+)

Loss of purchasing power (through inflation or deflation of consumer household income and assets impacting available consumer capital for purchasing including lost homeowner equity (from falling housing prices), lost household savings in retirement funds, 401k funds, college savings accounts through falling equity prices and speculation bubble bursts, and household credit contraction reducing purchasing power).

The importance of broadening the umbrella of persons counted in unemployment calculations related to economic misery and crime is an important one. There is a great cohort of unemployed or underemployed not counted in the general reported statistics of unemployed. The US Bureau of Labor Statistics only counts people as being unemployed if "they do not have a job, have actively looked for work in the prior 4 weeks, and are currently available for work."[24] Only workers expecting to be recalled from layoff are counted as unemployed, whether or not they have engaged in a specific job-seeking activity. In all other cases, the unemployed individual must have been engaged in at least one active job search activity in the 4 weeks preceding the interview and be available for work (except for temporary illness) to be counted in the pool of unemployed.

Under employment has many definitions and contexts. The International Labour Organization[25] created a policy to define (1) time-related underemployment, which is due to insufficient hours of work, and (2) inadequate employment situations, which are due to other limitations in the labor market which limit the capacities and well being of workers. A person can be simultaneously in these two forms of underemployment.

There is another group of unemployed individuals not captured by even the broader measure of unemployment and underemployment addressed above as U-6. For many small business owners, their companies might be ruined by the economic crises with sharp decrease in demand for products and services, yet these small business owners will not be counted in the unemployment category as they themselves are typically not eligible for unemployment insurance on their own account; only their employees may be eligible. This gap of statistical data reporting is important to consider more thoroughly on the contribution to crime opportunity, but is beyond the scope of further discovery in this book. The focus of crime opportunity in this book will center on the measured unemployment and underemployment captured by the US Bureau of Labor Statistics U-6 data.

UNEMPLOYMENT AND CRIME

Much has been written about the impact of unemployment on crime. <u>Studies show that there is a strong positive association between crime and unemployment at the individual level, a clear positive association at the cross-sectional level that gets weaker as the level of geographical aggregation increases, but quite an inconsistent relationship over time (or time series data)</u>.[26] One of the challenges of economic examination is that individuals and events are frequently more complex than the simple relationship being examined; so, while one can say there is a linkage between unemployment and crime, and that when unemployment rises crime also rises, there are additional variables at play that also influence the individual's economic and life choices concerning crime. Nonetheless, nearly all agree that there is a positive relationship between unemployment and crime and the two data points tend to move together. However, at the very outset it must be admitted that "joblessness is not the overwhelming determinant of crime that many analysts and the public a priori expected it to be."[27] There are other significant factors embedded in economic misery beyond unemployment that we will explore. However, we must start by examining just exactly what the research says, or does not say, about the linkages between unemployment and crime and go forward to delve deep into the extreme economic conditions of deep recessions or depressions.

The early academic research on crime focused on the economic relationship between the labor market and the unemployment level. These studies found that higher rates of unemployment are associated with higher levels of crime, but they tended to downplay the strength of the economic relationship of unemployment to crime, noting that many other variables are also linked to crime in the U.S. (Freeman, 1983).[28] When examining crime on an international geographic basis, Chiricos (1987) found that studies in the early 1980s gave a more positive assessment of the strength of the effect of unemployment on crime, noting even stronger results in the studies of the 1970s (during the time of the last deep economic recession). Chiricos found stronger evidence of a positive crime-unemployment relationship in studies that focused on property crimes such as burglaries and theft. Further, Pyle and Deadman (1994) found that when the relationship of unemployment and crime is focused on young people rather than aggregate population data, the statistical relationship gets stronger still.[29]

The subsequent research performed by other criminologists and economists continued to confirm an economic relationship between unemployment and crime. Indeed, most time series analyses find that crime rates rise with joblessness. Cantor and Land (1985) reported a positive effect of time-lagged unemployment on crime – meaning simply that **the attributable increase in crime following rising unemployment is time-lagged by a certain period, typically a period of months or years,** or to put it in other words, the onset of crime is delayed by a finite period of increasing economic misery, during which unemployed individuals presumably exhaust all other economic options before they willfully choose crime for their sustenance. Richard Rosenfeld, a sociologist at the University of Missouri-St. Louis, remarked quite significantly: "**There is a year lag between the economic change and crime rates. Every recession since the late '50s has been associated with an increase in crime and, in particular, property crime and robbery, which would be most responsive to changes in economic conditions.**"[30]

Just as joblessness varies from city to city and within cities, Land et al. (1990) demonstrated that the economic relationship between unemployment and crime is stronger "at the intracity level" compared to its corresponding intercity or national figures. Further, examining long-term changes (i.e., 10-year periods) in crime and economic conditions across 582 counties from 1979 to 1989, Gould et al. (1998) found that a one-point increase in unemployment raised property crimes by 2.2%. Other researchers such as Lee provide comparable results for 58 standard metropolitan statistical areas from 1976 to 1989 (an increase of 1.1 to 1.4% in crime rate for every increase of 1% in unemployment), meaning that for every increase in unemployment, there is a greater than one-to-one increase in crime.

Joblessness and crime do not appear to affect all groups in the same manner or to the same extent. For instance, unemployed youth without sufficient likelihood of meaningful employment are more likely to commit crime. Lugar (1978) commented, when speaking on delinquency and unemployment, that "there is no doubt in my mind that the growing feelings of despair, hopelessness, hostility, and self-destructive traits which characterized young delinquents are severely aggravated by their perception that they have no legitimate role or vocational satisfaction." The World Health Organization (1975) reported, "the poverty and frustration caused by unemployment debilitates, predisposes to fatigue and apathy, engenders despair, and increases not only psychological and bodily illness, but also crime, violence, drug abuse, and other forms of deviant behavior to which people resort to when they reject society or are rejected by it."[31]

Suppose increased crime follows unemployment incrementally, as identified above, by some time lag, say one year, and the rise in unemployment is significantly dramatic such as in our current condition following September 15, 2008, then the associated rise in massive unemployment, if unabated, would in time bring in a situation that will resemble a crime wave. Few are focusing today on the rapidly rising unemployment levels, thinking erroneously that they are not unduly bothered by that or in any way connected to it, and it leads easily to the assumption that massive job losses in the financial sector, or the auto sector, or name your own sector, will not impact us. Unfortunately, they are wrong–dangerously wrong. The economy is made up of many transactions of employers and employees, vendors and customers, providers and end users. Let us not forget that the autoworker out of work who cannot pay his mortgage or credit card bills impacts us all.

In this book, the author characterizes economic misery such as what the world has experienced since September 2008 and the Lehman Brothers collapse, followed by unexpectedly severe credit contraction, serially compiling massive job losses and loss of consumer and business confidence, as setting up the conditions for sharp, dangerous, downward-spiraling trends. This historic economic collapse is global and has no parallels in the past 100 years other than the Great Depression: all that remains to separate the two events are further collapse of economic stability, massive job losses, credit contractions, the widespread displacement and relocation of workers and families, and increasing public fear and outrage. Since September 2008, I have been amazed that people have not started thinking deeply or darkly enough about the current dire economic situation, perhaps thinking that someone or the government will be there for them. Although they are not aware of it, they are in serious error in not preparing for what appears to be a multi-year economic winter. It is time to assemble your own life raft for these tough economic times. What we are now witnessing is disruption and market collapse, but what we will see and experience is far worse – there is likely to be nothing but a "dead cat bounce" for the market for several years, as the trend is down with some 'L' shaped bottom while we work things out.

What we are going through now is a situation in which crime waves are being triggered by 'sharp crises' such as the sudden and unexpected deterioration of pre-existing conditions. The crises may be natural or man-made; however, the psychological impact of the man-made ones appear to create greater angst and carnage. A natural flood impacts all, but few blame an organization or institution for the flood, unless it is particularly responsible for keeping up the seawall, etc. On the other hand, when grave man-made crises occur, such as the failure of banks which can be attributed to a particular root cause or source, then crime waves may occur both on account of the consequent crime opportunity, but also in retaliation to those that appeared to have caused the crises. We need only look back into the days of the Great Depression to see what it means. Few would argue that the Depression Desperados robbing banks in the 1930s were doing wrong in robbing banks, since the banks, bankers, and insurance companies were viewed as the proximate cause of the stock market crash and economic misery, and many citizens reportedly turned a blind eye to these Desperados, or even committed acts of civil disobedience by thwarting law enforcement attempts to capture those criminals.

Consider, therefore, the ramifications of a prolonged and unabated spike upwards in unemployment from our current February 2009 non-farm unemployment rate of 8.1%, and compare this to Great Depression levels of 24%, and as high as 31% in some localities. The U.S. Department of Labor reported on March 6, 2009, that "non-farm payroll employment continued to fall sharply in February (-651,000), and the unemployment rate rose from 7.6 to 8.1 percent. Payroll employment has declined by 2.6 million in the past 4 months. In February, job losses were large and widespread across nearly all major industry sectors." If unabated, this trend could spiral into an economic tail-spin. And what if this happens? The first consequence will be that property crime could become as routine and ordinary as to make it a normal way of making a living. For an illustration of frustration and desperation, examine the following images.

ONE HOMEOWNER'S AMERICAN NIGHTMARE

For many people, a portion of the American dream is owning their own home. Now, all across America, this dream is becoming a nightmare as home prices are falling and many homeowners are 'underwater,' a phrase that denotes negative equity. This economic downturn impacted many homeowners' dreams and they are not alone. Foreclosures hurt the entire community. Like a brush fire, foreclosures burn equity value rapidly. For an illustration, consider the following typical home: a 3 bedroom, 2.5 bath single family home in the 400 block of Elm Street, Atlanta, GA 30314.[32] This home is located in a redeveloped area of Atlanta that experienced much investment and renewal during the real estate run-up that ended in 2007. At the market peak, this home was sold for $340,000 with the bank holding a note for $295,703. The real estate market for housing rolled over, home values collapsed, the homeowner equity was now negative, and they were technically 'underwater' on their mortgage, and they stopped paying their monthly note payments, and the bank foreclosed on them, and the homeowner was subsequently evicted from the property. This home is now on sale as a bank REO for $17,000.

Typical Atlanta Foreclosure

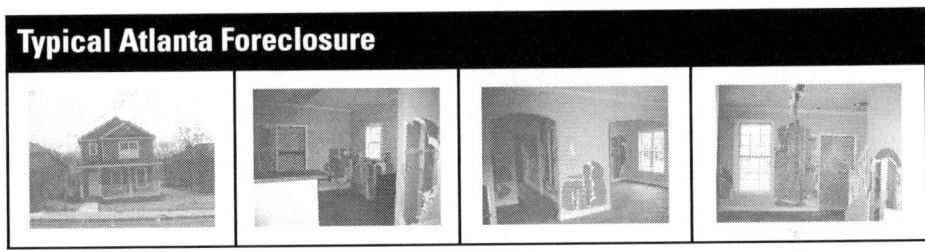

In just two years, the property deflated by over -72.4% to $93,501, per Realty-Trac. On exiting the property, the evicted homeowners or other vandals gutted the property of all appliances, plumbing, and wiring, leaving just a shell; this is now common place in Atlanta foreclosures. Now the bank holds the property note of $295,703 and is listing the property at Bank Real Estate Owned (REO) sale price of $17,000, or 5% of the original sales price.

Selling a foreclosed property for 5% to 10% of the 2007 peak pricing is gutting the housing market and homeowner equity of comparable home values in this neighborhood. What is happening to this one homeowner is being repeated over and over across the country. It is not just Detroit, California, Florida, Arizona, Nevada, and other locations – it is America that is having a fire sale on housing prices, and it is killing the life blood of the American dream, and encouraging 'moral hazard' as homeowners abandon property, either giving the keys back to the bank, or squatting at the property waiting for eviction, or worse, stripping the properties in their anger over lost fortunes and nest eggs. Sadly, until a price floor is put under housing, there is no end in sight for real estate price collapse in this market, as home buyers and investors are leery of offering any price beyond rock-bottom levels.

Recessions impact industries, but depressions impact everybody; the heat map leaves little doubt about our current state. This heat map shows home foreclosures by state. Michigan (Detroit), Florida, California, Nevada, Arizona, Ohio, and Illinois lead the nation in foreclosures. Gradually, the economic impact of the sharp contraction is working its way from the coasts to the center of the less populated states in the central plains.

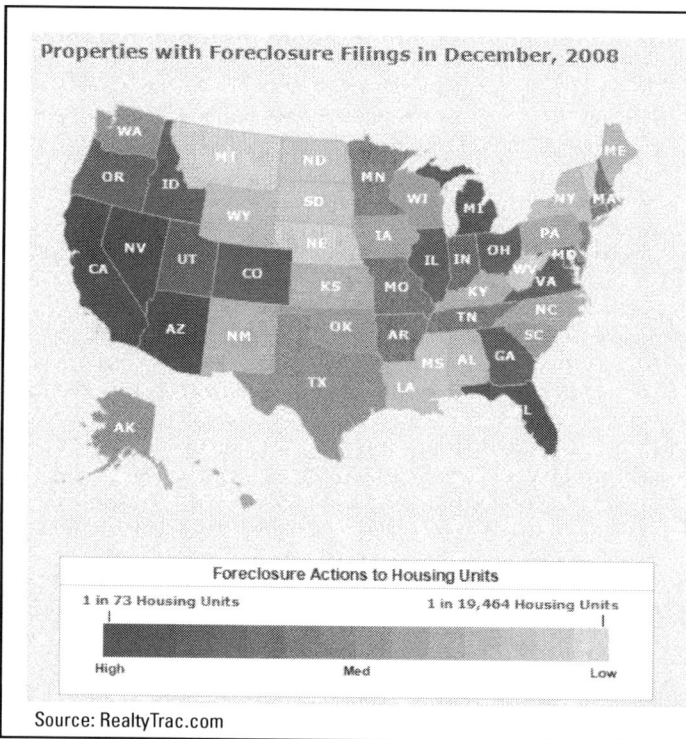

Recessions impact industries, depressions impact everybody; the heat map leaves little doubt about our current state. This heat map shows home foreclosures by state. Michigan (Detroit), Florida, California, Nevada, Arizona, Ohio and Illinois lead the nation in foreclosures. Gradually, the economic impact of the sharp contraction is working its way from the coasts to the center of the less populated states in the central plains.

Source: RealtyTrac.com

What is most disconcerting for our current condition, however, is the following: not in 100 years has the fall-off in demand in consumer goods, industrial goods or corporate purchasing occurred so rapidly as it has since the fall of Lehman Brothers, and the demand destruction caused by uncertainty, fear, lack of transparency in financial data, lack of access to capital, and negative economic outlook are strangling the economy, and with it the future employment prospects of a large segment of our generation. Economists will pull out data to show that typical cyclical crises do not significantly impact crime in a long-lasting way; however, this impartiality ceases in the presence of sharp crises such as that which we are having now. People are gradually being awakened to the reality that crime opportunity has increased considerably through this global economic collapse, and attention must soon focus on preparing for the coming crime wave. But there we are getting far ahead—what do the data say about the relationship of economic misery and crime?

Thus far we have considered the economic data of crime and unemployment in broad terms. The linkages get stronger when you focus on specific populations at highest risk or vulnerability to crime. Freeman and Rodgers (1999) report increasing propensity for crime among the youth. For instance, when unemployment increases by one percent, crime increases by 1.5% across states. Raphael and Ebmer (2001) found significantly positive effects of unemployment on property crime rates. Their estimates suggest that a substantial portion of the decline in property crime rates during the 1990s is attributable to the decline in the unemployment rate.[33] Cook and Zarkin (1985) argue that "robbery and burglary rates are sensitive to fluctuations in economic conditions. Recessions appear to cause increase in these two crimes… the magnitudes involved are not insubstantial. An increase in the unemployment rate from, say, 7 percent to 8 percent will result in a 2.3 percent increase in the robbery rate and a 1.6 percent increase in the burglary rate."[34]

In terms of violent crime, Engberg (1999) finds that the areas of a city where unemployment rises also show rising homicide rates. Elliot (1994) reports that persons who have engaged in "serious violent behavior" are more likely to terminate this if they are employed than if they are unemployed.

In several studies using pooled time series cross-city data, Levitt (1995, 1996, 1997) finds a positive relation between unemployment in an area and property crimes, including auto thefts. However, he did not find the relationship in all of his studies. Care should be taken in anticipating a one-to-one relationship between unemployment and crime as in some studies the relationship just does not hold – implying that increased unemployment does not make a criminal, rather, only the increased opportunity for crime does. In general, the data show a positive linkage between unemployment and crime.

When one begins to look more deeply into the data to find additional linkages, then the significance of unemployment as the only or key variable tends to weaken. People are complex and their situations are unique, so when one attempts to homogenize all people into the same research construct, the strength of the statistical relationship decreases. For instance, Butchdr and Pieht (1998) obtain a positive link in cross-area data but the strength of the relationship between unemployment and crime disappears when area fixed effects are added to the analysis. However, when considering the data on individuals, they find a positive link between crime and local unemployment rates.

Geography plays a significant role in providing crime opportunity. The same individual placed in two different locations with the same personal attitudes and unemployment conditions may make different choices based on the crime opportunity provided by the location. Just as location is important in real estate and marketing, so also is location important in crime opportunity. Economic research on crime amply bears this out. Some areas, where unemployment rates are high, just don't show much crime because of their geography or other variables. Butchdr and Pieht (1998) show time-series data between the 1960s and 1980s when the crime rate rose massively while unemployment moved up just slightly. The fact is that, in any given period, crime rates differ massively across geographies whose unemployment rates vary much less. Obviously factors other than unemployment must be considered in a full analysis; however, this is the work of others, and beyond the scope of the examination in this book.

Negative economic shocks (resulting in unemployment, loss of purchasing power, devaluation, inflation, etc.) preceding crime are not exclusive to the United States. Consider Japan, a country that has historically had low crime rates, where it has been largely thought that 'shaming' and cultural mores have kept crime in check. However, Leonardsen (2006) concluded that the crime situation in Japan deteriorated significantly following the financial collapse of 1990. They went on to show that though 'culture' might have inoculated the people against crime during economic expansion, when the economy suffered a significant economic shock, prior positive culture was an insufficient condition to thwart rising crime, particularly among the elderly offenders.[35] Headlines such as the following abounded: 'People are Scared,' 'Violent Crime Up in Japan,' and 'Increasing Youth Crime Problems.' Japan was not immune to the 1990 financial collapse; nor does it appear to be immune from our current financial troubles. Since 2007, crime is rising rapidly again in Japan, especially for the elderly population – not as victims, but as offenders who are shoplifting, stealing, and committing other crimes.

Since the 1991 Japanese economy meltdown crime has peaked among the elderly—no, not victimization of the elderly, but elderly offenders involved in numerous crimes such as pick pocketing, shop lifting and theft. Bloomberg reported on November 11, 2008, that "The latest [Japanese] elderly-crime wave comes after markets plunged and as Japan frets about a return of deflation. In 2007, a total of 48,605 elderly people were arrested or investigated for crimes other than traffic offenses, a fourfold jump from the early '90s." Besides theft and shoplifting, increased criminal activity by the elderly includes acts of embezzlement and assaults. The reasons cited for the increase in crime rates include financial troubles and isolation from families. Interestingly, three other indicators went up concomitantly with rising crime rates in Japan: (1) sales of security items to protect businesses and homes; (2) forming of neighborhood watch groups; (3) increasing crime survey reports of concerns with crime.[36]

Perhaps the author who offered commentary on the article, William Pesek, gave the most pertinent remark: "You don't need to be a criminal psychologist to see how this touches on many of the economic challenges facing Japan's 127 million people. It gets at everything from the gap between rich and poor to pressure on executives to how the government is dithering as the population ages. 'Elderly crime is a serious problem that our society must shoulder in the years to come,' the government report said. With baby boomers becoming elderly within five years, we have reached a state where we must make a fundamental review of anti-crime measures in a fast-aging society."

So whether we speak of Japan, the U.S., the UK, or Australia, there are many seriously concerned that the current economic downturn, if left unabated, may lead to conditions of increased crime opportunity and a potential crime wave. Linkage, however, does not necessarily mean causation in a scientific analysis, so we must look further at the research. There is a large body of academic support from data on individuals that crime is linked closely to unemployment. For example, look at what Freeman (1993) stated: "Nearly all studies find that persons prone to unemployment are more likely to commit crimes and that people who commit crimes are more likely to do so during spells of unemployment."

Freeman cited other researchers such as Thornberry and Christenson (1984) who found that in 1945, Philadelphia cohort unemployment had significant effects on crime, largely for African American youths and youths from blue-collar backgrounds. Using the same data set, Witte and Tauchen (1994) found that employment (but not wages) was related to crime. Sampson and Laub (1993) re-analyzed data from the Gluecks' 1939 Boston cohort and found that measures of job stability during early adult years (17-25) were inversely related to adult arrest rates for several crime types and that job stability during ages 25-32 had a significant negative effect on crime participation during later (32-45) adult years; it implied that job stability, especially during the early adult ages, had long lasting effects on the law-abiding behavior of these individuals into their mid-thirties.

However, it must be recognized that becoming unemployed, or being unemployed, does not make one a criminal – there is choice involved, and for many, being law abiding is the choice. Farrington et al. (1986) used interview data from the Cambridge Study of Delinquent Development, a longitudinal study of 411 adolescent males, to show that property crime rates were higher when subjects were unemployed, but also that crime was more likely only among unemployed youths who held attitudes more favorable to offending. Those who generally were law-abiding did not commit crimes during periods of unemployment. The crime-unemployment relationship was also stronger among youths with histories of low-status jobs. Farrington et.al. (1986) have provided strong evidence showing a "causal" relationship between unemployment and crime, particularly when the analysis is targeted at specific populations and attributes.

Freeman (1999) also examined studies with ex-offenders that show how unemployment (and lack of legal earnings) affects crime. In an earlier TARP program (not to be confused with the 2008 Paulsen TARP Program), the Transitional Aid Research Project (TARP), a randomized experiment that tested the effects of income supports for ex-offenders from Texas and Georgia released from prison in 1976-1977 was conducted (Rossi et al., 1980). Needels (1994) found that employment and (legal) earnings have strong negative effects on subsequent crimes following release from prison: in a ten-year follow-up of Georgia releases, criminal activity was markedly lower among those with higher legal earnings. So employment, especially meaningful employment, is a factor in reducing crime likelihood among repeat offenders, but there are also other elements at work.

Freeman (1999) draws attention to the "porous boundary between legal and illegal work." He points out, "perhaps the major reason is that crime and legitimate work are not exclusive activities. The border between illegal and legal work is porous, not sharp." There isn't any distinct line between being unemployed and committing crime, as many criminals have legitimate and illegal job incomes. Myers (1983) found that some people use their jobs to advance their illegal sources of income –such as the use of insider trading, market manipulation, protection rackets—while others look at crime as a second income. Peter Reuter, (1990) from Rand Corporation interviewed 'unsuccessful' street-level drug dealers in captivity who had been arrested and were incarcerated, to find out about their drug-selling behaviors. One of the many interesting findings was that many of these drug dealers had multiple jobs, and drug selling was a way of augmenting their income. Further, Reuter found that they would make rational judgments to sell drugs during times of greater drug selling whether their individual risk of getting apprehended was less, and the odds of defeating limited law enforcement response was greater.[37]

Fagan and Freeman (1997) found a number of studies that showed the doubling up of crime and work. Like the Reuters research, the Fagan and Freeman research shows that "experienced drug dealers often hold legal jobs, possibly to tide themselves over during periods when the drug business is especially dangerous; …youth shift between crime and work with some regularity; … employment has only a modest effect on whether or not they commit any crime." The fact is that individuals involved in illegal drug selling are frequently involved in other illegal activities from stolen-goods fencing, to auto theft, fraud, extortion, protection schemes, and burglary, in addition to their regular paying legal employment.

For those interested in following the unemployment and crime research, there appears within the endnotes a table summarizing the research studies by Steven Box (1987) that provides more insight into the nuisances of recession and crime that showed a positive correlation and no correlation by study performed.[38] Importantly, Farrington, (1986) found that career criminals commit crimes more frequently when unemployed, than when employed.[39] Besides exploring a linkage between unemployment and crime, there are other aspects to be considered: the level of sophistication, organization, and the seriousness of the crime.

Crime, however disorganized or organic at the grass roots level, if left unabated, can over time organize various structures that resemble big business. Consider organized crime—organized crime structures are similar to those of big business and involve continuous ongoing activities. During Prohibition in the 1920s and early 1930s in the United States, the unintended consequence of the social policy was to provide an opportunity for the involvement of individuals in the production and supply of alcoholic intoxicants. Like a business roll-up or consolidation, the numerous individuals were gradually replaced by large-scale criminal organizations with more efficient technology and business processes. Kunz (1976) wrote that the various steps of the economic process were horizontal market concentration, monopolization of political functions by the illegal organization, and the diversification of organized crime into both legal and illegal activities.

In the end, organized crime threatens even the legitimate power of the state because of corruption and bribery of public officials.[40] Crime opportunity, left unattended, will produce organized crime consequences if the opportunity is sufficiently large when aggregated. This has significant bearing on our situation today with all forms of criminal justice policy from marijuana enforcement to electronic financial crimes and other forms of embezzlement bundled up in the now famous credit default swaps.

WHAT ARE CRIME WAVES?

Definition

The Oxford Pocket Dictionary of Current English describes a crime wave as:

Crime wave, noun, a sudden increase in the number of crimes committed in a country or area.

In this book, we shall use Fishman's (1978) definition of a crime wave as follows: "When we speak of a crime wave, we are talking about a kind of social awareness of crime, crime brought to public attention."[41] This attention may surface as a result of a catastrophic criminal event such as a particularly violent crime or spree of crimes, repeated hashing or rehashing of crime data, a particular news story of crime news or events, or some other shady calculation or notion brought to public attention. The data may show a peak-to-trough pattern of crime, but public perceptions and the fear of crime is a greater barometer of crime waves in terms of public thinking.

The underlying economic supposition of this book is that people are rational maximizers and that their choices are guided by economic opportunities available to them under conditions of scarcity and self-constraint, guided by rule of law, conventional norms, and moral character and personal integrity. Economic misery--unemployment and inflation (and loss of purchasing power) — may make one more open or susceptible to corruption or crime opportunity when presented. Hard economic times can lead some to rationalize crime opportunity. Indeed, in hard economic times there may be an erosion of moral high ground as economic necessity persuades some to take the waiting out of wanting, and they commit crimes of opportunity to meet their basic needs.

Still others might be persuaded by the masses that the laws are wrong, and that crime is not crime at all. Under conditions of severe economic hardship, it is not uncommon for some individuals to turn a blind-eye to the law, or turn away from the law, or exercise civil disobedience and abandonment of the rule of law. Consider the huge public civil disobedience during the time of Prohibition, or in our day, the large number of people who smoke marijuana though it remains illegal; both Prohibition of alcohol and criminality of marijuana make criminals out of civil disobedient offenders; more distressingly, however, these same 'crimes' create economic opportunity for illicit income and feed criminal organizations with operating funds.

A great danger in this environment is when rational risk-taking Robin Hoods become entrenched in their condition and become more severe criminals, as these patterns are hard to break free from even in good economic times. The mob did not turn to legitimate businesses just because Prohibition was announced. Crime patterns can take many generations to wean from a family once ensnared. This is why the words of Euripides have such meaning – "the parents have eaten sour grapes, but it is the children's teeth that are set on edge to the third and fourth generation." Stopping this cycle of criminal dependency is very important before the onset of crime, or crime may become a systemic and familial pattern not easily combated. Indeed, the research shows that crime can be habit-forming and may lead habitual criminal offenders to more serious crimes if not controlled.

The problem with crime is that once it takes hold, it tends to keep a lock-grip on the individuals, particularly if they gravitate to more serious crimes. If individuals are introduced to crime when they are down and out, why is it rational to assume that when conditions improve they will abandon their easily learned ways of committing crime? The fact that criminals who are experienced in crime choose rationally not to seek law-abiding income activities in good times, does not necessarily mean that generally law-abiding individuals in good times are not tempted to augment their incomes by crime in bad times.

CRIME WAVES AND TIME LAGS

1. Tsunamis and tidal waves, and their parallel to crime waves

2. Crime wave time lags from economic event to crime wave

3. Consequence timelines

As mentioned previously, "When we speak of a crime wave, we are talking about a kind of social awareness of crime, crime brought to public attention."[42]

Some persons become 'criminals,' not because their basic motivation differs from that of other persons, but because their benefits and costs differ" (Becker 1976, 14). Factors that influence the benefits and costs of criminal activity include legal employment opportunities, deterrence (police, prisons, and capital punishment), education, social policies, and social insurance (that spending provided by the government to lessen the financial misery of individuals, a byproduct of which is reduced crime motivation likelihood).

Within this book, crimes that enrich a person, whether property crimes or violent crimes, are examined as the primary focus and these may include theft of property or violent, predatory, or retaliatory crimes such as arson, workplace violence, intimidation, drug and gang territorial disputes, kidnapping, extortion, etc. The author recognizes that there are many crimes that, by their very nature, do not enrich a person, and these types of crimes may include the litany of domestic disputes, hate crimes, and other forms of such crime. Quite naturally, these do not come into the focus of this book though it stands to reason that some hate crime may increase due to heightened tensions, animosity, and angst targeted at those the public thinks most likely responsible for their economic misery.

There is considerable debate among scholars and criminal justice leaders on the linkage between negative economic shocks and crime waves. Studies show that there is a strong positive association between crime and unemployment at the individual level, a clear positive association at the cross-sectional level that gets weaker as the level of geographical aggregation increases, but quite an inconsistent relationship over time (or time series data). Further, the underlying thesis of this book implies that as the magnitude of the negative economic shock increases, the data show stronger linkages between sizable negative economic shocks and crime waves. The recession of the early 1980s fostered an environment of increased street-level drug selling, which was further exacerbated by new entrants following "Black October" 1987, when the stock market crashed, crime surged, and illegal drug markets flourished flagrantly on our city streets.

In the late 1980s, the advent of 'crack', a derivative form of cocaine, made distribution easier, and in an environment of hard economic conditions in low-income neighborhoods, illegal drug selling created marginal market income opportunities for many young people seeking additional income beyond their lawful employment if they had any, as drug selling became a moon-lighting position for the majority of street-level drug dealers. In this environment the public policy mantra went from 'just say no' to drugs, to specific interventions, and thereafter the war on drugs was declared to curb drug and demand supply at the source points, and to renewed focus on demand reduction and intermediation through intensive treatment therapy. In our current situation, unless deliberate action is taken now to decriminalize marijuana and provide remote diversionary program for unemployed inner city youth, we are likely to witness another violent drug and crime wave in our city streets.

During the buildup of the 1974 deep recession, the crime rate was sufficiently high that it led to the abandonment of many city neighborhoods. Robberies skyrocketed throughout the 1970s, peaking in 1981. The dislocations caused by high densities of home foreclosures in our nation's cities may cause further decay and crime milieu in our day.

Another expected crime fall-out of our current economic condition is a rise in fraudulent bankruptcies, and insurance frauds including arson, corruption, and other risk-prone measures, to keep firms from bankruptcy. Enforcement efforts need to be increased to address the increased fraud opportunity and to reduce moral hazard and the temptation of the general population for committing fraud as a means of support or asset recovery in this economic downturn.

Summing up, we can say that crime is a multi-variant outcome of many factors including the spatial relationship of the offender, victim, crime object or target, time, place, laws, and specific settings. Economic conditions are not the only, or the strongest, determinants of crime. Criminal offenders may be impacted by many other variables that may include seemingly exogenous variables such as rising temperatures, moon light and other background features. Rising temperatures[43] are correlated with increasing crime rates,[44] and in some locations in New Orleans exceedingly hot weather is often correlated with increased homicides, shootings, and violence. So, the author is far from suggesting that economic factors are the exclusive contributor to the rise in forecasted crime, but the current economic misery cocktail impacting the human condition now is most likely to be responsible for changes in crime patterns going forward through this deep recession.

SHARP ECONOMIC CONTRACTIONS, RECESSIONS, AND DEPRESSIONS

In this book we are concerned particularly with what are known as "sharp" economic crises, those economic contractions that are most severe as their effects on economic misery are great and most noticeable; sharp crises, if unabated, can turn into economic depressions as experienced from 1929 to 1933, and relapsed in 1937 to 1938. The sharper, deeper, and broader contractions are more economically impactful.[45] Economic contractions can be characterized by the 3-Ds

– duration, depth, and diffusion.[46] Duration is measured in months. Depth is measured by percent decline in GDP and by the unemployment rate . Diffusion is measured by the percent of economy experiencing declining employment.

Economists typically define recessions as two quarters of negative Gross Domestic Product (GDP) growth. However, the National Bureau of Economic Research (NBER), the official body that calls economic cycles, defines recessions thus: "a recession is a significant decline in economic activity spread across the economy, lasting more than a few months, normally visible in real GDP, real income, employment, industrial production, and wholesale-retail sales."[47] Since the end of the Great Depression there have been eleven recessions[48] and their average duration is ten months from start to finish, or "peak to trough", and of these six have been "sharp" economic contractions. Besides the economic contractions lasting several quarters, in this book we are also concerned with economic shocks, such as the Black October 1987 where the stock market crashed, or singularly significant events such as the terrorism assault of the World Trade Center on Septmber 11, 2001.

Sharp Economic Contractions, Recessions, and Depressions (1929-2009)			
Negative Economic Contraction	Start (Peak)	End (Trough)	Months
1929 Stock Market Crash; Banking and Insurance Industry Collapse; Protectionism contracted trade by greater than half between 1929-1933; Worldwide Economic Depression	August 1929 (Q3)	March 1933 (Q1)	43
1937 Recession, also known as the "Roosevelt Recession"; contraction of New Deal Spending, and Taxation before unemployment was not resolved; Relapse into Economic Depression	May 1937 (Q2)	June 1938 (Q2)	13
Sharp Economic Recession; massive human toll and trauma, World War II, war ends; 8-15-45; contraction in spending; inflation concerns; monetary policy tightening	February 1945 (Q1)	October 1945 (Q4)	8
Sharp Economic Recession; Post Korean War Recession	July 1953 (Q2)	May 1954 (Q2)	10
Sharp Economic Recession	August 1957 (Q3)	April 1958 (Q2)	8

Sharp Economic Contractions, Recessions, and Depressions (1929-2009)			
Negative Economic Contraction	**Start (Peak)**	**End (Trough)**	**Months**
Sharp Economic Recession Quadruple Witching; (1) OPEC Oil Embargo I (1973); (2) Stock Market Crash (1973-74); (3) Vietnam War Spending Drag; (4) Stagflation	November 1973 (Q4)	March 1975 (Q1)	16
Mild Economic Recession; OPEC Oil Embargo II (1979); Iranian Hostage Crisis	January 1980 (Q1)	July 1980 (Q3)	6
Sharp Economic Recession Early 1980s Recession Inflation fighting; era of tight money supply	July 1981 (Q3)	November 1982	16
Black October 1987; stock market crash; real estate overleveraging and bank failures; RTC emerges			
Sharp Economic Recession; NASDAQ Bubble Burst; Terrorism of 9/11/01; Accounting Scandals (Enron, etc)	March 2000 (Q1)	November 2001 (Q4)	8
Sharp Economic Recession; Speculation Bubble Bursts; Housing market collapse; Credit-Default Swaps (CDO) and toxic illiquid debt; stock market crash; Rapid commodity inflation followed by rapid deflation in commodity prices	December 2007 (Q4)	Unknown?	16+ months and counting

When considering these economic contractions, it is not difficult to understand the macroeconomic impact these contractions have on consumer and business sentiment and, by extraction, on employment. Consider the following charts on percent of employment during the 1930s, and from 1954 until present for white males.

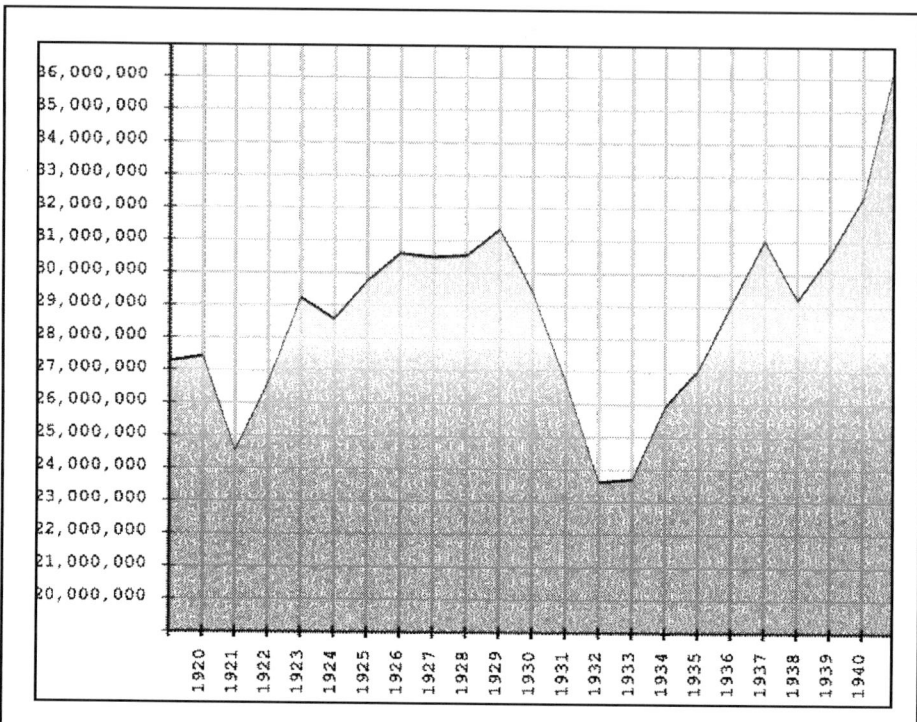

Source: Mark J. Lu Source: US Unemployment Rates During the Great Depression, Wiki Great Depression

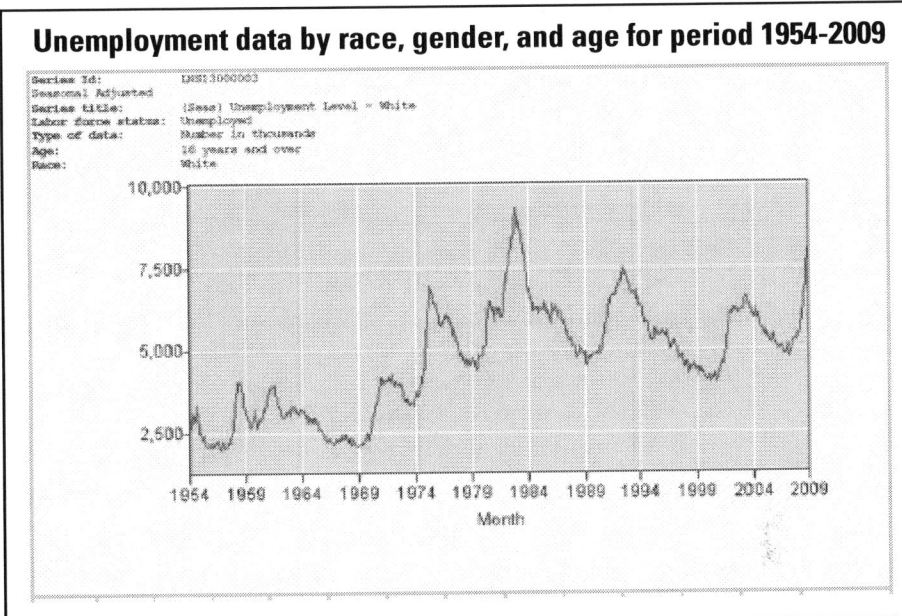

Unemployment data by race, gender, and age for period 1954-2009

Series Id:	LNS14000003
Seasonal Adjusted Series title:	(Seas) Unemployment Rate - White
Labor force status:	Unemployment rate
Type of data:	Percent
Age:	16 years and over
Race:	White

Source: US Bureau of Labor Statistics; http://data.bls.gov/PDQ/servlet/SurveyOutputServlet;

CRIMINAL JUSTICE DATA IN THE PAST 30 YEARS

It is true that every sharp economic contraction since 1954 has been followed by a crime wave. However, criminal justice researchers in the past 30 years have observed that with increasing expenditures on criminal justice manpower and programs, and increased drug related arrests and incarcerations, there has been a noticeable decline in violent and property crimes, particularly since 1993, emerging from the recession of 1991. During this 30 year period there were crime spikes that occurred during recessions and sharp crises; however, these crises did not lead to economic depression, and the more noticeable evidences of crime were in increases in illegal drug trafficking and street-level sales. History will record that these spikes were ameliorated in time by continued spending on targeted prevention, intervention, intensive treatment and adjudication programs. Further, the run-up in criminal justice expenditures also parallels the run-up in the US market during the rapid technology growth and prosperity of the mid to late 1990s, and this prosperity continued by massive switching of speculation bubbles from NASDAQ stocks prior to the NASDAQ bubble burst, and they switched to a massive housing speculation bubble made available by cheap money (at low interest rates) and federal programs encouraging homeownership for low-income and moderate-income households.

The charts below show the concomitant increase in U.S. criminal justice expenditures at the federal, state and local level; increasing corrections population; increase in drug-related arrests of adults; and general reduction in violent and property crime. There have been many studies performed to determine 'what works' in criminal justice programming and the reader is directed to Sherman (2002) **Evidence-Based Crime Prevention** for specific programs and successful outcome based research.

What is most noticeable to this author as an economist viewing the data at a macro level is the strong relationship between criminal justice expenditure and reductions in crime, even during times of recent economic contractions. In this author's view, what challenges law enforcement in our present economic crisis is the dangerous trend of state and local governments reducing law enforcement expenditure due to current budget crises on grounds (using data from past periods) showing decreases in crime during periods of relative economic affluence, just as these criminal justice social control mechanisms are about to be challenged by a surge wave of crime related to our current sharp economic contraction that will surely come.

On January 31, 2009, the Police Executive Research Forum (PERF) released results from a survey of 233 law enforcement police chiefs, including many of the major city chiefs and found the following: "Nearly two out of three police agencies responding to a new survey said they are currently making plans for cutting their budgets, according to the Police Executive Research Forum (PERF), a Washington, D.C.-based independent research organization made up of local and state police officials. And 44 percent of the police departments report increases in certain types of crime which they believe can be attributed to the economic crisis… 63 percent said they are preparing plans for an overall cut in their total funding for the next fiscal year. In a large majority of cases, the police officials indicated that they are not merely making contingency plans or thinking about cuts as an academic exercise; of those who said they are planning cuts, 88 percent said they have already been told to expect cuts by their mayor, city council, or other governing authority."

People simply cannot close their eyes, and hold hands over their ears, and ignore the sights and sounds of current negative economic events, and hope that by decreasing criminal justice expenditures (and services) they will provide an adequate safety net for their citizens as they face rising demand of criminal justice services, and find themselves unprepared for the surge wave of increasing numbers of likely offenders. It was true when Rudyard Kipling first spoke of the wolf and its strength, and it is true now; the strength of the wolf is the pack, and likely offenders are emboldened to commit crimes when their numbers greatly outweigh social control resources. Research shows this and common sense tells us that one cannot simply allow a rising tide of likely offenders to go unattended, or indeed, leave the criminal justice system short-handed as the likely offenders may overrun the social control resources designed to defend us in times of non-crisis. Perhaps this is yet another reason why hand gun sales have skyrocketed during this economic recession.

Felson and Clark[50] described a 'routine activity' approach to crime prevention wherein three elements must exist for a crime to occur: (1) a likely offender – anybody who has reason to commit a crime – (2) a suitable target—anybody or anything of interest to the likely offender – and the absence of a capable guardian, the individual, agency, or institution that maintains order of place. For those known to be repeat offenders, additional supervision is required in the form of an 'intimate handler.' The absence of the capable guardian and intimate handlers create a condition ripe for crime when the rising numbers of likely offenders may pick and prey on vulnerable likely targets.

That economics and crime are invariably linked together is a reality. The fact that these variables do not run up and down together in proportional units suggests that there is some 'stickiness' to crime making that once started, if not abated in early onset stages, criminal behavior is habit-forming and may be difficult for repeat offenders to entirely clear from their behavior even when good economic times return. This pattern evidences itself repeatedly in the history of organized crime.

3   October 1929 Market Collapse and the Ensuing Crime Wave

"The strong do what they can and the weak suffer what they must."
– Thucydides, *History of the Peloponnesian War,* Book IV, 108.

"No one can possibly have lived through the Great Depression without being scarred by it. No amount of experience since the depression can convince someone who has lived through it that the world is safe economically."
– Isaac Asimov

The scene and setup:

- The Hoover Era – Roaring Twenties and the age of over consumption

- Prohibition and civil disobedience

- Speculation and leverage bust the banks

- The bubble bursts, the market collapses

- Run on banks, rising unemployment, and other misery indicators

- Economic misery index

- Leading economic indicators

- Animal spirits and mob action

- Oil swindling

- Police corruption

- Prohibition "Desperados"

- Public enemies

- Taking the market away from organized crime – lessons learned from the abandonment of alcohol prohibition

- Beer-Bill passage and release of small-time operators from jail

- The 1930s timeline of market collapse, fear, crime wave, and recovery

Sharp negative economic crises like a stock market crash, natural disaster, war, terrorist attack or other civil unrest, can create disequilibrium between normal operating requirements for law and order control systems, and capacity overload of these same systems during sharp crises, and this happened during the 1920s, during the run-up to, and during the Great Depression. Economic misery—that cocktail of increasing unemployment, reduced purchasing power, whether by inflation, or deflation and reduced asset-based purchasing power—can create situations which, if unaddressed, may gradually result in conditions where people turn a blind eye to petty crime, and if left unchecked for long, these crimes can turn into more serious crimes. Essentially, increased crime opportunity is found to be linked to increasing civil disobedience with moral Robin Hoods turning to petty crimes to feed their families and meet their needs. However, if these forays into crime remain unchecked, these same individuals can become ensnared more deeply into serious crime, creating graver problems for the society. This is a vital lesson people learned—and learned the hard way—from the Great Depression.

From the early colonial period through the late nineteenth century, the primary role of law enforcement had been community-service-oriented policing, doing such things as feeding the hungry, caring for the homeless and the travelers passing through their towns, and returning drunks to their homes. Though initiated in the 1870's, investigations didn't become a major aspect of police function until the crime wave of the 1920s.[51]

The age of Prohibition in the 1920s and early1930s was the period that fostered unintended consequences of public policy in terms of crime, corruption, and violence. Strife between states and federal law enforcement became common. Relations were also much strained by conflict between political machines, graft, and diverse local reactions that ran the local crime sets. Where liquor was considered evil, the federal agent was glorified. Where liquor was accepted, the federal agent was an unwanted intruder. This division of public interests created an environment rich in corruption, gangsters, excessive violence and murders, intimidation and coercive tactics.

It also fostered an environment where localized criminals became regionalized by making broader networks beyond their local geographies. Policing was slow to recognize or adapt to these events. Bootleggers and organized crime had better technology (faster cars), organization, and communications that gave them the leg-up on outwitting law enforcement. Another problem highlighted during this period was the consequences of the passage of a law that a great number of people objected to – Prohibition. This opened up a period of civil disobedience and tolerance for crime, as many people frequented the liquor houses and clubs. With the collapse of the stock market in 1929, greater crime opportunity presented itself as an ever increasing number of likely offenders overwhelmed the crime control structures built for a quieter time.

The Great Depression was sparked by the collapse of the stock market in 1929, and the downward pressure on the market continued for some four years, before forming not a 'V' bottom with rapid rise back upward, but more of an 'L' bottom where a bottom was found but little upward pressure seemed to be in sight to restore former market ranges. John Kenneth Galbraith (1954) wrote a seminal book on this period, *The Great Crash, 1929*,[53] where he provides a wonderful narrative of the build-up to the crash through unbridled optimism, leverage, risk taking, and financial market development, the risks placed on the economy by unchecked speculation and leverage, and the play-by-play downfall of the economy that occurred through the Great Depression. It is very instructive to read it, and it is highly recommended as a source of crucial information on the background of what happened, and the consequent results of the actions or inactions.

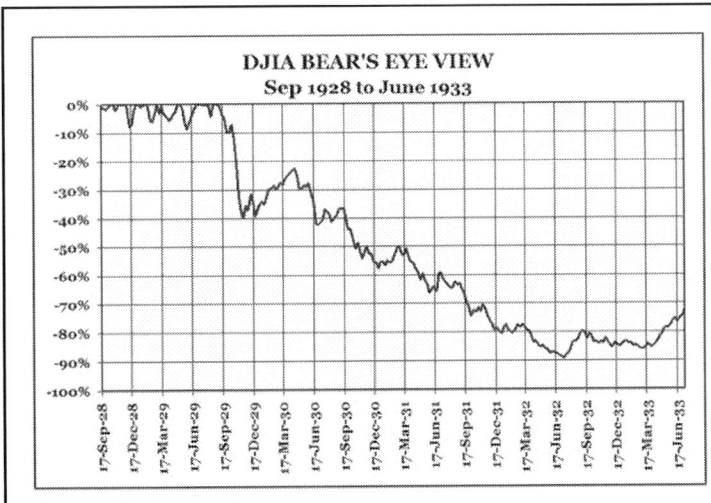

DJIA BEAR'S EYE VIEW
Sep 1928 to June 1933

This chart shows the US Stock Market crash from 1929 to 1923 and the reduction in overall stock price equity value, which fell some -89% to the trough some 3 years from the onset of the market crash. The chart is normalized with "0" being the peak for DJIA closing prices.

Source: Mark J. Lundeen

It took 12 years for the stock market to return to its pre-crash 1929 level. During that period of time the economic system collapsed with great hardship on people in North America, Europe and Asia. It is usual today to look back at this period to reflect on what happened. One author, Lawrence Reed, put it this way:

> How bad was the Great Depression? Over the four years from 1929 to 1933, production of the nation's factories, mines and utilities fell by more than half. People's real disposable incomes dropped by 28 percent. Stock prices collapsed to one-tenth of the pre-crash height. The number of unemployed Americans rose from 1.6 million in 1929 to 12.8 million in 1933. One of every four workers was out of a job at the Depression's nadir, and ugly rumors of revolt simmered for the first time since the Civil War.[54]

During that era corruption was rampant in the major cities. Crime organizations ran the politics and controlled the polling places. A newspaper article from April 10, 1928, "Chicago votes in terror,"[55] printed in the Columbus Evening Dispatch, describes the situation in plain words: "in the first four hours of Chicago's voting in the primary election today the following disorders were reported to police:

- One alderman was released after he was said to have been kidnapped

- One political worker was shot

- Four election workers were kidnapped

- Three election workers were beaten

- Seven reports were received of ballot box stuffing

- Eleven polling places reportedly invaded by hoodlums

- The entire election board, officials and clerks, of a precinct police place on the West side were reported kidnapped by gangsters today and the ballot boxes wrecked."

It is wickedly ironic that as time passes on, the more things change, the more they stay the same in terms of political corruption. Is it any wonder how an Illinois governor would be accused of doing business as usual with his 'pay for play' scheme as he attempted to sell the open Senate seat vacated by President Obama on his election to the U.S. presidency? I think one blogger captured the sentiment best with these words: "Those who think Rod Blagojevich is the worst person in the world should be careful. He's not even the worst person in

Chicago or Illinois. He's just the fall guy for the political system that doesn't like all this attention on the way business is done and the game is played."[56] This blog provokes many questions for further exploration, but that is beyond the scope of this book.

Suffice it to say that there were many grave crime events during the Great Depression that marked turning points in American history where the crimes were so heinous and violent that the public outcry changed the course of history as people began fighting back at what they had turned a blind eye to. Arguably, the most serious crime associated with Prohibition was the St. Valentine's Day Massacre that included the execution style murders of six Chicago bootleggers and one wannabe groupie by rival gangsters disguised as police. The massacre occurred on February 14, 1929, and sparked a public outcry that made a turning point for Chicago law enforcement; now Prohibition, speakeasies, and corruption were seen to be causing a greater problem.[57]

Beyond the bootleggers and organized criminals, there were the disorganized, dislocated, wanderers. Homeless, wandering men, dislocated and unemployed, wandered the countryside following railroads and other highways, looking for work. Family abandonment, youth runaways, and other disruptions in the family unit led many young people in the early years of the Depression to leave home in search of work and new frontiers, striking out on their own. In Los Angeles, free flophouses and midnight missions gave asylum in 1932 to more than two hundred thousand. Many homeless left the cities in search of opportunities elsewhere. For instance, along the Missouri Pacific Railroad, homeless men and freight-car migrants increased from 13,000 in 1929 to nearly 200,000 during the Depression. This was not a one-of-a-kind phenomenon in this era. By 1932, most railroads added additional box cars and left the doors open to prevent individuals from breaking into "sealed cars". Over time, these homeless nomads were viewed by railroad operators, social workers, and police, as neither criminals nor vagrants, but petty criminals stealing only for food and, excepting the circumstances of the Depression, would have been law abiding and in school or at work.[58]

It was against this backdrop that Franklin Roosevelt spoke at the Governors Conference in 1929 and told the governors in attendance that the states must accept the responsibility for enforcement, clean out their antiquated machinery of justice, meet new kinds of crime with new kinds of laws, and initiate these reforms in all states, not just a few, so that geography cannot be used as a tool by criminals.

The economic misery of the Great Depression exacerbated crime conditions and new forms of crime emerged. Moreover, as the government took control of the illegal vice markets, organized crime looked for other revenue-creating crimes. By the summer of 1933, a rash of kidnappings occurred in different pockets in the country. The targets of the kidnappings were bankers, financiers, organized crime family members, corporation executives, and politicians. The federal government responded with new legislation and a federal police force to handle kidnapping cases, as well as legislation focused on anti-racketeering.

Besides kidnapping, crime organizations moved into other crimes such as selling drugs and bank robberies. Racketeering became an additional focus. The federal government thrust was going after the most heinous public offenders' labeled 'public enemies.' John Dillinger, Baby Face Nelson, Pretty Boy Floyd, Machine Gun Kelly, and the Barker-Karpis gangs and criminal co-conspirators became public enemies as they, through their violent actions, claimed too much public attention, popularizing the notion of a crime wave that must be combated, and this development turned a whole nation against the desperados. Ironically, of the gangs mentioned above, only the Dillinger and the Barker-Karpis gangs were highly organized, while the others operated as gangs but were more frequently co-criminal conspirators.

It was widely believed that the severe economic conditions and unemployment would create a crime wave. So, in addition to going after serious criminal offenders, Roosevelt had a desire to work on the social aspects of crime. Importantly, Roosevelt tied "crime to economic recovery" and said that the foundations of "agriculture, industry, and finance had been secured, and now we must eradicate the crime menace."

When economists examine crime, they frequently use a theoretical assumption that criminals act 'rationally' to maximize their reward, and minimize their risk. Consequently, criminals frequently search for soft targets of crime opportunity that hold treasures that cannot be nailed down, or that can be pried loose. Economic hardship appeared to usher in more brazen attempts of crime. Some soft targets that were identified within the US were seeking to steal or swindle the oil property rights of Native Americans, and more precisely, the Osage Indian Tribe.

Criminals from outside the tribal community used multiple means to swindle and cash in on the new found Osage wealth by marrying into a family that had land rights, and then separating the remaining relatives from the endowment through multiple means including murder. This tactic took a shocking and heinous turn in 1921 when a white man named Ernest Burkhart married into a land-grant family and with the help of his uncle and brother conspired to murder those who would inherit the land rights. This became known as the Osage Indian Murders and the case went so far as to receive attention from federal law enforcement. This violence finally caused Congress to pass legislation limiting inheritance of land rights to only those with Osage Indian blood and required those with no degree of Osage Indian blood to sell their shares to the tribe. Today, land rights have become split up among the Osage descendants of those who originally possessed them, although it is estimated that 25% of land rights are owned by non-Osage people. [4] The social consequences of the oil boom for the Osage Nation have been depicted in John Joseph Mathews' semi-autobiographical novel *Sundown* (1934).

Mark Twain frequently quoted Disraeli's saying that there are liars, damn liars, and statisticians.[61] That is the problem with examining crime data from the Great Depression era. Mainstream criminologists examine sterile statistical data and make general assumptions about human behavior and crime based on this data. However, frequently, there are misnomers in the data that render the conclusions of the data invalid. Consider the category of crime called "floating bodies," under which the Ecorse Police Department of Michigan recorded dead human bodies pulled from the river that float down from Detroit and drifted north in the early 1990s. This had the effect of hiding the data; as there is no Uniform Crime Report (UCR) category called "floating bodies" this item is unlikely to get into the local UCR homicide statistics.

Unfortunately, crime data from the 1930s have been, in a more heinous manner, scrubbed of real meaning, leaving the blatantly erroneous picture that crime actually went down during the Great Depression—leading some to falsely assume that we should expect no crime wave from the current economic downturn. A report that was broadcast on National Public Radio[62] on November 20, 2008, titled, "Experts: Bad Economies Don't Cause Crime Waves" concludes in these words:

> The Depression years had very little crime. "With the economy's current troubles, many people assume a crime wave is just around the corner. But criminologists say that's just an American myth. Just look at the 1920s," says David Kennedy, director of the Center for Crime Prevention at John Jay College of Criminal Studies, "It was a period of booming economic prosperity, the Roaring '20s, and very high crime," he says. The 1950s and '60s were the same. The economy was great, but crime rates rose every single year.

Where is it written that there must be a linear relationship to crime and econom-ic misery such that when economic misery goes up, crime goes up, and vice versa in equal proportions? The fact that unemployed and underemployed persons may commit more crimes during times of heightened economic misery, does not necessarily mean that these same individuals would choose not to commit crimes of opportunity in times of prosperity, especially if during their economic misery they were exposed to crime opportunity, committed crime, and have become habitual criminals. Criminal habits are hard to break once formed. Both criminal justice and social psychology literature report a consistent theme that exposure to, or participation in, criminal activity, however minor, can create a baneful pattern of crime-making, wherein people may become habitually disposed to more serious criminal activity as a way of life. Such individuals may not be expected to return to lawful ways during economic good times, but might see increased crime opportunity in times of plenty. Indeed, organized crime did not "go legit" when Prohibition was vacated, but rather adapted to the times and chose additional crimes such as public corruption, fraud, extortion, kidnap-pings, and other racketeering schemes to take the place of bootlegging activities. Consequently, the fact that some criminals do not reduce their criminal behavior in times of prosperity at the same ratio that they increased criminal activity during times of severe economic misery does not negate a linkage or relationship; it just means that the relationship is not linear.

There is a meaningful difference between crime and what is reported as crime, just as there is a difference between the past and history of the past. The past is the past, but the history is what is written. Not only was there a huge crime wave that started in the 1920s and spread with astonishing speed and reach in the 1930s with the onset of the Great Depression, but the crimes were so severe that it overwhelmed the existing crime control structures designed to maintain law and order during more peaceful times. Crime peaked in 1933 and only started retreating with the onset of new crime control forces, institutions, laws, and New Deal programs. Government leaders created a strategic crime control plan of sweeping breadth that will easily rival the Paulsen Financial Plan of today. In this context we should recall that the U.S. government took giant strides to combat crime in the 1930s, including the strengthening of the FBI; elimination of Pro-hibition, stripping organized crime of illegal gains from liquor sales; and, most formidably, the creation of the Civilian Conservation Corps (CCC), a program that served to greatly reduce the likely offender population by removing nearly 25% of the "at-risk" unemployed young males from the inner cities from 1933 through the remainder of the Great Depression. Not only did the CCC provide valuable employment opportunities for the "at-risk" population, the program simultaneously served as an effective crime demand reduction initiative for the young male unemployed population living in the cities who were sent to rural work camps managed by the U.S. Army.

When some historians look at the Great Depression era, they mistakenly misinterpret facts when examining crime data that was both underreported because of the sheer size of petty crimes, and underrepresented in that 25% of the likely offender population of at risk unemployed males were extracted from the population and sent to remote CCC camps. The facts about crime during the Great Depression that are not in dispute are these: "youthful crimes against property generally rose when relief measures slackened; and offenders under twenty-one made up a third of all arrests for major crimes in New York City in 1939. Including both young and old, the prison population of the United States numbered a hundred and eighty thousand in 1939, an increase of nearly two fifths during the decade."[63]

There is a strong linkage between crime on the one hand and negative economic shocks, economic hardship, unemployment, and loss of purchasing power on the other—and the relationship is stronger with more significant economic shocks. The crime wave that was prevalent during the 1920s and early 1930s was significant and brutal, and was only brought under control after the strengthening of the federal powers of the FBI and the extraction of serious habitual offenders from the general population along with a large cohort of young unemployed men who had the greatest propensity for crime. Modern researchers fail to understand the significant crime environment of the 1930s and falsely claim that statistical reports of reduced crime during the Depression showed a natural condition. But, in retrospect, we realize that crime went down during the Depression precisely because over 500,000 unemployed young men with the greatest propensity for crime involvement were taken out of the cities and placed into 2300+ work camps managed by the Civilian Conservation Corps (CCC).

The CCC statistics show that in 1934, young men between the ages of 18-24 comprised only 6% of the population, but accounted for 51% of arrests for auto theft, robbery, burglary, rape, and assault; one-third of larceny arrests, and two out of every ten homicide arrests. It was necessary for the U.S. Government to proactively remove a significant portion of the unemployed population at greatest risk of crime involvement, and they were duly placed in work camps in rural areas managed by the CCC. This was the primary reason why crime decreased—there were far fewer likely offenders. The impact of a huge targeted diversion program, taking the unemployed males at the greatest risk out of the city and sending them to camps in the rural areas, had a huge, explicit impact as it reduced the number of likely offenders significantly.

It may be instructive to look at the history of the CCC. It was created by President Franklin Roosevelt on March 23, 1933, just three weeks after his inauguration. The CCC would operate as many as 2,650 rural work camps engaging up to 500,000 young high-risk unemployed males. The "enrollees" were removed from the general population and were geographically isolated so that they could not be a risk to the people remaining in the cities. The camps operated with military discipline under the supervision of the U.S. Army. Free time was provided for enrollees but generally there was no access or transportation to leave the work areas. These camps provided the geographical containment of a prison through their isolation. Wector (1948) described the CCC as follows: "The CCC was voluntary, but its discipline and spirit were mildly military, though drilling, saluting and marching were taboo. The war department directed the building of camps and also supervised the boys' health, morale and welfare. The administration of the corps, however, became wholly civilian."[64]

Beyond targeting aid for populations at greatest risk of crime, President Roosevelt also targeted aid to the general working population through national infrastructure goals – with projects of sufficient length and size to last through the Depression era. President Roosevelt spent some $11.4 billion in Works Progress Administration projects that built useful roads, bridges, utilities, public buildings, etc. From 1935 to 1943, the WPA put 8.5 million people to work and through these projects paved 651,087 miles of roadway, erected or repaired 124,031 bridges, built 125,110 public buildings, and constructed 853 airport runways.[65] The challenge for Roosevelt then, and Obama now, has been to create meaningful employment opportunities without crowding out free market enterprise; goals must be far-sighted enough to get us through the economic depression, but reachable enough that the programs can wind down when the economy recovers. Further, wherever possible, goals should be leveraged with private sector initiative, enabling the private sector to both fund and benefit from participation in projects, thereby extending the ability of government to provide stimulus in difficult economic times.

So in the end, both the WPA and the CCC were instrumental in helping the federal government reduce the 'demand' for crime; i.e., reduce crime opportunity by purchasing 'social insurance' – the investment that would be made on the public works projects, and the same spending of which would increase economic well-being and reduce the likelihood of crime for specific individuals and families. This relationship was recently examined by several researchers who found that "relief spending during the 1930s lowered property crime in a statistically and economically significant way."[66] In an examination of 83 American cities, these scholars found that for every 10 percent increase in per capita relief spending, there was an associated lowering of the crime rates by roughly 5.6 to 10 percent at the margin. This typically implies at least two things: (1) there was a need for purchasing 'social insurance' to reduce economic misery and the demand for crime; (2) researchers examining the Great Depression cannot look at criminal justice data without considering the huge and sweeping impact of the New Deal Programs.

Franklin Roosevelt, in an address on April 12, 1939, spoke about the crime prevention drive in these terms: "[T]hrough a broad program of social welfare, we struck at the very roots of crime itself... Our citizens who have been out of work in the last six years have not needed to steal in order to keep from starving. Of course, when we instituted those [New Deal] activities we did not have in mind merely the narrow purpose of preventing crime. However, nobody who knows how demoralizing the effects of enforced idleness may be, will be inclined to doubt that crime prevention has been an important by-product of our effort to provide our needy unemployed citizens with the opportunity to earn by honest work at least the bare necessities of life."[67]

Trends in Relief Spending for 114 U.S. Cities, 1930 to 1940				
Year	Unemployment Rate (Entire U.S.)	Per capita relief spending (1967)	Annual average relief benefits as a percentage of annual manufacturing earnings	Federal share of relief spending
1930	9.0	$3.74		
1931	16.3	$9.06		
1932	24.1	$18.06		21%
1933	25.2	$29.71	21.7%	51.8%
1934	22.0	$47.93	31.2%	78.9%
1935	20.3	$51.03	33.3%	78.9%
1936	17.0	$61.78	42.4%	74.7%
1937	14.3	$52.24	37.6%	72.1%
1938	19.1	$69.61	39.3%	62.0%
1939	17.2	$63.32	38.3%	62.5%
1940	14.6	$52.93	34.9%	57.4%

68

Besides stimulating the demand to create more jobs, Roosevelt also worked to narrow the scope and focus of law enforcement to those crimes of greatest consequence to the country. Combating organized crime and civil disobedience were a few of the aims of Prohibition. The declassification of crime, or Repeal of Prohibition, along with the de facto non-reporting of petty crimes during the era, allowed the government to redirect law enforcement efforts to the most serious crimes and offenders. Within weeks of Inauguration, President Franklin Roosevelt put forward his "Beer-Bill" message to Congress, using an economic argument that $35 per barrel of beer could accrue to $100 million in annual tax revenue, and at the same time, take money away from the crime organizations. Along with the bill, Roosevelt advocated pardon and release from jail or prison to low-consequence criminal offenders engaged in small-time bootleg operations, as it would relieve the criminal justice system.[69] On December 5, 1933, Congress passed the 21st Amendment, which repealed the 18th Amendment, ending Prohibition. This bold action enabled scarce law enforcement resources to focus on larger crime problems, reduced civil disobedience, and repatriated untaxed monies from bootleggers and organized crime and turned it into the U.S. general treasury. Such bold action could easily be repeated today on similar grounds with marijuana, a controlled substance that is trafficked illegally on the streets and college dorms, and that employs the underbelly of organized and disorganized crime in America.

New York City Deputy Police Commissioner John A. Leach, right, watches agents pour liquor into a sewer following a raid during the height of Prohibition [70]

Library of Congress Photo

Beyond combating illegal alcohol sales, Roosevelt focused on more serious criminal offenses that exacerbated with increasing economic misery in the Great Depression. During the Great Depression, violent crime increased with able support from organized crime and disorganized criminals that included "kidnappers, gangsters, racketeering, and collective violence."[71] Therefore, a core crime control strategy of this era was targeting and incapacitating the most serious violent offenders.

From the crash in 1929, it took some four years to get crime under control. By the end of 1933, Al Capone was in prison, Prohibition was ending, and President Roosevelt's New Deal – beyond creating jobs – had declared 'war on crime.' The strengthened Federal Bureau of Investigation (FBI) was empowered to attack the organized crime problem. A new problem emerged for the criminal organizations as these 'federal outsiders' did not turn a blind eye to the gangster lawlessness as did the Chicago police or other local law enforcement agencies in the past. These G-men, without the ties that bind or cause men to turn a blind-eye to crime, were highly effective in rooting out the most serious criminal offenders. However, it is to be remembered that while the face of crime may be taken from the limelight, so long as criminal opportunity exists, and the market-place is not tended, new criminals will take their place; indeed, it is frequently the case that the upstart criminals turn in their older competitors to law enforcement, thereby clearing the market using any means available.

There was more to the crime story in the Great Depression than the headlines on Prohibition or the round-up of the Desperados. Higher population density was equated with higher crime rates. More crime occurred in the cities in areas with diverse heterogeneity of populations and incomes, and in areas with too many unemployed young males. Those seeking a safe haven from crime victimization were more likely to find peace in the less densely populated areas or rural areas. In reviewing Depression-era crime patterns, Block (1949) found that the closer the proximity to the farm or the small village a certain community is, the less likely is the possibility of producing rising rates of major and minor criminal offenses.[72] From 1934 onwards, throughout the Great Depression, crime rates subsided as programs designed to address the underlying conditions of crime opportunity were put into place.

However, it must be remembered that once-serious criminal behavior becomes entrenched, like taking the cowboy out of the country, it is difficult to take the man out of the mob when this has become his way of life. This same theme is pronounced repeatedly in the criminal justice literature where once-casual criminals of opportunity become more serious habitual criminals, if their pattern of law-breaking goes unchecked, and they are not turned back to law-abiding behavior swiftly. Wector (1948) captured some of this in his book on the Great Depression when he says: "The most spectacular crime wave, which reached its crest between 1932 and 1934, had nothing to do with juvenile delinquency and bore only an oblique relation to the Depression. It was the work of racketeers turning from rum-running and other activities of waning profit to the kidnapping of children and adults. An aroused Congress passed severe laws against interstate abductions in 1932 and 1934, with penalties involving death if the victim were harmed."[73]

The most famous of kidnapping cases involved the kidnapping and murder of the famous Aviator, Charles Lindberg's son, just 3 years old, Charles Augustus Lindbergh, Jr. In 1932, the toddler was abducted from his family home in East Amwell, New Jersey. H.L. Mencken, the famous newspaperman, called the kidnapping and trial "the biggest story since the Resurrection."[74] The culprit was found, tried, and executed, and an outcome of the trial was a new law making kidnapping a federal crime in the United States.

Take just one look at the border between the U.S. and Mexico today and one can see reflections of the same malady, with reported kidnappings on the rise, and untold numbers of unreported kidnappings happening right in our own backyard.

In review, the following measures were necessary for the crime wave to be abated during the Great Depression:

1. regime change – laws were changed, structure of response, new criminal justice institutions formed (e.g. FBI was created, Prohibition ended, etc);

2. serious habitual offenders causing greatest crime impact were targeted and incapacitated;

3. crime demand reduction programs were instituted to reduce the pool of likely offenders, particularly those most vulnerable to crime opportunity;

4. broad scale employment programs were designed as crime demand reduction programs, increasing the outlook of normalcy and the value of law abiding behavior, with the government investing in the economy, providing meaningful employment that led to contributions to household incomes, eventually leading to a decrease in need and an increase in the opportunity cost of illegally produced income.

We can expect that some of these very solutions will be taken up to address the coming crime wave in our day. However, we will need to look with new eyes as several key conditions have changed. Our population size is greater. Our technology, access, and speed of transportation and communication are greater now. We are more interconnected than ever before with the rest of world.

4 September 2007-2009 Market Collapse and the Coming Crime Wave

"Burgeoning quantities of long-term derivatives contracts and the massive amount of uncollateralized receivables" reflect a "megacatastrophic risk."
"Derivatives are financial weapons of mass destruction, carrying dangers that, while now latent, are potentially lethal."
– Warren Buffett, 2002 Letter to Shareholders, Berkshire Hathaway

The scene and setup:

- The Clinton / Bush Era – and unbounded possibilities of the Internet

- Internet age, market bubbles, irrational exuberance, and moral hazard

- An impatient consumer, financing the American dream, taking the waiting out of wanting

- Homes as ATMs

- Moral hazard

- Household leverage and declining housing prices

- Credit default swaps and swindles

- Paralyzing myth – too big to fail

- Paralyzing myth – the government will bail me out

- Paralyzing realization – crime pays, the bag holders are the honest people; those who should not have gotten loans are rewarded, while those who were credit-worthy and repaid their loans were shafted with lower housing prices and future tax burden

- Paralyzing realization – the stimulus package does not help me personally
- The Newest Deal with ever-changing strategy
- Nationalization of banks
- Politics and puppetry, big government returns with a vengeance

In this chapter the author reviews the setup to the coming crime wave, the economic crises we find now, and the glide path of economic misery leading up to the crime wave, and hopefully some sign of a way out.

The columnist James B. Kelleher wrote poignantly on September 18, 2008: "When historians write about the current crisis, much of the blame will go to the slump in the housing and mortgage markets, which triggered the losses, layoffs and liquidations sweeping the financial industry. But credit default swaps – complex derivatives originally designed to protect banks from deadbeat borrowers – are adding to the turmoil."[75]

"This was supposedly a way to hedge risk," says Ellen Brown, the author of the book *Web of Debt*: "I'm sure their predictive models were right as far as the risk of the things they were insuring against. But what they didn't factor in was the risk that the sellers of this protection wouldn't pay…That's what we're seeing now."

In 2002, billionaire investor Warren Buffett called derivatives a "time bomb." He asked his listeners to be wary of these "financial weapons of mass destruction" and directed the insurance arm of his Berkshire Hathaway Inc. to exit the business. In the Berkshire Hathaway annual letter to its shareholders, one reads this grave warning from Buffet: "We try to be alert to any sort of megacatastrophic risk, and that posture may make us unduly apprehensive about the burgeoning quantities of long-term derivatives contracts and the massive amount of uncollateralized receivables that are growing alongside. In our view, however, derivatives are financial weapons of mass destruction, carrying dangers that, while now latent, are potentially lethal."[76]

Gerald Celente wrote: *"Beyond the $1 trillion subprime problem that has been erroneously targeted as the prime culprit behind the credit crisis are more serious financial catastrophes that are barely reported, mostly overlooked and cannot be remedied. The Fed cannot print enough money to paper over the $531.2 trillion in deriva-*

tives and credit swaps, the trillions in the overbuilt commercial real estate market ready to collapse, the multi-trillions in leveraged buyouts going bust, and other exotic financial instruments that have turned toxic. Yesterday's lowering of interest rates and **the continual Fed action to flood the markets with money will lead to an era of hyper-inflation, the likes of which no living American has ever seen. Gold prices shot up some $24 after being down over $20 earlier in the day. We continue to forecast gold $2000**. *And once again, we urge you to take precautionary measures in view of a worsening global market meltdown."* [77]

The current sharp economic contraction that was so noticeable commencing September 15, 2008, actually started in November 2007, the peak of the bull market run. What economists now call our current Deep Recession started in December 2007, and when we emerge from this crisis period the historians will surely rename it the Second Great Depression. Our current great economic crises did not start with a particular event, but the steps downward have been exacerbated by seminal events such as the collapse of the houses of Lehman, AIG, Fannie Mae, Freddie Mac, Merrill Lynch, Countrywide, etc., that created their own economic shocks with rapid loss of confidence, credit contraction, and runs on equity. These events can be viewed graphically on the chart showing our current economic descent from November 2007 through March 2009, with no forecast in sight of a confirmed bottom. While we should expect bear market rallies, they may be short lived as retesting the lows is almost a foregone conclusion held by technical market analysts. What is also not in dispute is that we are in uncharted territory with our only point of comparison being the Great Depression of the 1930s.

So how did this happen? What can we do to arrest the pattern? What other societal costs will come as a result of this sharp economic contraction? How can we keep this from happening again?

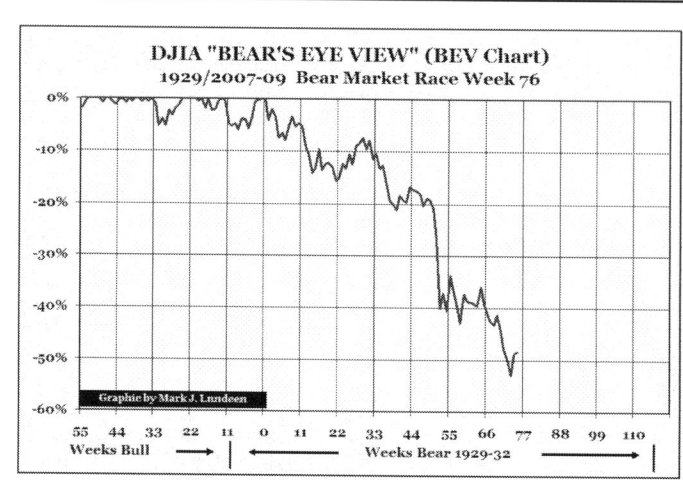

DJIA "BEAR'S EYE VIEW" (BEV Chart)
1929/2007-09 Bear Market Race Week 76

This chart shows the parallel Bear Market tracks of the 2007-2009 Great Depression, wherein Equities (Stocks) have lost over 50% of their value in the current Bear market. Outside of the 1929 Stock Market Crash and Great Depression, no other recession has broken the -40% barrier until now.

Source: Mark J. Lundeen

THE TIPPING POINT

Concomitant events

- The sub-prime market collapse[1]

- The CDS shoe drops, credit contracts, banks fail, deleveraging accelerates, commodities and equities fall, and the market collapse begins

- Banks do not trust each other and credit facilities shrink

- Commercial loan defaults

- Regional bank defaults

- Fear takes new place on the front page and television sets

- Federal action necessary, but insufficient as we blindly go where no market has gone before

- Capitalism fails as an unregulated entity in the crisis

- Trillions of dollars of equity and bonds unwind, taking cash out of economy

- Central bankers and national governments intervene to support banks and financial industry

---

[1] Ironically, it is the sub-prime loan candidate, the largely undercapitalized, low or moderate income homeowner that is placed out of their home that becomes the greatest risk of unbridled crime opportunity when eating is more important than adhering to laws and social rules

TRUST BROKEN, CONFIDENCE LOST

- Emergency management actions made to curb collapse of market and restore trust

- Ad hoc rule changes move investment from an educated art form to speculation, and flight to cash and treasury bonds ensues

- Changing rules of market to protect what remains

- Market confidence further weakens and flight to cash and gold ensues

- Huge sell-off in assets to raise cash; erodes gold's safe haven status and price falls

- Corporate and consumer spending contracts

- Municipal and state governments fail to fully fund debt financed spending, encouraging further belt-tightening, city budgets cut

- Their lips support the market, but their hips are moving to protect capital, to reduce spending, and hunker down for the cold winter

- Credit card companies and banks contract credit unilaterally, further damaging consumer confidence and capital availability

- Additional bank closures

- Massive layoffs and unemployment rises

- "Recession is when a neighbor loses his job. Depression is when you lose yours." – Ronald Reagan

- Increased homelessness and need for personal financial aid

- Insurance companies fail

- The economic misery cocktail index rises, being the broader measure of economic misery

CRIME WAVE STARTS, FIRST GRADUALLY, THEN SUDDENLY

- Random increases in violent and property crime observed, not a trend, but outside norm

- Poor with least preparation hit first

- Elderly with least resistance hit second

- Low income housing crime wave and lawlessness
- Small business victimization and rise in protection rackets
- Online crime increases with fraud, trafficked stolen goods, and vice crimes
- Organized crime crowds violently back into street level illegal drugs distribution
- Organized retail crime targets major companies at unprotected points, and becomes more bold and violent in their tactics
- Rule of law continues to weaken, and civil disobedience increases
- "Whatever is not nailed down is mine, and whatever I can pry loose was not nailed down"[78]
- Robin Hoods and other hoods emerge, and the theft of private property is rampant
- Racial discord increases, hate crimes increase, dehumanizing victims providing rational basis for crime
- Rise in self-protection and vigilantism
- Rise in community based self-protection
- Internal insurrection in pockets possible
- Public outcry over crime begins with a seminal heinous criminal event or series of events
- The "crime wave" bottom is put in

THE TURNAROUND BEGINS

- A national crime control and nuisance abatement strategy is prepared
- Law and order institutions are modernized to meet the new needs of crime fighting and crime prevention
- Serious habitual offenders are incapacitated and removed as instigators of criminal organization and riot-setting
- Laws are changed to take the money out of crime, denying criminal organizations of their life blood – money to proliferate; Marijuana is decriminalized

- Situational Crime Prevention methods are used to combat crime at specific places

- Individuals protect themselves

- Businesses fortify and strengthen their own security and safety

- Local, municipal, and state governments spend money to protect citizens

- Gradually the crime wave is abated by specific targeted interventions, including massive public relations campaign to fight crime, be civic, and re-build sense of ownership and responsibility in communities

- Demand for income support through crime diminishes with federal and private support for long-term strategic investment goals that improve infrastructure, energy and solve severe problems, gaining support enabling funding for long-term national policy goals, achieving 10-year aims requiring consistent commitment and vision for turnaround

- Targeted intervention education and treatment is focused on families where crime became a way of life during this economic downturn, helping them turn a corner, bury their instruments of crime, and rebuild lives within the bounds of society; expectations once more.

Everywhere in the world people have learned the sad but compelling truth that the global economy is contracting rapidly with many developed nations now in declared recessions, and most of the developing nations at great risk from economic dependence in terms of trade with developed nations. During this downturn, which was as quick as a flash of lightning, what shocks us most is the fact that the speed and depth of the downturn surpass that of past debacles – the post 9/11 downturn, the 1991 recession, the 1987 stock market crash and the 1974 deep recession. Each time the bar was lowered as the market continued to retract faster and more severely than in past instances.

The only past experience comparable to our current market is the Great Depression of the 1930s, sparked by the dramatic collapse of the stock markets in the fall of 1929. Those were extraordinarily horrible times nobody is likely to forget and no one in his right mind would like to see its resurrection. Optimists who subscribe to the theory that the current situation will not be as bad as the Great Depression point out that we have learned from the Great Depression and have pulled out all the stops to create a soft landing for the economy, and hopefully to declare that the Second Great Depression is off the table for the following reasons:

1. More responsive monetary policy and interconnected or correlated international banker actions including massive coordinated interest rate cuts to spur investment and liquidity.

2. U.S. Federal Reserve policies to provide needed liquidity to markets through multiple tools introduced since the 1930s with advantage of lessons learned.

3. U.S. Federal government responses like the US TARP provide liquidity and capital to financial markets.

4. FDIC insurance safeguards individual depositor accounts in banks up to $250k preventing runs on banks.

5. Federal and state unemployment insurance for employees losing jobs preserving a modicum of income for households for the first few months of unemployment while workers find new work opportunities.

6. Many other New Deal policy actions of the federal government.

Some also comment that since we are not now at Depression levels all talks about and comparisons with that difficult period in the past are irrelevant. Take, for instance, this post commenting on the parallels between the Great Depression and today, and how times are somehow different now:

"By the afternoon of March 3, scarcely a bank in the country was open to do business," FDR said in his March 12, 1933, fireside chat (now available on a very cool podcast at the Federal Deposit Insurance Corp.'s Web site). In 1933, some 4,000 commercial banks failed, causing depositors to take huge losses. (There was no FDIC back then.) The recession that started in August 1929 lasted for a grinding 43 months, during which unemployment soared to 25 percent and national income was cut in half. By contrast, through mid-November 2008, only 19 banks had failed. The Federal Reserve last week said it expects unemployment to top out at 7.6 percent in 2009. Economists surveyed by the Philadelphia Federal Reserve Bank believe the recession, which started in April 2008, will be over by next summer. (Of course, back in January the same guys forecast that the economy would grow nicely in 2008 and 2009.) But don't take it from me. Take it from this year's Nobel laureate in economics. "The world economy is not in depression," Paul Krugman writes in his just-reissued book The Return of Depression Economics. "It probably won't fall into depression, despite the magnitude of the current crisis (although I wish I was completely sure about that)." This quote and more on this line of thought can be found at **http://www.outsidethebeltway .com/archives/not_the_great_depression/**

Balderdash. What can one say to that! From a factual frame of view, no economic downturn in the past 100 years has occurred more sharply or deeply as the current one. Perhaps it is our electronic broadcasting, rapid news transfers, or speed of transactions and movement of capital, or perhaps our recollection of history that have jointly caused this downturn to hit with more speed than any other in recorded history in the last century. The scary facts are this: the stock market collapse, an indicator of market sentiment and store of value, has now reached market levels not seen since the 1929 stock market crash. While it took more time for the market to reach its current levels than in 1929, there are many existing conditions that portend extremely stormy weather ahead. Here are some trends that bespeak more negative news for the future.

First, despite the political leadership's continuous declarations throughout last year that "the fundamentals of the economy were sound," we now recognize the alarming truth that they clearly were not. It is now generally and emphatically confirmed that we are already one year into the recession that started in December 2007, as reported by the National Bureau of Economic Research on 12 January 2008: **http://www.washingtonpost.com/wp-dyn/content/article/2008/12/01/ AR2008120102771.html**

We cannot be such willing subjects as to believe our political leaders when they facetiously try to prop up the markets with their unbridled optimism when the facts speak otherwise and there are negative facts galore. Political leaders are cheerleaders and hope not to yell "fire" in the theater causing greater mayhem; so while we need political leaders to carry the show and to take stringent actions for the benefit of the general public, to rely on their boldfaced statements will be just as wise as to put your head in the sand.

Secondly, housing prices continue to slide downwards rapidly, impacting individual wealth and prosperity and wealth-making options in the United States. Massive unemployment and layoffs announced during the past 90 days, if continued, may cause a would-be housing bottom in summer 2009 to fail, and we could be headed further down if more home loan defaults occur. Home equity is one of the primary vehicles used by entrepreneurs, small business owners, and new business start-ups to provide cash for their businesses whether the homes are used as collateral for business loans, or more simply as credit lines in the form of home equity loans. When housing prices are expected to continue falling, the amount of capital that banks are willing to lend on an asset-backed basis is cut drastically.

As a small business owner since 1994, the author too has used the equity in my home(s) as a backstop for my business enterprises both as collateral for loans and performance bonds, as well as home equity loans. The appreciation in real estate values in the 1990s and early 2000s enabled me to provide capital to my company relatively easily and quickly. And when business cycles impacted my business, such as the NASDAQ market crash in 2000 or post-9/11 terrorism events, I was able to use my home equity to create a soft landing and recovery means for my business to conduct a business-cycle recovery that would not otherwise have been available to me or my employees. Falling housing prices erode banker confidence necessary to sanction loans against the equity of the home, and consequently, homeowners are locked out of capital that, in goods times, was plentiful.

Thirdly, massive unemployment announcements continue to weigh down on the overall market, suppressing consumer views of the economy and market, and reducing expectations. There has been much written on this topic elsewhere. The important thing here is that unemployment impacts other variables, and lack of income creates crime opportunity for those who would otherwise be law abiding. "The national unemployment rate rose last month at the fastest pace in 26 years, foreshadowing what economists fear could be the biggest increase in joblessness since the recession of the 1970s. There are now more than 10 million Americans out of work, nearly 3 million more than a year ago, with manufacturing, construction, and retail sectors particularly hard-hit." **http://www.boston .com/news/local/massachusetts/articles/2008/11/08/unemployment_rate_ in_us_surging/**

Fourthly, another shoe to drop in this centipede market is the credit card bubble and the contraction of consumer credit, just at a time when many employees are losing their jobs. Credit cards have been viewed falsely by individuals as a store of value, safety, or safe haven for consumers to smooth the periods between financings. I have openly chastised financial planners such as CNBC's *On the Money* analyst for encouraging individuals to pay-off all of their credit card debt with available cash, when she fails to tell these same individuals that once they pay-off their credit cards, the credit card companies can unilaterally cut their credit availability and they would end up with no credit and no cash – the worst of the situations in an economic downturn. On an individual basis, the only prudent move is to hold as much cash and credit available to make it through the rough patches ahead – if you spend all your cash, you are prone to paying higher prices as you have fewer options ahead.

On this note, the Motley Fool cited: "Meredith Whitney – bank analyst extraordinaire – predicting that the credit card industry may slash more than $2 trillion of existing credit lines – 45% of the total – over the next year and a half. Yikes! The obvious outcome here would be a huge risk reduction for companies that issue consumer credit, such as JPMorgan Chase (NYSE: JPM), Bank of America (NYSE: BAC), and Citigroup (NYSE: C), while kicking an already-bloodied consumer – and to a lesser extent, card processors Visa (NYSE: V) and MasterCard (NYSE: MA) – while they're down." Read more on this at: **http://www.fool.com /investing/dividends-income/2008/12/01/the-death-of-credit-cards.aspx**

Fifthly, residential and commercial lending crises in regional banks could be a future shoe to drop. Regional banks have financed home loans and loans for small businesses and construction loans throughout the U.S. Reuters reports that "Regional banks exposed to deteriorating home equity loans are facing a greater risk of bankruptcy, possibly extending a U.S. credit crisis to 2010." Wall Street bank exposure to subprime mortgage debt and structured finance products already has resulted in more than $400 billion of write-downs and losses since last year. Now other consumer debt, such as credit cards and auto loans, may be the next source of busted loans. See **http://www.reuters.com/article /InvestmentOutlookMid08/idUSN0964320080609**

The next possible scenario is that the commercial real estate bubble will burst in 2009. Massive unemployment of white collar positions in banking, advertising, and other traditional salaried positions will be leaving huge amounts of commercial real estate empty. Of the trillion notes to be refinanced in 2009, approximately 1/3 are underwater, meaning they cannot be refinanced at former values. One blogger posts: "Fitch has been saying since last April that commercial real estate was exhibiting the same sort of frothiness as subprime. CMBS spreads started widening sharply last August. Investors started pulling back from purchases in September, expecting prices to fall considerably. In November, Nouriel Roubini added commercial real estate to his list of impending financial train wrecks, estimating the damage at $100 to $150 billion." **http://www .nakedcapitalism.com/2008/03/surprise-commercial-real-estate-woes.html**

The seventh trend is that government receipts from tax collections are impacted significantly and will be another source of serious harm in the economy. California has warned of the danger of running out of operating capital in 2009 without significant financial assistance. Perhaps the only consolation available to them at present is that they are not alone. "Led by California with a $28 billion hole in its budget, 41 states are in financial trouble, and many of their leaders are looking to Congress to bail them out." **http://www.idahostatesman.com/1425 /story/571171.html** Not only are the states in trouble, but many cities are in financial trouble and looking for ways to cut services and costs at a time of peaked needs. It is not just the tax revenues that are down, but also the state and local governments' ability to borrow as many tax-based finance bond auctions have gone under-subscribed since 9/15/08.

State Government FY2009 Budget Deficits		
State	**Total Budget Short-fall (Deficits) by State; reported in Billions ($)**	**Total Shortfall as Percent of FY2009 General Fund**
Alabama	$1.80	22.20%
Alaska	$0.36	6.80%
Arizona	$3.50	34.80%
Arkansas	$0.11	2.40%
California	$35.90	35.50%
Colorado	$0.60	7.70%
Connecticut	$1.90	11.00%
Delaware	$0.44	12.20%
District of Columbia	$0.49	7.80%
Florida	$5.70	22.20%
Georgia	$2.40	11.50%
Hawaii	$0.23	4.00%
Idaho	$0.22	7.40%
Illinois	$6.10	21.40%
Indiana	$1.10	8.00%
Iowa	$0.48	7.60%
Kansas	$0.19	2.90%
Kentucky	$0.72	7.80%
Louisiana	$0.34	3.70%
Maine	$2.65	8.60%
Maryland	$1.50	10.00%
Massachusetts	$3.60	12.70%
Michigan	$0.67	2.90%
Minnesota	$1.60	9.20%

State Government FY2009 Budget Deficits		
State	Total Budget Short-fall (Deficits) by State; reported in Billions ($)	Total Shortfall as Percent of FY2009 General Fund
Mississippi	$0.27	5.20%
Missouri	$0.34	3.80%
Nevada	$1.40	19.60%
New Hampshire	$0.25	8.00%
New Jersey	$6.10	18.80%
New Mexico	$0.45	7.50%
New York	$6.60	11.70%
North Carolina	$2.00	9.30%
Ohio	$1.90	6.80%
Oklahoma	$0.11	1.70%
Oregon	$0.44	6.60%
Pennsylvania	$2.30	8.10%
Rhode Island	$0.80	24.50%
South Carolina	$1.10	16.30%
South Dakota	$0.27	2.20%
Tennessee	$1.40	12.00%
Utah	$0.62	10.40%
Vermont	$0.14	11.60%
Virginia	$2.30	13.80%
Washington	$0.51	3.40%
Wisconsin	$1.20	8.80%
TOTAL	$100.60	15.20%

Source: Iris J. Lav and Elizabeth McNichol, State Budget Troubles Worsen, discussion of raw deficits data reported 9/08/08, as discussed on http://www.cbpp.org/cms/?fa=view&id=711, published March 13, 2009

I could go on, but you have already got the gist of it. The confluence of the above negative events, if unabated, will create an economic death spiral for the economy that will lead to the Second Great Depression and the other concomitant ills that such an economy entails. Our leaders are using the playbook of lessons learned from the Great Depression, and that book of experience has its limits. Communication is faster, transportation quicker, capital moves electronically, news reaches a boiling point more swiftly, and the world is more interconnected. Criminals are more sophisticated and using complex instruments and technology to dodge responsibility and capture. Add to this milieu the fact that we live in a troubled world of anarchists, terrorists, pirates, and extremists, and you have a cocktail of misery for the next year and, unfortunately, for several years to come. Consequently, not talking about the Second Great Depression will not forestall it. We do, however, need to focus attention on solutions, as being a town-crier on its own does not solve the problem. Even then, the recognition of our current dilemma and its gravity is necessary to proactively combat the economic forces that weigh us down today. Only the collective genius of all working in harmony to make active change to our current circumstance will make a difference.

Unfortunately, a hard landing is in the offing, and if you live in the pockets of misery such as Detroit, the heart of the automotive industry, what was already bad is about to get unbearable: **http://www.youtube.com/watch?v=ufexZnViDiU**. Follow this link and you will see that Detroit Free Press published on November 16, 23, and 30th of 2008, the following section of foreclosures (including property tax foreclosures) totaling 137 pages of property foreclosure notices, and only 4 pages of employment opportunities – and the massive layoffs from the automotive industry have not occurred in any meaningful way yet. Many of the tax foreclosure notices were on properties that are underwater or homes that cannot sell in this market. This story also illustrates the loss of working capital of state and local governments that need funds to operate.

The data from Detroit highlights another characteristic about crime waves – they are not evenly distributed, but rather are geographically distributed to areas of greatest economic misery. Consider that home foreclosures are not randomly distributed, but geographically distributed in clusters throughout the US, with some regions seeing higher incidence of foreclosures. The current wave of foreclosures has been over-represented by middle-class and revitalized neighborhoods where speculation, sub-prime, alt-A, and no-document loans fueled the housing boom and these are the first loans to unravel in foreclosures. From criminal justice research the warning has come that, as homes become vacant in these neighborhoods through foreclosures or abandonments of under-water mortgages, residents in these abandoned neighborhoods face increasing risk of burglary and robbery, especially as these neighborhoods fall into disrepair. Community decay, broken windows, and the crossing of the 'tippingpoint' are all concerns facing high-impact neighborhoods with potential long-lasting impact of crime opportunity in economically deprived communities. All these may easily lead some to say caustically: "Will the last one leaving Detroit please turn the lights off?"

Researchers in Charlotte, North Carolina, have noticed a similar phenomenon of community decay and crime conditions increasing as foreclosures rise along with vacancies in their communities. In Charlotte, researchers found that their high foreclosure neighborhoods shared a characteristic of being priced just below the average price for homes in their area, and these neighborhoods were considered 'affordable housing' neighborhoods. These neighborhoods tended to be renter neighborhoods, not home-owner neighborhoods. Further exacerbating the vacancy rates and impact on crime, they found that as the many foreclosure homes become rentals, non-owner occupied dwellings following foreclosures. Renters have less community buy-in and are more difficult to organize in crime prevention activities. Charlotte Police Department (CMPD) has examined their own data in these neighborhoods and has reached the conclusion that foreclosures lead to higher crime rates. The Department examined crime data from 2003 to 2006 and found that violent crime rose in the higher-foreclosure neighborhoods as compared to the lower-foreclosure neighborhoods for all years but one. [79]

The phenomenon observed in Charlotte, and likely to occur in Detroit, has parallels to the famous "Broken Windows Theory" of James Q. Wilson and George L. Kelling (1982). They theorized that neighborhood physical and social disorder can lead to further decay if left unchecked and such decay can lead to conditions that foster more serious crime. These signs or markers of community decay included such noticeable things as broken windows, graffiti, garbage-strewn lots, abandoned cars, vacant buildings, etc. These signs also included behavioral signs of disorder such as homelessness, panhandlers, etc.[80] We might add to this list problems like illegal drug selling, street prostitution, and gambling. The greater the number of markers, the weaker the community fabric and support for lawful activities. Hence, fixing broken windows early, or in the case of housing, filling up vacant homes with law-abiding occupants, is essential to fostering reduced crime opportunity. Otherwise, these broken windows and vacant dwellings will create their own entropy and decay within the communities where crime can bud and grow.

Market fluctuations are natural, and recessions happen, but we as an advanced society have an obligation to make things better – history is not what happens, history is what we make happen, and it is imperative that the future history of the second great economic depression should show that we used our collective genius to build a new future, a better world, a world where we did not abandon our peers living in other communities, a world where we were kind to each other, where we remembered the poor, and together we lifted each other up. For without that kind of commitment to humanity, life will truly be "nasty, brutish, and short" for the multitudes living in these pockets of economic depression within the U.S., and our society will regress, not progress in modernity.

Preparations for the coming economic misery-led crime wave are being made by world leaders at the IMF and World Bank, and in Australia, UK, and in parts of the United States. Others will join the preparation bandwagon as unemployment rises in the coming year.

Australia's Victorian police sound warning as hard times spur crime wave

The Australian reported on December 27, 2008: "Police are bracing for a new wave of economic crimes driven by the financial crisis and rising unemployment, such as theft and burglary, after studying crime patterns from the previous downturn. Senior officers have drawn on crime statistics from the 1990 recession, when so-called property crime jumped sharply, to pinpoint the types of offences expected to rise as the financial crisis deepens."

The Australian went on to add:

> "By tracking crimes over the past six months, police have found offences such as theft of valuables from motor vehicles, house burglaries, street robberies, handbag and wallet theft, shoplifting and other types of theft have begun to rise, as they did in 1990. Victoria's Deputy Commissioner of Police Kieran Walshe told *The Weekend Australian:* 'We are starting to see crimes against property beginning to trend upwards. We have also seen an increase in petrol theft and those sorts of things. Those are the kind of things potentially that are going to increase if you have a slowing economy. Particularly as unemployment starts to rise, that's going to cause people in some circumstances to seek other means of getting money.' "

Later in the article, *The Australian* reports: "Crime figures show that, in 1990-91, there was a sharp jump in property crime in Victoria compared with the previous year. Theft rose 13.6 per cent, robbery 12.3 per cent and burglary 8.1 per cent. The rates of those crimes began falling again as the economy began to pick up in following years. Victoria Police this month arrested a gang that had carried out eight ram-raids on retail outlets in Melbourne's northern and western suburbs in recent months, resulting in $700,000 in stolen and damaged property. About $150,000 in stolen goods was recovered. Mr. Walshe said research on previous economically driven crime sprees would help develop preventative strategies, such as increasing police patrols in certain areas or encouraging the community to be more vigilant."

UK public officials prepare for crime wave

Martin Gill, Ph.D., the well-respected criminologist and practitioner, wrote the following in one of his monthly *Perpetuity* newsletters to industry colleagues: "Will crime rates rise with the failing economy? The Home Security Secretary, Jacqui Smith, certainly thinks so, warning that violent crime could grow by nearly a fifth based on increases seen during the 1991-2 recession. But the academic evidence suggests that won't be the only crime type that's set to rise; fraud, forgery, burglary, robbery, theft, and arson have all been linked to recession and unemployment. So what does this mean for you? It's clear that at a time when budgets are being reduced, cutting back on security is not an easy option; with crime rates set to rise cutting back on security could result in rising costs of crime. Instead it's a good time to review your existing processes to identify any opportunities to improve efficiency and work smarter to cut costs, achieving greater value for money."

U.S. law enforcement prepares for crime wave, not uniformly, but in noticeable hotspots

Within the U.S., police chiefs are preparing for a coming crime wave of sorts, from the experienced professionals such as Chief Bratton of LAPD, to others that are dealing with increasing crime rates in south Florida, the Midwest and other locations impacted by economic misery more profoundly than most.

United Nations crime chief sees increasing crime problem during financial crises

Antonio Maria Costa, Executive Director of the United Nations Office on Drugs and Crime (**http://www.unodc.org/**), said the global financial crisis is making it easier for organized crime groups to launder profits from narcotics, human trafficking, and other illegal activities. Costa told the Associated Press that crime groups were using the financial crisis "as a golden opportunity" to launder funds through bank deposits and the buying of shares. He declined to single out any institutions but said it was "certainly happening across the board." He went on: "The money is available and the need for that money is there." In Costa's expert opinion: "I think the whole system is infected." Costa said he was basing his claims on contacts with prosecutors in various countries, as well as on consultations with banking representatives and on his years of experience tracking organized crime.[81]

.

CHAPTER 5
Lessons learned from combating past Crime Waves

"Vice is a monster of so frightful mien,
As to be hated needs but to be seen;
Yet seen too oft, familiar with her face,
We first endure, then pity, then embrace."
— Alexander Pope, *The Essay on Man*. Epistle ii, Line 217.

Sharp crises, particularly sharp, downward-spiraling economic crises, create conditions that, if not soon reversed, can create further economic misery leading some to the throes of crime, not as a matter of first choice, but of survival. Again, reflecting on lessons learned from the Great Depression, we had better remember our past lest we repeat it. Hans von Hentig , a criminologist, made this insightful comment in 1947: "Human beings are not made to resist lightning bolts…We must acknowledge similar configurations of our cultural life when extreme want, extreme provocation, or extreme frustration wrings an unlawful act from an otherwise law-abiding individual. Most of our criminals are milieu-made. They are law-abiding while the sun shines, while economic life goes on undisturbed, and their ability of adjustment is not taxed excessively. When social storms are brewing, depressions set in, prices tumble, and the army of unemployed swells, the average law-abiding individual yields to extreme pressure and becomes a law-breaker."[82] It is important to address emerging crime problems early, particularly in terms of blocking crime opportunity, as too much familiarity with crimes of opportunity arising from civil disobedience, if unchecked, may spill into more serious habitual criminal behaviors.

An analysis of the literature and the practice of combating crime waves since the Great Depression leads the author to assert that in the face of our sharp crisis, a deep economic downturn and forecasted crime wave to follow, to do nothing, to let economic markets correct on their own with great harshness and cruelty to individuals and families, would, quite naturally, exacerbate the underlying conditions that create increased crime opportunity, and a spiraling decay of social order may occur. With hindsight from our past, foresight from our lessons learned and the trends that have become so evident now, we must act to intercept the coming crime wave in meaningful ways that include both supply-side and demand-side measures. Individuals and institutions are simply unprepared for the surge wave of crime that is coming.

It has been proved time and again that economies in sharp crises of escalating negative proportions create conditions of economic misery that impact crime opportunity in a decisive manner. Increased unemployment creates conditions of reduced income, increased unsupervised time, painful individual economic disruption, and even very acute psychological impact. If unemployment remains over a prolonged period, the standard of living of ordinary households must drop precipitously, or the income must be resupplied from alternate sources. However, humans are not machines; nor do all individuals possess the kind of emotional maturity required to rationally assess their diminished income situation, real-locate their scarce resources, reduce their cost of living, reduce their life demands by paring back wants from needs, and satisfy the individual and family needs which rapid reductions in household income have made extremely difficult to meet. For Radzinowicz (1977), the choice of crime by some unemployed in downturned markets "may imply a failure in adaptation to changed conditions, an acquired rigidity in habits which have grown during better times, a sudden shock, a weakening of social ties, or simply a latent disposition reinforced by economic pressure."

Unfortunately, whether by miscalculation of their own situation, accident, or choice, some individuals and families in hard economic times will switch to crime for sustaining their household income. Early warning of crime patterns might be crimes of opportunity such as borrowed items not returned (e.g. taking a few stamps at the office, borrowing from the petty cash box, or a neighbor's tool box), or theft of something that was not tied down (e.g., typical crimes of opportunity such as an unattended cell phone, a dropped wallet, a car with keys left in it, an unlocked home, etc.), and, if this pattern is not checked and positive, legal income-producing patterns are not restored, the crime pattern may progress to more serious habitual patterns of disorganized to organized crime or more violent crime. Should this regressive crime lifestyle pattern occur, the unintended consequence of this pattern may impact the individual and the family unit to the third and fourth generation. Individuals, families, communities, businesses, and governments must do whatever they can to thwart the progression of crime lifestyles by restoring meaningful opportunities for gainful employment, as, for most, crime is not the first choice, but usually only the last resort of the helpless and the hopeless.[83]

Employment, not just restoration of income, must be an integral aim of any criminal justice plan to combat crime in downturned economies, as there are great psychological benefits to employment employment, such as improvements to individual self-esteem, life balance, stability, personal integrity and law-abiding behavior, in addition to reducing unsupervised time. Work is therapeutic for many disorders including depression, anxiety, stress, and health problems including marital stress. Boardman, Grove, Perkins and Shepherd (2003) made this very pertinent observation: "Employment helps maintain good mental health and in turn promotes recovery."[83] Unemployment is not equally distributed, and while the news today may report massive job cuts or layoffs at banks, automotive manufacturing facilities, and infrastructure development areas, it is frequently the case that unemployment and inflation hit hardest the individuals that appear most frequently in the crime statistics: the poor, racial minorities, the young, the inner-city dwellers. It is painfully ironic for the poor that inflation impacts them harder than others in terms of escalated prices of food and fuel. Likewise, the poor spend a proportionally higher percentage of their working day to pay for these life essentials, and so, any remedy we have in mind must also address these core basic needs.

In retrospect, during the Great Depression, public officials moved to do several things worth repeating: first, they identified their greatest crime problems, recognizing that structures of the past were insufficient to resolve current problems; secondly, they reorganized or built new criminal justice organizations, tools, and laws to combat the crimes; thirdly, they focused on the supply side of crime by targeting serious habitual offenders, 'public enemies' who were Depression desperados, and organized crime; fourthly, by repealing Prohibition, the government eliminated the revenue streams afforded by bootlegging and related criminal activities, preferring to tax and control spirits, and, thereby, eliminating a great source of organized crime and not-so-organized bootleggers; and lastly, they controlled the demand side for crime by reducing the number of potential offenders, whose likelihood of participation in crime was increased through economic misery, by means of relocation and through employment and jobs programs (e.g., the CCC). In time, these strategies would serve to increase law and order, increase law-abiding behavior, reduce civil disobedience and law-breaking, and strengthen social institutions within a nation suffering through the Great Depression. None of these strategies alone were sufficient, but together they created a framework for focusing on real problems identified at the outset of the crime wave.

There are other lessons learned from our past in dealing with economic crises and crime. In 1974, amidst the deep recession of the early 1970s, the United Nations convened a workshop of criminal justice and economic experts[85] to examine the unholy nexus between 'economic crises and crime.'[86] A severe and deep recession was impacting Western Europe, Japan, and North America. Inflation and monetary exchange rate fluctuations and supplies were problems, so also was an energy crisis and oil embargo. Crises were characterized by sudden, unexpected events that served to deteriorate pre-existing conditions. 'Sharp crises' included natural catastrophes, wars, other armed conflicts impacting civilian areas, the collapse of major industrial enterprises, and abrupt market disruptions. Macro-economic losses from sharp crises include property losses, commodity shortages, loss of housing, loss of purchasing power, and unemployment. Today we would add the rapid loss of income or net worth through burst bubbles impacting household incomes, employment, home equity, 401k retirement funds, and loss of asset value through deflation.

Interestingly, the scholars who gathered around the UN roundtable in 1974 did not seem to think much about economic crises creating more crime, but rather about how increased crime opportunity due to economic crises created more likely offenders that in turn incapacitated existing control structures, and thereby created a tipping point or dam-break wherein more crime occurred. Excepting cases of "sharp crises" including seismic economic events, immediate disaster scenes, and the associated relief fraud and mismanagement, the 1974 UN scholars reported no strong relationship between economic crises and crime that is not accounted for by other variables.

The "overall conclusion" made by the 1974 UN workshop was that "economic crises do not directly entail any significant or alarming increase in serious offenses, except for dislocations of resources related to the economic disloca-tions" such as, black market rationing schemes. However, the crime workshop participants concluded that there was a risk of civil disobedience and minor crime spilling over into more serious crime if the control systems did not ac-commodate the crisis-led change of dynamics that served to increase crime op-portunity. Consequently, these scholars posited that it was not essential that the economic conditions of crime had changed, but rather that the control system management under the conditions of crises were overly stressed, and this break-down or incapacitation created uncontrolled crime opportunity. Interestingly, the UN workshop scholars postulated that when economic crises occur, and the social control systems are not adjusted to accommodate these changes, then the control systems can become overburdened and cease functioning effectively, contributing to a milieu of decay, increased crime opportunity, and gradual progression to more serious crime if left uncontrolled. This decay or progression to more serious crime is a result of sub-system overloads.

Another fascinating revelation of the 1974 economic crises workshop was the focus on the long-lasting impacts of sharp crises and their deleterious impact on the individual, families, communities, etc. Anyone interviewing someone who lived through the Great Depression can tell you stories of how the deeply negative experience of that period shaped their entire lives, including their spending habits, work habits, expectations, family life, and their dreams. Scholars find that there are indeed lasting impacts from such sharp crisis and these must be examined before conjecturing about any solution to the problem. One can assume that with any sudden sharp crises, physiological trauma, along with the disruptive patterns associated with catastrophes, will be reflected in behavioral changes and the health of the impacted individuals. Evidence shows physiological impact (liver and cardio-vascular stress) and increased mortality rates due to increased suicide risk and other health-deteriorating, stress-induced aliments. Prolonged crises impact not just individuals, but families, communities, and broader social structures and one can predict increased unrest, alcoholism, petty crime, and juvenile delinquency even to the second generation.[87]

Another observation from the past is that during economic downturns, states and local governments collect less revenue and services frequently are cut back, and this may include law enforcement and other supportive services serving or 'handling' the unemployed. Under conditions of increased need for services, and a lack of financial resources to provide 'capable guardianship', criminal offenders may swamp or over-tap the resources of the system, creating a systemic crime control problem. However, one of the lessons learned is that all of these individuals must commit crimes in place or space, and these locations can be altered to make crime making more difficult.

Since the 1920s, economic disruptions and sharp downturns have been followed by crime waves, with one exception, and there the crime wave had started much earlier, in the early 1920s with Prohibition, but it was exacerbated by the economic crisis of the Great Depression. In examining the historical responses to these successive economic shocks and crime waves, there appear to be some patterns of public policy and criminal justice response that are suitable now: examine the problem; identify key factors contributing to the problem on the supply and demand side of crime; control and minimize civil disobedience and change laws when existing laws are inadequate to deal effectively with the crime situation; and adapt crime justice organizations throughout the criminal justice process from investigations, enforcement, adjudication, incarceration, and parole.

Individual criminal events must be understood in the broader framework of a number of underlying factors. While economic misery can lead to conditions creating a greater number of likely offenders, economic misery does not account for the complete calculus involved in the crime wave equation. There is an environmental criminology to particular criminal events even in times of increased economic misery that are characterized by a greater number of likely offenders. The Brantinghams' (1991) put it this way: "Individual criminal events must be understood as confluences of offenders, victims or criminal targets, and laws in specific settings at particular times and places." Outside of everything that is happening at the individual level creating the personal opportunity for crime, there is a place where crime occurs that can be altered to mitigate the increased risk of crime happening at that place, to push off, repel, deflect, deter, delay, or reduce crime opportunity. In other words, the likelihood that a crime wave is coming does not mean that crime necessarily needs to happen to us, our homes, communities, businesses, and localities. We can protect ourselves, fortify our respective domains, and be on our guard against the oncoming epidemic of crime.

If we understand the underlying context of crime and criminals, then we can more reliably use blocking strategies to manage crime, and redirect resources to curb crime most harmful to society, while at times letting other lesser crimes go unattended, shifting priority of law enforcement resources to the most serious and harmful crimes to individuals and our communities, and indeed to our society and government. When the number of likely offenders surges, the likelihood of criminal offenders being successful in their illegal enterprise increases through their reduced likelihood of identification (or anonymity). In other words, if 100 illegal street-level drug dealers are working at the same hour and there are only four police officers, their likelihood of continued operations is higher than at a time when only 12 drug dealers are working and the same four police officers can more adeptly focus their limited resources on the specific individual offenders, settings, and locations of crime.

Examining crime through a framework of environmental criminology – not environmental law, but the environmental settings in which crime thrives – we find that criminal offenders exploit particular settings, times, and places to commit their crimes successfully; unsuccessful criminal offenders violate these rules and get caught. Nowhere is this principle more clearly demonstrated than in illegal street selling of drugs. It remains illegal to sell dangerous drugs (cocaine, crack, heroine, methamphetamines, etc) and less harmful drugs (marijuana, and other controlled precursor drugs) at the street level in open-air drug markets or without controlled, pharmacy distributed medical prescriptions. Yet illegal drug markets thrive all over the world, and have ebbed and flowed over the decades, increasing more broadly in difficult economic times. For these criminal markets to exist they must have buyers and sellers, a place to exchange, and a currency (real or electronic) or barter to take place. But these exchanges do not occur in a vacuum and require specific contextual environmental conditions in order to be successful.

Having examined the 'cat and mouse' game that law enforcement and criminals play in street-level drug markets, there are some particular environmental criminology factors that must be in place for successful illegal drug selling operations to occur, and it is imperative that law enforcement agencies understand and attack these market-influencing factors to disrupt the likelihood of successful drug markets. Attention should be paid to the following disrupting conditions:

- Place (street corner, curb, bar, tavern, campus, laundromat, motel, etc.)

- Location (specific street address or GPS lat/lon)

- Setting (stage set with costumes, props, and backdrops)

- Time (hour, date, week, season, and community calendar)

- Offenders (dealers and supporting cast)

- Co-offenders (buyers)

- Victims (non-combatants)

- Crime target (drugs)

- Distribution method

- Place management (administration, sales, security, maintenance, communications)

- Law enforcement efficacy (combination of law enforcement structure, resources, rules of engagement, enforcement priorities, and adjudication system capacity)

From 1994 through 2002, the author led a series of Crime Prevention through Environmental Design technical assistance and training programs for the U.S. Department of Housing and Urban Development (HUD), wherein he, along with his team of criminal justice analysts, examined crime in public and assisted housing settings throughout the US. Part of this process includes performing ethnographies (a social scientist's word for in-depth street surveillance studies) to determine at the ground-level what was happening, and why, where, when, and by whom, in order to make significant improvements in the quality of law enforcement response to improve the general health, safety, and welfare of the residents of public housing. We conducted many assessments of illegal drug markets and criminal behavior and street ethnographies including interviews on the streets of 'successful' drug dealers – those not in jails.[88] From all of these research experiences we created a core body of knowledge in terms of situational crime prevention factors impacting low-income, high-density housing settings, and these observations and lessons learned have been applied to minimize crime opportunity throughout the United States.

One of the favorable attributes of situational crime prevention is that it targets specific places and criminal events that need not get the support of criminal offenders to work effectively. Shaping, reshaping, modifying, and altering en-vironments to reduce crime opportunity along with capable place management can greatly reduce crime opportunity in long-lasting ways. Successful criminals seek to maximize their performance by exploiting the environment to take asym-metric advantage of the crime 'set' – that combination of place, location, time, setting, etc. where crime occurs. Situational crime prevention starts with identi-fying the 'set' and determining the factors needed to increase the effort needed to commit crime, increase the risks associated with committing the crime, reduce the rewards of crime, and remove excuses for crime – all at specific places.

Analyzing criminal 'sets' or locations where crime occurs is not difficult, but it does take observation and thoughtful analysis of what is going on under the cover of routine activity. For example, what appears to be an auto repair operation to the casual eye of passerby might actually be a coordinated communication system of street-level narcotics dealers using the stage props of the natural environment to communicate an open and closed market (i.e. front hood up, market open; trunk hood up, market closed, come back in one hour). What appears to be a teenage hoax of athletic shoes hanging by their laces on the overhead power line might actually be the turn-right, turn-left direction way-finding system of drug-sellers leading customers to their illegal drug market. These and other telltale signs of criminal sets can be identified and the markets disrupted by careful observation to take away the means of routine communication or operations. When these telltale signs are amalgamated, they can provide an operation play book for the opposition that can be quite useful in closing down the market, suppressing it, and driving it away. An illustration of this point is the following – in April 1999, the author was invited to present a paper at the John Jay School of Criminal Justice in New York City at the International Workshop on Drug Markets. I used the occasion to teach criminal justice students how criminal offenders use or exploit settings to create optimal career-lengthening choices, and how to use these same findings to combat these markets. In a tongue-in-cheek presentation titled, "22 Immutable Laws of Successful Illegal Drug Market Trafficking,' I outlined specific ways that criminal offenders exploit environments, and what to do about it.[89] In a similar manner, I strongly recommend that situational crime prevention strategies and tactics can be used to prevent or curb the crime opportunities we are likely to face in the coming crime wave.

Ronald Clarke, the author and capable guardian of *Situational Crime Prevention* has found through examining numerous crime prevention studies that "crime is not spread evenly across all places, people or times and, to be effective, preventative measures must be directed to where crime is most concentrated. Focusing on 'hot spots' – those places with a high rate of reported crimes or calls for assistance – has proved useful in directing police patrols and crime reduction measures. Similarly, giving priority to 'repeat victims' of crime has proved to be an effective use of prevention resources."[90] John Eck (1997) put it this way: "Most places have no crimes and most crime is highly concentrated in and around a relatively small number of places. If we can prevent crime at these high crime places, then we might be able to reduce total crime."[91] So, in addition to reducing crime opportunity through increasing effort, increasing risk, reducing rewards, and removing excuses – we need to focus on hot spots, those places of greatest risk for crime.

One of the early lessons of fighting crime in the 1930s was the essential requirement to reduce organized crime opportunities of the sort that were allowed to flourish during the age of Prohibition. The essential strategy used to protect the public then, was a concept characterized in criminal justice research as "opportunity blocking". This same method is used as the deliberative hampering of activities of organized crime groups through interrupting or eradicating the supply of illicit goods and services, most notably narcotics. The "opportunity blocking" approach has been coined by Ronald Goldstock (1990) as a method that "seeks to change the social, economic, physical, or organizational environment so that particular crimes become impossible or at least very difficult, to carry out…"

"Opportunity Blocking" is a concept that needs to be considered more fully when dealing with highly motivated criminal offenders in our day. John Eck (2002), in "Preventing Crime at Places," writes: "blocking crime opportunities at places reduces crime in many circumstances. Over 90 percent of the interventions [examined in his metastudy of criminal justice studies] reported evidence of crime reduction following the installation of an opportunity-blocking tactic."[92] Again, Eck (1997) wrote: "Opportunity blocking does not have to be done at places. It can also be built into targets (for example, designing anti-theft devices into automobiles [Clarke 1995] or printing holograms and photos on credit cards to curtail forgery and fraud)."[93]

More importantly, while drawing clues and best practices from history, let us not for a moment forget that our time is radically different in terms of crime opportunity made available through the Internet and communications methods. Any thinking about crime control in our age must combat these increased challenges with specific, measured, and targeted approach to cut off the means and instruments of crime used particularly in international organized crime, from the low-level crimes of stolen goods sales on eBay, to the great frauds perpetrated upon the public in financial crimes. In whatever plan that is prepared to combat this crime wave, policy makers must add crime opportunity blocking to the list of directives within the national crime control strategy. Policymakers and practitioners should focus on the crime opportunity market, and in the words of Goldstock (1990), seek to "change the social, economic, physical, or organizational environment so that particular crimes become impossible, or at least very difficult, to carry out."

It is perhaps here, when exploring the concept of "opportunity blocking", that we find the greatest insights for the new challenges that will face us in our current sharp crisis. Situational crime prevention is most likely to find success in reducing crime opportunity by blocking, denying, limiting, and curbing opportunities to commit crimes through four distinct strategies and their many subcomponents. Blocking opportunity is an effective strategy where the target or market is constantly moving, and can be likened to maneuver warfare, where the objective may be to continually persist in increasing the difficulty of committing a crime – and this is what is required to combat organized crime where there are highly motivated offenders that are not likely to be persuaded to return to law-abiding activity merely by being blocked at one opening for crime.

Situational Crime Prevention is an opportunity blocking strategy that seeks to:

1. increase the effort needed to commit crime at specific places;

2. increase the risk associated with crime at specific places;

3. reduce the rewards for crimes committed at specific places;

4. remove excuses for non-performance, non-cooperation, and even loitering at specific places, thereby blocking opportunity crimes; in some cultures, this might include shaming to discourage participation in crime, or encourage positive behavior.

From 1994 through 1997, the author worked with Professor Ronald Clarke, John Hayes, Ellen Walsh, Nikki Bellamy, and Marina Myhre, to adapt Situational Crime Prevention to low-income, high-crime neighborhoods with much success. A situational crime prevention model was adapted to these high risk environments where getting community support from stakeholders is sometimes hardest, particularly in drug and crime ravaged neighborhoods. The result of the crime opportunity blocking program was discernible reductions in UCR Part I Crimes between 17 % to 76%. Since the Situational Crime Prevention model was modified to address crime in low income communities, the structure of the model can be adapted with creativity to other settings with success; indeed, there is a great body of literature on successful case studies of situational crime prevention in diverse settings, times, and places.

Sixteen Techniques of Situational Crime Prevention in Public Housing

(Adapted from Severin L. Sorensen and Ronald V. Clarke, Situational Crime Prevention and High Density, Low Income Housing, 5th International Seminar on Environmental Criminology and Crime Analysis (University of Tokyo: Tokyo, July 1996).

Increasing Perceived Effort

1. Target hardening
- Inspection of premises, security, and maintenance
- Locks, tough glass, key control
- Remove trees that enable access to upper-level units

2. Access Control
- Limit # & monitor entrances
- Perimeter fencing, self-closing gates and doors
- Electronic access
- No exterior handles on exits

3. Deflecting Offenders
- Bus stop and metro station placement and stop times
- Traffic routing & street closures
- Limit interior pedestrian routes
- Steep slopes near windows to prevent entry

4. Controlling Facilitators
- Gun control and alcohol ban
- Alter payphones for no incoming calls
- Secure vacant units
- Controlled spray can sales
- Removal of shopping carts

Increasing Perceived Risks

5. Entry/exit screening
- Visitor sign-ins and expiring badges
- Resident registration & ID badges
- Entry-phones, PIN number, entry metal sensors, Apt. door peepholes
- Locked gates, lighting

6. Formal Surveillance
- Police & security patrols, bike patrol
- Police substation on-site
- Resident and employee screening
- CCTV, video surveillance
- Remove shrubbery obstructions

7. Surveillance by Employees
- Front desk clerks, maintenance, management offices face the front
- On-site residence for PHA employees
- CCTV systems, pay phones in visible locations
- Daily "drive around," weekly inspect.

8. Natural Surveillance
- Neighborhood Watch, hotlines
- Free phones for block watch organizers to report crimes
- Improve interior & exterior lighting
- Remove greenery obstructions
- Replace solid fencing w/ see-through picket fencing

Reducing Anticipated Rewards

9. Target Removal
- No-cash policy manager's office
- Tokens for laundry & vending machines (or removal)
- Off-site food stamp distribution
- Secure maintenance equipment

10. Identifying Property
- Vehicle and bike registration
- Equipment ID, education prog.
- Property marking, Operation ID
- Property serial # database
- Greenery to define private areas

11. Reducing Temptation
- Gender-neutral phone lists
- Rapid repair of vandalism
- Replace metal signs w/ wood
- Hide graffiti-prone walls behind shrubbery or thorny bushes
- Close play areas at night

12. Denying Benefits
- PIN for car radios
- Rapid graffiti removal
- Anti-graffiti paint
- Forfeiture of lease for aiding offenders

Removing Excuses

13. Rule Setting
- Drug-free housing zone
- Evictions & One Strike signage
- "Call 577- TIPS" to report crime
- Local laws and polices posted
- Define public & private spaces

14. Stimulating Conscience
- Public posting of trespasser names and pictures
- Postcards to suspected drug purchasers

15. Controlling Disinhibitors
- Asset forfeiture drug dealers
- Enforced lease forfeiture for tenants who deal drugs or commit other crimes
- Enforced open container laws
- Relocated liquor stores & bars

16. Facilitating Compliance
- Trash bins
- Frequently posted signage
- Established ground rules
- Threat of eviction

Table - 16 Situational Crime Prevention Techniques for Blocking Crime in Low Income Communities

Situational crime prevention has many potential applications for our current and emerging crime situation. When choosing techniques, the author suggests revisiting 'Evidence-Based Crime Prevention,' as put forward by Lawrence Sherman, et al. (2002) since it is essential for our future planning of place-specific crime prevention. The work is still fresh, with poignant insights, and it is yet to be implemented on a broad scale. The reader is directed to the book in its entirety, but particularly to the tables at the end of Sherman's book wherein the much needed clarity about what works, and what does not work in crime prevention is provided: see particularly table 10.2 prepared by Welsh and Farrington (2002). What the reader will find is that convention does not necessarily mean best practice in terms of crime prevention. Highlights from "what works"[95] in crime prevention include the following:

- Parental education plus day care / pre-school for young children to establish norms for behavior for crime, alcohol, etc.

- Cognitive behavioral therapy, moral resonation therapy, and reasoning skills development

- Community employment

- Mentoring and tutoring with work study for anti-social behavior and drop-out/truancy problems

- Intensive residential training programs for at-risk youth

- Nuisance abatement statutes and practices (focusing on crime disorders, drug dealing, property crimes, graffiti removal, etc)

- Improved street lighting in open public places

- Problem-oriented policing

- Increased directed patrols in street-corner hot spots of crime

- Proactive drunk driving arrests

- Reinforce school and discipline management

- Incapacitating offenders who have high crime rates

- Proactive arrests of serious habitual offenders

- Ex-criminal offender job training for older males no longer under criminal justice supervision

- Vocational education for adult offenders and juvenile delinquents

- Target specific problems of offenders; provide intensive treatment

- Prison-based therapeutic community treatment of drug-involved offenders

What was found not to work in crime prevention includes the following:

- Drug market arrests do not prevent drug markets from re-emerging; the market must be disabled by other means to prevent drug crime

- Community policing without clear crime-risk factor focus is ineffective and does not prevent crime

- Adding additional law enforcement to cities regardless of assignment or activity is meaningless, and does not prevent crime

- Gun buy-back programs were found to be ineffective to reduce criminal deaths or injuries, and do not prevent crime

- Neighborhood watch programs, without a capable manager and financial support are too cyclical in wind-up and let-down to prevent crime in a lasting way

- Summer job programs or work programs for at-risk youth – they are too short term and non-intensive, and do not prevent crime

- Home / community parent training alone, with child involvement, does not prevent crime

- Self-control competency instruction for alcohol and drugs have been shown to be insufficient

- Counseling, social work, and other therapeutic interventions are only effective if undertaken outside of the disciplined school environment

- Mentoring, tutoring, and work study were ineffective for preventing alcohol and drug problems, and do not prevent crime

- Short-term non-residential training programs for at-risk youth do not prevent crime

- Diversion from court to job training for adult offenders as a condition of court dismissal does not prevent crime

- Specific deterrence interventions such as shock treatment shock treatment and "scared straight" programs do not have lasting impact, and do not prevent crime

- Rehabilitation programs that use non-directive, unstructured counseling are ineffective in reducing crime

- Intensive supervised probation and parole do not prevent crime

- Home confinement does not prevent crime

- Community residential programs do not prevent crime; they may have other merits, but crime prevention does not result from them

- Urine testing does not prevent crime

- Increased referral, monitoring, management in the community by courts and corrections do not prevent crime

- Correctional boot camps using traditional military discipline do not prevent crime

- Juvenile wilderness programs do not prevent crime

Continually seeking to identify what works and why is essential to improving our ability to resolve crime problems, and prevent them. There is much written about what works, and what does not work, and some of the crime problems anticipated in this economic downturn have old remedies that might be pulled out or dusted off, but more likely, we are to find that our new age has new challenges, new technologies, and new communication forms that require new strategies. An environmental criminology framework is best used to prevent crimes in places, both mobile and fixed positions, that take place in our modern age.

Beyond blocking crime opportunity through the use of Situational Crime Prevention techniques, there are other important lessons from our past that require revisiting. An important lesson from the Great Depression was that in an era of reduced tax receipts for governments, the government had to do more with less. Already in this chapter, the author has highlighted how state and local governments are trimming law enforcement and other support services due to reduced funding. In such times, it is important to focus on what is most important to the greatest number of citizens, and to target precious and increasingly scarce resources at the problems that exert the most deleterious impact on society.

In the Great Depression, this meant ceasing to use techniques that were not working. The repeal of Prohibition meant a reduction in ineffective policing, denial of monies to organized crime, and an increase in tax revenue for the government. It is time to look at our own laws and stop doing what we know is not working today. Marijuana decriminalization must be addressed, as it wastes huge resources of law enforcement time, and makes criminals out of millions of Americans who are quiet users of the substance. The substance itself, while harmful to the individual, is not the proximate cause of the majority of drug-impacted crimes; it is rather cocaine, methamphetamine, PCP, and heroin that are known to be linked with crime of greater violence and safety risk to society. Taxing the product, regulating the market, making the consumer of marijuana safer, providing public education to reduce marijuana demand, while simultaneously eliminating dangerous street-corner selling, drug trafficking, and funding criminal organizations, are positive ends. This does not mean that the author supports marijuana use – I know and affirm it is a drug and it is bad for you, and I would not want any children to use it – what it does mean, however, is that the social cost of criminalization of the drug for adults exceeds the benefits to society, and now, at a time when crime is anticipated to increase, and specifically vice crimes, it is time to take the revenue opportunity of illegal marijuana distribution out of the hands of organized crime, drug cartels, and street gangs. Licensed, regulated, taxed, and controlled distribution of marijuana at a price approximating street prices of illegal marijuana, will serve to wipe out this market, and with it much violence in trafficking and crime milieu associated with street distribution.

In an era of financial crisis, we must learn to be lean and do without whatever is not absolutely necessary, and take stock of what we are doing that is not working, and stop doing it, as these would be good steps in the right direction. We should revisit laws, statutes, ordinances, law enforcement programs, methods, and means to achieve peace on the mean streets that accompany crime waves.

To sum up, the lessons of our past teach us that we must adapt our control sys-tems to meet new challenges of technology, change our laws when they are not working, target habitual offenders and incapacitate them, and target crime prevention and employment programs for the unemployed population most likely to be ensnared as likely offenders in crimes of opportunity during the economic contraction. We must be as bold as the problems we face, and think of new heights to create the barriers needed to block the challenges that face us now, the sea walls we prepare to hold back the crime wave, designed, ensured, re-measured, and supported to combat the coming crime wave.

6 Limits of the past experience, and new challenges to be confronted in the coming Crime Wave

"We cannot solve our problems with the same thinking
we used when we created them."

— Albert Einstein[96]

There is no steady state; we live in an age of continual change. Our own ignorance (not knowing what works) and unwillingness to abandon what we know is not working, may keep us from reducing economic misery and preventing crime in our new age. There are many, perhaps even the great majority at the time of this writing, that seek not to look at things as they are now, but as they would like them to be, or perhaps they are stuck in the past, remembering that glorious past or actively desiring that past period to re-emerge. We must look squarely at our current financial crisis and take bold action to protect our families, businesses, communities, and countries, by gathering our collective genius to create a new future. The past is the past, but history is what is written subsequently, and we have yet to write the history of this global contraction.

This is not the time for inaction. We are indeed in great peril, ruining not only our economy for our generation, but also the lives of our children and their children for decades to come. Those who say that this current economic contraction will not be as bad as the Great Depression frequently claim that we are different now, as our economy is bigger, our economic safety net is better, and we have lessons learned from our past to help us. It is clear that our past experience has helped guide the footsteps of Federal Reserve Chairman Ben Bernanke along with his Treasury colleagues to move swiftly to implement significant actions to accelerate financial interventions and forestall another Great Depression. But, although the Stimulus package is passed, we are still unconvinced as massive job losses are still occurring, credit contraction persists, and consumer and business saving has spiked upwards with few spending money in a market where the amount of money spent can be the life blood of a free market economy.

It is time to ask, what next? After the honeymoon of President Obama's first 100 day plan, what next? Will there be a second 100-day plan, and a third; most definitely they will be needed. President Obama will leave the Oval Office as a much older man and he will surely need his youth, his vigor, and his optimism to see him through. Under no circumstances will we repeat the Great Depression of the 1930s because we have the playbook from this era and have been on a crash course implementing the lessons learned with deliberate speed. The Second Great Depression will have new challenges. We face different struggles now and it is important to highlight them in order that they will remain in our focus and the lessons we shall hopefully learn from them are included in future interventions to curb likely economic downturns and the consequences of those crises. The circumstances and factors that make us and our times will be discussed in the following sections.

GLOBALIZATION

For centuries Americans have been largely protected by their coastal waters that prevented easy access into the country. Passage was by boat which took days to cross the Atlantic. It was not until 1927 that Charles Lindbergh[97] made the first historic airborne passage non-stop across the Atlantic Ocean in an aircraft covering 3,610 miles in 33 1/2 hours from New York to Paris. In 2009, that same flight takes only 7 hours and 16 minutes and thousands take that flight routinely every day.[98] Globalization has been facilitated by great improvements in transportation including air transportation, making us different from prior generations as travel expands our life experience, our commerce and the ability to trade, as well as family relations, but globalization also increases our exposure to those who would seek to harm us. Our border control and port strategy are far more important today than ever before to prevent crime and terrorism. Air travel and migration patterns have created increased opportunities for cross-cultural marriages, international educational experiences, global business, long-distance friendships, and distributed peer networks that create new challenges for security. Our own transportation networks are used against us and frequently deliver to us the very goods we seek to keep from our shores. Car travel is facilitated by major networks of roads, thruways, and freeways, and the freedom to travel creates its own risks of crime opportunity, allowing determined offenders to practice their frauds in multiple jurisdictions with ease.

COMPUTERS AND INFORMATION TECHNOLOGY

The first commercial typewriter was invented in 1867 by Christopher Sholes, Carlos Glidden, and Samuel W. Soule in Milwaukee, Wisconsin. For years this had undoubtedly been the workhorse of written communication for commercial industry. In the early 1980s, the electronic word processor for personal computers was born with the early entrants of Wordstar, Wordperfect, and MS Word. These word processors and the hard drives that would store their data revolutionized industry and a new age of productivity was born. Within a short time, whole libraries were put on electronic disk, opening up many publications that were previously bound in hard copies only. The Encyclopedia Britannica was founded in 1768, the best seller for over two-hundred years, but it was disrupted by a free online Wiki Encloypedia started in 2001 that has seemingly unlimited resources of knowledge through thousands of voluntary contributors. Take the personal computer, add online data from millions of sources like Wikipedia, and run analyses using business intelligence engines, and you have actionable intelligence that, if used as intended, beckons individuals everywhere to fascinating facts and figures, but if used for illicit or illegal means, it can be used easily and efficiently to steal, beg, barter, and erode prior barriers to entry protected trade secrets, military secrets, business secrets, financial information, personal information, medical records, etc. Increasingly faster computers and software tools have created amazing possibilities in information technology, but motivated criminal offenders do find many ways of exploiting computers and information networks for their criminal ends.

COMMUNICATIONS AND SPEED OF THOUGHT

Just as the horse-drawn carriage was replaced by the barge and the railroad, so also had the telegraph and fixed line telephone been replaced by the mobile phone, text messaging, and pervasive computing. It took four years for the peak-to-rough collapse of the Great Depression, owing largely to the new experience with the deep contraction and slow communications. Many rural areas appeared unimpacted 12 months after the crash, but within months thereafter, the impact was felt throughout all developed nations. The rapid means of communication enable communications in many forms, written, electronic, radio frequency, and other signals. These tools which have traditionally been used for so much good can be used for harm as well, and it is important to safeguard these technologies for our own protection. Frequency-hopping radios, availability of cash-and-carry mobile phones, and increasingly powerful computing networks, make it difficult for law enforcement to keep up with determined criminals. More research and work need to be done to protect privacy and electronic security to combat the sizable advantage with which the criminals, seem to operate with impunity worldwide. Only when the light of justice is shone on the criminal operation does it get illuminated and placed before public attention, but there are other seemingly limitless frauds, extortions, and organized crime rackets to keep law enforcement busy for years.

GLOBAL POSITIONING SATELLITES

The GPS device, enabling cars to navigate with visual and audio voice directions, has changed the way we commute and work: when traffic gets backed up, we can take alternative routes with confidence, increasing workplace productivity and safety. The GPS technology that allows UPS trucks to deliver packages more efficiently, and UAV craft to fly their coordinate navigated routes, is also the very same technology used to exploit geography for dead drops and rendezvous appointments with crime. GPS has broadened the definition of place, enabling space to be put between buyer and seller, increasing the difficulty of law enforcement to combat serious trafficking crimes. Robots and other unmanned craft are increasingly being used for trafficking contraband, placing additional distance and a veil of anonymity between offenders and their customers or victims.

WEAPONS AND ELECTRONICS

In the 1920s and 1930s, it was the automatic machine gun that was a game-changer, giving the Depression desperados a lead up on their less armed law enforcement chasers. The technological advantage of faster cars and better technology allowed the criminals to excel for a season until law enforcement was improved with modern technology. Today, weapons have improved in terms of firepower, but it is electronic commerce that seems to have taken great losses for the markets. It is incredible that bank robbers continue to risk capture and exposure through physical theft, whereas organized crime has assessed the risk of exposure for electronic theft that seems so minimal given the electronic terrain. The Madoffs and other fraudsters have exploited technologies for confidence games and to keep ahead of the not-so-watchful-eyes of auditors, regulators, and the general public taken in by these frauds.

LEVERAGE AND COMPLEX FINANCIAL TRANSACTIONS

Another grave challenge today is the complexity of financial transactions that have the ability to obfuscate the truth through smoke screens of data so that frauds can be perpetrated without detection by the untrained eye. The Madoff scandal appears to have been created by one of the founders of NASDAQ who had the trust of many key players in the market, and the Madoff fund appears not to have purchased an equity for over 13 years, yet they were issuing statements, collecting money, paying dividends, etc. Other frauds will soon be revealed one by one or in multitudes. However, more significantly, credit-default swaps and other complex financial instruments have created new risks to the broader market, and new forms of leverage, the collapse of which have created catastrophic losses for many. An army of criminal justice-trained forensic accountants, auditors, and inspectors and their vigilant inspections need to be cultivated to meet the challenge of the new financial criminal profile.

ENERGY DEPENDENCE

Energy dependence creates systemic weakness and places supply chains and our country at risk from foreign influence. Most of the fossil fuels are extracted in countries that are hostile to the United States, or must be harvested in hostile terrain. This cost and risk creates challenges for law enforcement. For too many years the U.S. has pursued an oil-based energy policy, putting off to the future the requirement to capture and use more sustainable sources of energy. The policy has left us open to two oil embargos that contributed to two recessions, and successive oil shocks have led to conditions leading up to military interventions. While we are down economically, look for our enemies to kick us, seeking to inflict maximum pain at our moment of vulnerability; this was surely the case with the two OPEC oil embargoes of the 1970s, and this is happening again today.

TERRORISM

On the front page of the *Washington Post* on November 15, 2008 was an article titled, "Experts See Security Risks in Downturn: Global Financial Crisis may Fuel Instability and Weaken U.S. Defenses." The article warns that two forces are colliding with potential harmful effects to U.S. security and global safety: (1) economic downturns in global economies are causing increased economic hardship and political instability (in terms of food price inflation, rising unemployment, etc.), giving rise to the vulnerability of insurrection and the influence of extremist groups like Al-Qaeda, or new political alliances not in line with U.S. interests as those that hit hardest in third-world countries and seek money (and by reference new political economic relationships) from those with funds, with China being the most likely financier; and (2) the governments globally, but particularly in the U.S. are preparing to downsize their expenses in military, intelligence, and criminal justice in line with budgetary concerns, or new Obama presidential administration interests, just at a time when crime and terrorism opportunity are on the rise.

Key highlights of the article by Joby Warrick, *Washington Post* staff writer, on Saturday, November 15, 2008 (Page A01) include the following: "Intelligence officials are warning that the deepening global financial crisis could weaken fragile governments in the world's most dangerous areas and undermine the ability of the United States and its allies to respond to a new wave of security threats. U.S. government officials and private analysts say the economic turmoil has heightened the short-term risk of a terrorist attack, as radical groups probe for weakening border protections and new gaps in defenses. A protracted financial crisis could threaten the survival of friendly regimes from Pakistan to the Middle East while forcing Western nations to cut spending on defense, intelligence and foreign aid, the sources said." Read the entire article at **http://www.washingtonpost.com /wp-dyn/content/article/2008/11/14/AR2008111403864.html?hpid=topnews**

The author of the article has focused his attention on terrorism, but what is much more likely is insurrection, economic misery, and increased crime occurring in these locations that can create environments where terrorists can thrive with impunity. The world economy has fallen into a deep global recession, and if it is not curbed quickly, history books will have to describe it as the second coming of the Great Depression. In third-world countries particularly, many people are hungry, unemployed, and feeling miserable, and the World Bank has correctly assessed the risk.

Joby Warrick writes: "As bad as economic conditions are in the United States and Europe, where outright recessions are expected next year, they are worse in developing countries such as Pakistan, a state that was already struggling with violent insurgencies and widespread poverty. Some analysts warn that a prolonged economic crisis could trigger a period of widespread unrest that could strengthen the hand of extremists and threaten Pakistan's democratically elected government—with potentially grave consequences for the region and perhaps the planet. Pakistanis were hit by soaring food and energy prices earlier in the year and the country's financial problems have multiplied since late summer. Islamabad's currency reserves have nearly evaporated, forcing the new government to seek fresh foreign loans or risk defaulting on the country's debt. The national currency, the Pakistan rupee, has been devalued, and inflation is squeezing Pakistan's poor and middle class alike."

As the world leaders from the G-20 met in Washington, D.C. in March 2009, it is becoming increasingly apparent that a deep freeze has hit the global economy, and one of the negative consequences of the downturn is increased economic misery, crime opportunity, and terrorism threats. The world has changed, but how much we do not yet know, but when the dust ultimately settles, it will look like a different place.

Thinking about crime on an international scale, an international crime control strategy report[99] phrased the challenges this way:

> International criminal activity has increased in scale and extent in the wake of globalization, becoming a complex worldwide threat. International criminals today engage in a wide range of illegal activities, including drug trafficking, terrorism, alien and contraband smuggling, fraud, extortion, money laundering, bribery, economic espionage, intellectual property theft, and counterfeiting. Many also resort to extreme violence to advance their criminal enterprises.

> International criminals ignore borders, except when seeking safe haven behind them. They move sums of money through the international financial systems that are so huge they dwarf the combined economies of many nations. They are often organized in multi-crime businesses, and they have capitalized on growth in international communications and transportation to expand their criminal operations and form potent alliances.

> The corrosive activities of international criminals in the post-Cold War era no longer threaten particular countries or regions. They threaten all nations, including our own. International crime is not only a law enforcement problem, it is a formidable and increasing threat to national and international security.

On February 12, 2009, top U.S. intelligence officials told Congress that the financial crisis spanning the globe is a significant security threat. Dennis Blair, Director of National Intelligence, told Congress that "the global financial crisis was the primary near-term security concern of the United States...the longer the crisis drags on, the greater the threat it will pose to political stability." He went on to give dire warnings: "Economic crises increase the risk of regime-threatening instability if they are prolonged for a one- or two-year period." He also predicted a possible scenario of the immediate future: "Instability can loosen the hold that many developing countries have on law and order, which can spill out in dangerous ways into the international community." Blair told Congress that U.S. allies and friends may be unable to meet defense and humanitarian commitments at home and abroad because of the economic crisis. He further added that the crisis may exacerbate with a wave of destructive protectionist trade measures by countries under economic pressures.[100]

Whether we speak of the U.S., UK, Australia, Japan, or other developed nations, the dramatic contraction in consumer and business spending has now hit the markets for a second round of pain; it was not so long ago that we suffered the first round with the credit contraction following the Lehman Brothers collapse. Now we must consider more grave consequences and move to mitigate these risks.

But is it just the capitalist economies and developed nations that must be concerned? China and other major nations of the world are also confronting serious contractions of their economies. China's economy has slowed down more rapidly than many others, and with a population of about 1.3 billion, the sharp contraction, if prolonged, may create crime opportunity difficult to thwart.[101]

By February 2009, there was a growing chorus of world leaders, economists, futurists, thought leaders, and radio talk show hosts, raising the specter of concern that this contraction may be the type of serious negative sharp contraction that causes much disruption, crime waves, and worse – civil unrest.[102] These include Pascal Lamy, the head of the World Bank, who in February 2009 said: "the global economic crisis could trigger political unrest equal to that seen during the 1930s…the crisis today is spreading faster [than the Great Depression] and affects more countries at the same time…This crisis weighs heavily on politics and puts peace in danger."[103]

In December 2008, Dominique Strauss-Kahn, the head of the International Monetary Fund, gave this serious warning: "Advanced nations will be hit by violent civil unrest if the elite continue to restructure the economy around their own interests while looting the taxpayer…social unrest may happen in many countries, including advanced economies…violent protests could break out in countries worldwide if the financial system was not restructured to benefit everyone rather than a small elite." Strauss-Kahn warned gravely "that civil unrest could arise, specifically in the U.S., as a result of the wholesale looting of the taxpayer and the devaluation of the dollar."[104]

When I started writing this book in September 2008, it was as a voice of warning trying to get people to focus on the likely consequences of the economic collapse and the tsunami-level fallout to come. Unfortunately, now in March 2009, as time has progressed and the writing of this book has developed, I am afraid, the predictive nature of the book has almost given way to the reporting of current events, and it is for this reason that a good book, not a great book, is written. For good is the enemy of the great, and I have not time to be a voice of warning if a great book is what is required; I will leave it to successive editions of this book to correct the errors, clarify the context, and write more precisely with the assistance of hindsight. For now, there is urgency and a call to action.

It is time for governments everywhere to consider how best to manage the next phase of this crisis – the phase where we realize that the stimulus, government financial interventions, and coordinated central bank efforts, while important, do not bring immediate relief to individuals and fail to alleviate the suffering of the people in any manner; in these conditions local distress may escalate to global unrest. In 1974, the UN called together economists and criminal justice experts to review data and the lessons learned from sharp past contractions and they found that a great contributor to crime opportunity was the unprepared states, indeed the under capacity of social control systems to hold down order during surge waves of crime; in time the social control systems respond and meet needs, but at first they are overwhelmed when much havoc can happen, ruining many lives and fortunes. It is not too early to prepare.

President Obama and world leaders everywhere need to revisit our crime control plans, and the plans need to be as big and bold as the problems we face now, and will face in the future. It is a boldfaced myth that the Great Depression saw falling crime rates requiring inaction on the part of government – that somehow crime went down on its own. On the contrary, crime conditions were great during the Great Depression, and crime as a systemic problem was deliberately tackled by President Roosevelt through specific measures to: (1) strengthen criminal justice institutions to meet new crime needs; (2) target and incapacitate serious habitual offenders; (3) eliminate laws not obeyed by the people (exercising civil disobedience) to concentrate focus of attention on laws designed to reduce most harm; (4) take the money out of crime (and tax undesirable commerce if possible); (5) reduce demand for crime, and, more specifically, provide long-term intensive employment for the most likely offenders – unemployed young males. At one point in the first Great Depression, over 25% of the young male unemployed population was working in rural work camps in the nation's state and national parks. This and many other lessons we should be reviewing now for their relevance.

7 Stemming the Tide of the Coming Crime Wave – a proactive crime control and risk mitigation strategy

> "I have yet to be in a game where luck was involved.
> Well-prepared players make plays. I have yet to be in a
> game where the most prepared team didn't win."
>
> – Urban Meyers, University of Florida football coach and multi-national champion title winner

Truly the "parents have eaten sour grapes," and it is the children's teeth that will be set on edge to the 3rd and 4th generation. This age of debt, unbridled avarice, and taking the waiting out of wanting, has left our economy and our children's heritage much poorer. How long can a nation continue to promise that the enterprises are 'too big to fail', pushing off into the future the repayment of debt obligations that far exceed our ability to repay?

It will be foolish to take comfort from periodic pauses in the financial storm: it took four years for the market to reach bottom during the Great Depression and while our stock markets have raced to the bottom, unemployment and other measures have not fallen as quickly and may reasonably be expected to fall further in course of time. If one stops to think about it, through October 2008, the speed of the stock market collapse was exceeded by only two previous economic events: the 1974 deep recession and the 1929 stock market crash and Great Depression. In November 2008, the market broke through the 1974 downturn levels, only to rise in an abrupt government-financed run-up (with the public financed bailout of Citibank), yet as it happens in many bear market rallies, the rally peaked and faded in weak volume. Technically, with the 1974 lows breached, we have only the Great Depression as a comparable bottom now. Keep your fingers crossed that we do not repeat the Great Depression.

Times are different now and we have many measures that can act as an economic cushion to the hard landing of the kind experienced in the 1930s. However, these social cushions were built as a response to a different time, and we hope they are more supportive than mere whoopee cushions of bailouts. It was Charles Dickens who made this illuminating comment on a period, "these are the best of times, and the worst of times," and the same can be said of today, except for the fact that in order to return to the best of times, we need to focus on the worst of times, and make life better, safer, kinder, gentler, and more humane in our day.

Actually, in 2009, our economy is larger and more integrated with other nations, where trading is swifter, transportation is faster, borders are easily crossed, and crime has new pockets and niches not available to previous generations. The brief honeymoon of the new Obama administration will provide some elixir for those optimists who go on chanting that the sky is not falling, however, when the first 100 days eventually transform themselves into bleak reality, they too will reluctantly admit that all the king's horses and all the king's men cannot put the king dollar back on the wall again. The Rest of the World (ROW) will not continue to allow us to beggar them with our insatiable wants without making payment for them.

Sadly, the first baby boomer has now retired, and this occurs at a time when we need more taxpayers, working many more months, not less. The public cry for handouts now will in time turn to tax revolts in a few years as the burden of this debtor economy is passed on to our children.

We are witnessing the death of Pax Americana. We can no longer afford to be policemen to the world for free, as freedom isn't free. Others must pay their fair share of the burden of peace-making. New leaders will emerge. New challenges will need fresh approaches, and more reflections on our past may unnecessarily bridle creative responses to our current problems.

We must avoid, in policy and action, succumbing to future shock and information overload that accompany the barrage of economic misery and crime that is bombarding us daily, and must focus squarely on the great task before us to bring together our collective genius as a society to wrestle with our current condition, and decide best how to regain control and bring about a future that we want our children to live in. On no account must we be paralyzed by fear, but rather we must channel our fear into action. We must move now to wrestle with the uncomfortable, the unthinkable, the unfathomable, for to do otherwise will only usher in an end that will definitely leave us much weaker when the dust settles.

Just as sea walls[105] alone are insufficient to hold back the tsunami tide,[106] preparing for a crime wave requires a complimentary and coordinated set of strategies beyond first defenses; one must prepare for a "defense in depth" strategy. "Defense in depth" is a defensive strategy adopted by militaries and security professionals to combat complex security threats, vulnerabilities, and risks, where it is more difficult for an enemy to combat a coordinated multi-layered defense, than to simply overwhelm an adversary at their weakest point and pierce a single barrier of protection. Defense in depth strategies use multiple security measures and countermeasures to protect the assets (people, places, processes, and valuable objects), detect intrusions, and safeguard assets.

Defense in depth strategies minimize the likelihood of success for the determined offenders and will deter them from succeeding in their assault and capture of the protected assets. A well-designed defense in depth strategy will provide early warning systems to detect intrusions and probes into the system. If an intruder or virus is infecting the system, the early warning system will identify, isolate, and then incapacitate the risk, and inoculate the system from further threats of the same type. Importantly, defense in depth creates space and time distance between an offender and his target, allowing coordinated security measures and countermeasures time to respond, raising the defense shields and releasing the hounds to prevent successful assault on the fortification.

Sharp crises can create surge waves of demand for services, especially for law and order services, that systems built for normal times cannot possibly hold. These surges can overwhelm institutions and create additional problems. In terms of prevention, one of the primary differences between sharp crises like an earthquake, flood, or tornado, and sharp economic crises that may trigger an economic depression, is that the natural disasters come and go relatively quickly, though the clean up may take many years, whereas sharp economic crises creating economic depressions have lasting psychological impacts on individuals, communities, economies and institutions for many years, or even generations, to come.

Surging waves of massive unemployment and sudden wealth losses can create situations of desperation at the individual level. Resolving employment and income problems must be an integral part of any systematic drive to prevent crime. Merely suppressing the crime likelihood through defense shields will not dissuade and hold back the likely offender from searching for another target if their core basic needs are not met. Hacking at the roots of the problem necessitates an environment where crime opportunity prevention and employment opportunity creation work hand in hand. A defense in depth approach to handling increased crime vulnerability and threats due to this economic depression must include meaningful opportunities for employment for the potential offenders, work activity, and reduction of unsupervised free time when unemployed. A balanced approach to crime prevention requires strategic planning, a theoretical framework for situational crime prevention, reassessment of risks under conditions of threat, coordination of stakeholders in crime prevention, communication mechanisms, and resource utilization. The prepared comprehensive strategy will then be used to coordinate the implementation of a broad array of tactics which will be deployed following defense in depth modalities.

CRIME CONTROL STRATEGY AND TACTICS

Strategy

Master planning for defense in depth strategy

Review of laws and focus on crimes of greatest impact on society

Review of criminal justice systems, their structure and performance

Focus on situational crime prevention at specific places

Think maneuver warfare, where crime 'opportunity blocking' is the objective

Understand that restoration of meaningful employment is an important key to getting the train of society back on track again; public officials should recognize that work has value unto itself. Support payments are important, but it is not the same as employment since meaningful employment has increased positive psychological benefits. Let us put this nation to work in some great unifying effort, plan, and vision.

Plan, and work to the plan; include within the plan...
Assessment
Coordination
Communication
Resource utilization

Evaluate what is working, and be quick to jettison that which is not.

Tactics

Target and incapacitate serious habitual offenders

Target crime hotspots and honey pots (attractors) and reduce crime opportunity

Target fraud-related crimes that are known to increase during times of sharp economic crises, related to relief aid, insurance, bankruptcy fraud, diversion of aid, etc.

Target organized crime markets and take the money out of crime; tax the trade if possible, and remove crime opportunity from criminal organizations; decriminalize, regulate, and tax marijuana.

Actively divert young male unemployed individuals most vulnerable to criminal involvement and steer them into lawful and meaningful employment opportunities in geographically remote areas.

Remove "moral hazard" as an economic incentive to commit crime, and strive to keep a bright and clear line between what is right, and what is wrong, reinforcing ethics through example, regulation, and training.

Educate and train governments, businesses, communities, families, and individuals on how to detach themselves from crime opportunity through implementing situational crime prevention in places most vulnerable to crime.

Increase the effort needed to commit crime
Target hardening
Access control
Deflecting offenders
Controlling facilitators

Increasing the risk associated with crime
Entry and exit screening
Formal surveillance
Surveillance by employees
Natural surveillance

Reducing the rewards of crime
Target removal
Identifying property
Reducing temptation
Denying benefits

Removing excuses (and encouraging shaming)
    Rule setting
    Stimulating conscience
    Controlling dis-inhibitors to crime
    Facilitate compliance
    Promote victimization prevention education
    Implement Crime Prevention Through Environmental Design (CPTED)

Target hardening
    Access control
    Surveillance
    Image and maintenance
    Location specific activity support

Monitor performance and develop the technical body of research that examines and broadcasts evidenced-based crime prevention measures.

Beyond these broad strategies and tactics, here are some specific things that governments, businesses, communities, and individuals can do.

7.1 What governments and public officials can do

We must address our current situation, and squarely deal with the upcoming crime wave condition, in terms of tackling the supply and demand of crime opportunity with determination and conviction, to reduce not just the unsightly symptoms, but the very roots of the crime condition.

A balanced plan must embrace both the offender and the victim, the spatial geography of criminal place and location, the laws and their enforcement, and opportunistic times and settings whence crimes occur.

Environmental criminology and situational crime prevention must become the normative theoretical framework from which to address this problem and its place-based variations.

We must recognize that economics and 'rational choice' play a vital role in crime opportunity, and economics should be used to reduce the reliance on crime for subsistence.

Economic events that are cataclysmic can bring on rapid massive unemployment conditions that exacerbate civil disobedience and imperil the adherence to good behavior and the rule of law.

Since 1954, sharp negative economic shocks have been a leading indicator of crime waves with approximately a 12-month time lag.

Multi-disciplinary approaches are most likely to be effective to get in front of the problems to reduce the velocity as well as the depth of the crime wave.

In reviewing history, we recognize the apparently odd fact that one of the causes for unabated crime opportunity following sharp crises was the control institutions that were inadequately prepared, equipped, or staffed for the surge force of increased criminal offenders or likely offenders at peak force, and this in turn offered little resistance to additional crime as the crime wave washed over the few controls set up for normal times.

A balanced supply and demand crime control policy should be prepared for these times with increased focus on attacking the roots of the crime problem, by targeting serious habitual offenders (SHOs), preventing victimization, inoculating places for particular crimes, and reducing crime opportunity through law enforcement and meaningful job creation. The vast majority would naturally work at lawful jobs than operate in the streets in illegal enterprises, but the option for work must be kept out there for hope of a better way.

We should stop doing what we know is not working, and dedicate resources to crime issues of greatest negative impact in our society. When the greater part of the public ignores a law through civil disobedience, perhaps it is time to review the law. For instance, the unintended consequence of Prohibition was to give rise to civil disobedience and funds that facilitated increasing organized crime. Its solution was to repeal the law itself.

Taking the funding sources from organized crime was vital, as was crafting laws that the people would support. Ending prohibition was essential to narrowing the focus of law enforcement on crimes of most serious negative consequence to society. Today's continued enforcement of marijuana is a comparable problem. Obviously, it is a drug with harmful personal consequences, but not a substance causing malicious violent crime, and so it should be decriminalized, regulated, and taxed; and that would be tantamount to denying organized crime and drug cartels the crucial income accruing from traffic in the substance.

Resolving the macro economic problems is integral to resolving conditions that enable good people to rationally accept crime as a lifestyle, while no other meaningful work opportunities exist. We as a society must realize that there is value in employment beyond money – work can provide self-respect, a foundation for self-definition, and a meaning in itself that mere money handouts cannot provide.

Thinking of Keynes, for centuries leaders have fought wars, built pyramids and great walls to employ their people. We could do all these things to spur employment with little lasting benefit outside of new tourist sites, or if we have even less vision or no vision, we could, as Keynes suggested, bury money in old salt mines and seal the mines up, and then let the free market entrepreneurs go down and employ people digging up the money.

Employment for employment's sake is alright in the short-term, but it would have far greater impact if the employment were meaningful, being a multi-benefit investment in our future, with a long-term benefit for our children and their children. The broad range of time spans between the economic soft landing and hard landing scenarios ranges from 3-5 years to 8-12 years. When the economy recovers, and it will, the government will need to get out of the way of commerce or it will crowd out enterprise and risk over-stimulating the economy with excess demand for services, creating inflation on many fronts. So, whatever is done should last long enough to see us through the economic depression and short-term enough to terminate once the crisis is over.

In the author's view, what are immediately called for are big, audacious national goals – projecting a vision far greater than the next speech, next month or quarter. What are called for are bold national economic and science policy goals that will take at least 10 years to achieve, with far-reaching impact extending well into the future. Only with these long goals can we hope to create a sustained economic impact to change an economy and gain the investment outcome we desire. President Obama's pledge to build a new power grid to bring back the power from the new renewable sources of power is a worthy and practical goal, but it will be achieved only at great expense and with marginal impact on the planet. We can think bigger, and we must, for the benefit of human kind.

While it is difficult to calculate the net multiplier effect in advance, it is, nonetheless, significant that the inventions created through these targeted national science policy goals sprung our nation forward in discoveries and applied science. Consider the national science goal of putting a man on the moon. It seemed like such a 'far out' impractical idea – putting a man on the moon? Why? But what resulted was a 7:1 economic multiplier bringing us the microwave, communications, Velcro, and many other useful spin-offs. Yet another beneficial spin-off was to put in place a unifying vision in response to the then-threat—the Soviets who beat the U.S. into space with Sputnik, and this launched a race for the high ground.

Today we need another equally large, seemingly impossible task, and the author has one for you to seriously consider. For Kennedy, putting a man on the moon was seemingly impossible, but we did it and it paid huge dividends and supplied our civilian army with jobs, both white collar and blue collar. For Obama, rather than put a man on the moon, why not send our nuclear waste to the Sun? The great obstacle to using the efficient and clean energy source of nuclear power is the waste product that is makes, and nobody wants to store it. A whole facility of tunnels has been prepared at Yucca Mountain to contain the waste for more years than we will be alive, but no state wants to allow this waste to cross its borders. Not even Nevada wants the waste stored at their site. What respectable environmentalist thinks that storing that hazardous nuclear waste on this planet is a responsible action?

Why not think bigger, better, farther, higher, and in a more visionary manner and send this hazardous nuclear waste to the sun where it will be burned up efficiently? Imagine the jobs that would need to be created worldwide for nuclear waste management and permanent disposal to handle the robotic collection, containment, distribution, launch, security, emergency recovery, insurance, engineering, and the list goes on. With many propulsion options available including an electromagnetic cannon requiring no flammable propulsion source, the waste could be propelled out of the earth's atmosphere and directed to the Sun, and somewhere along the way the gravitational pull of the sun will welcome the toxic payload, drawing it ever so welcomingly into its grasp, returning the waste to its natural form of energy. Now that would be an example of thinking big.

Before you say this is just too ridiculous, ask yourself a harder question. Why not? It would provide tens of thousands of jobs, and would be a great benefit to this planet, and a lasting legacy of a generation known only for its wasteful spending; that we might turn this reputation around and do something for future generations beyond saddling them with debt would be a worthy goal. Whether or not this is the right solution now or in the future, remains to be seen, but it is a pertinent example of the way in which thinking big can be helpful in times of crisis.

Meaningful investment in the U.S. that leads to employment, income, and prosperity is what is needed. It matters not who owns the company, but the workers themselves perform the work in these examples. In an age where protectionism looms large, Congress and other world governments should focus on economic stimulus that creates many jobs to the 3rd and 4th level of demand. Modify the ultimately unhelpful imperative to "Buy American" to focus instead on requiring the use of indigenous steel for bridges made from metallurgic coal mined from Appalachian Coal, transportation on U.S. rails, smelting by U.S. steel companies, tooling by U.S. machine systems, engineering by U.S.-based engineers, and construction by U.S. workers – leverage must be turned to lever every public dollar spent on investment into more creating U.S.-based jobs. All countries should pitch in and create demand-oriented industrial projects in their own countries. This is not to say that foreign companies or workers will be denied work opportunity, but rather, if the government is the financier, then the work opportunities should remain here where the taxes were raised to finance the work.

Beyond work opportunities for meaningful employment, educational opportunities for retooling the mind and providing new techniques and trades for the body are important. Any crime control bill should surely have within it some demand reduction component targeted at creating better life opportunities for individuals at greatest risk of crime involvement. Governments should consider endorsing a massive grant program to train or retrain people on education grants to graduate in math, engineering, and sciences. We beggar our nation and our children's futures when we do not focus on those tools that will leave them better prepared for their future – and math and sciences are critical.

We must attack 'moral hazard' and civil disobedience of laws. We must rid our society of what will surely return as a popular notion that civil disobedience is good not bad, particularly when civil disobedience and crime is targeted at paying taxes, or injuring big banks, insurance companies, mortgage financiers, and big businesses, that stripped the common man and woman of their American dream. In the tale of Robin Hood, the reader is introduced to a merry band of outlaws that found good reason to steal from the Sheriff's lands.

Unfortunately, once a life of crime is undertaken, it may be difficult for some to return to their former modes of legal employment when economic conditions that encouraged the taking vanish. The sooner we act, the fewer law-abiders turned criminals we will have to return to law-abiding behavior.

Erosion of the rule of law and morality impedes law enforcement. Examine laws that create the opportunity for civil disobedience, and eliminate enforcement temporarily or otherwise, focusing on reducing risk, and handling extremes and outliers. This may mean relaxing written laws that are frequently not enforced, or not obeyed by a majority of the public, to reduce the enforcement burden, and removing the excuse-setting trend that holds that if a little crime is alright, then a little more crime won't hurt either – and this attitude is important to avoid early to prevent further onset and to cement the poor values in individual's minds and behavioral patterns.

We need a diversion program to keep likely offender candidates – particularly young unemployed males – out of crime and to guide them into career paths contributing to society. We need a significant program comparable to the CCC of the 1930s, and here are several ideas along these lines. Revamp the Peace Corps, create an Environmental Corps and send unemployed high-risk males to undeveloped nations to work on wells, irrigation, infrastructure, etc. The work is meaningful and contributive, a career can be learned, and the young participants will be too far away to return home on weekends, thus creating the temporary reduced crime opportunity through reduction in the number of potential offenders in our inner cities. In hindsight, the attributes of the CCC program that worked for crime opportunity reduction in the 1930s was that 25% of the unemployed male youth population was extracted from the inner cities and relocated to rural encampments that were sufficiently isolated that the 'volunteers' could not return to the cities on weekends. To achieve the same end today would require that the program be international and that we set up encampments for do-good environmental construction projects in third-world countries, digging wells, constructing irrigation systems, cleaning up sites, and other similar reconstruction programs.

Lastly, and not least importantly, we must recognize that economics and crime opportunity are linked. A healthy economy reduces the rationality of crime for many. We also need to understand that all of these programs need to be paid for. Some ideas on payment for these crime prevention measures include increased asset seizures of law breakers, more "workfare" contributions from minor criminals instead of prisons alone that cost us money, taxing and regulating marijuana distribution in the manner of tobacco industry, and risk-adjusted tax assessments to 'places' for their crime opportunity contribution to the community.

Besides the revenue measures specific to criminal justice, this author recommends that we should strongly consider a gasoline tax to support infrastructure to pay for switching to more energy-efficient technologies. We must recognize that energy policy is national security policy. Building nuclear power plants takes decades but it is the type of energy policy that is sustainable and friendly to the planet. As for those who think we cannot ship the nuclear waste across state lines to store it in earthen vaults, then let's get creative and think not on where to bury the waste, but rather how to ship it permanently to the sun, eliminating it permanently from being a problem for mankind.

In addition to these strategic and policy issues, governments can and should create strategic crime control master plans that include the "crime control strategies and tactics" outlined earlier in this chapter.

7.2 What businesses can do

Businesses are the life blood of the economy and they are obviously the most severely challenged sector in this economic crisis.

Protect assets of people, places, processes, and things; conduct assessments in light of new risks, and safeguard the enterprise. Use situational crime prevention techniques to protect people, work places, supply chains, and assets and use specific measures from the 16 prevention techniques.

Think virtually, removing geography and place from the workplace; consider extended or virtual work as options for a greater part of your workforce; this will reduce costs and overhead, and will reduce travel commuting requirements for employees.

Protect the supply chain and place additional safeguards to protect from piracy and leaks in the supply chain that will emerge with greater frequency in difficult economic times, as piracy is likely to occur with greater frequency as economic conditions worsen.

Internet crime and organized retail crime will increase during this period and you will need to increase your preparedness level for these events.

Beware of protection rackets, intimidation, bullying, and potential violent and property crime risk that may be rising in this diminished economy.

Plan for the long term, be decisive, view this as an 8-12 year cycle, and spread financial resources accordingly and appropriately.

Check your company "lifeboats" and ensure they are ready for sailing; secure the future of your company by getting yourself and your company's core business into the lifeboat.

Be a community citizen and pitch in and help others; think of 'mutual aid' relationships and share resources, information, and intelligence to make everyone safer.

Be sensitive to needs and the ways in which your company resources can add value or bring comfort to your community.

Spread your work opportunity around; consider shorter work weeks engaging more resources to give the firm added flexibility.

Conduct a security and vulnerability assessment, and prepare a strategic plan. Create your own written crime control strategies and tactics using items identified earlier within this chapter.

Participate in trade association and industry groups to share experiences, information, intelligence, and best practices to ensure that you get timely information and early warning of potential problems impacting your firm or industry.

Examine and inoculate your business from Internet-based frauds and scams; see the appendix for specific guidance on this topic.

Keep your eyes wide open to subtle changes in your marketplace or among employees, vendors, and customers, which will give you telltale signs necessary to adapt to changing conditions of crime opportunity at your place of business.

7.3 What communities can do

Share information with each other just like we are doing now.

Prepare situational crime prevention assessments and plans for your communities, and implement site-specific measures from the list of 16 prevention techniques.

Place your "eyes on the street", watching each other properly and cautiously, and observing activities that are out of the ordinary. Respond with a watchful eye when the dogs bark.

Repair the "broken windows"[107] and other visible signs of community decay to display a sense of ownership, place management, and in order to present a visually harder target to criminals who frequently select targets that are less organized.

Be friendly, courteous and curious with strangers on the streets. Research shows that a smile and eye-to-eye contact can unnerve criminal offenders because they might be concerned you could remember them later, and most probably they may push off to a softer crime target.

If your neighbor is out of town, pick up their newspapers and other objects that might show that they are out of town and store them out of site. When you have to be away for a few days, you can also coordinate with your neighbors to let them know that you will be gone.

Improve the outdoor lighting of your property. Be sure not to cast a glare into your windows to blind yourself from being able to see outside; however, lighting against the home is useful to silhouette individuals walking on the lawns or approaching the homes. When you plan the lighting system, consider motion sensing lighting and use halogen, metal halide, or other bright lights with immediate responsiveness.

Improve the lighting outside your property; trim bushes below your windows so that you can see the outside more clearly.

Get a 'barking dog' – notice I did not say biting dog. This can provide advance warning and give you greater protection on account of being a harder target than the community or households without a dog.

Consider security "scarecrows" such as alarm signs, dogs on the premises, etc. Consider the use of timers inside your home or business to light a few rooms while you are away, to give the impression that somebody may be home. When you are away, you might consider parking your car locked outside instead of in the garage to give the impression to people observing from the street that somebody is home.

Ensure that your doors and windows are locked. Change the code on your garage door opener if you have not done so in the past year – or 20 years. Recheck the quality and suitability of your door locks.

Inside your house, disperse your valuables so that they are not all in the same place. A determined offender will succeed in committing crimes, but by reducing the size and quantity of items they might take, you can greatly reduce your risk potential.

Unless you are trained and comfortable with firearms, it is better when confronted to let intruders in and give them what they want, as survival rates are higher in that kind of responses. In such conditions, let them have one, not the entire cache of your valuables.

If crime persists, neighbors might consider fencing the sides and rear of all their properties, creating a virtual stockade requiring visitors to enter and exit along clearly visible pathways.

Further, if the crime issue becomes a much greater problem in the future, each of our community entries could be retrofitted easily to create gated communities with a minimum of fuss. Gated communities can be automated, manless or staffed. You could have a camera at the gate and decide from the comfort of your home whether to let guests in. We certainly do not need this now; however, in course of time, if the threat of crime opportunity rises, it might be an option.

For other ideas you might consult
http://www.ncjrs.gov/celebrate_safe_communities/

7.4 What individuals and families can do

All of the advice given already in this book is aimed at assisting individuals involved in rulemaking for safety and security in our government institutions, law enforcement, businesses, the broader community, and the society as a whole. This section speaks personally about the safety and security of individuals and their families, particularly of those who may be feeling concerned about their own livelihoods and the health, economic viability, and safety of their own household, and who are looking for some guidance about what to do, or where to go, particularly in this utterly confusing environment.

Focus on situational crime prevention and the 16 prevention techniques at specific places where you live, work, go to school, etc. Seek to strengthen the places where you work, live, and where your children study or play, to make them relatively invulnerable to criminal attempts. Then, once you have raised your level of security measures, help your neighbors do the same, and continue to increase the symbolic barrier walls that insulate and protect your places from the broader community and from the rest of world. In small communities, this may mean banding together to create your own crime watch organizations, perhaps gating your communities, posting your own forward posted guard, concierge, bell man, or volunteer. Just as on an airplane where you are instructed to put the oxygen mask on yourself first, and next help others, do the same in situational crime prevention.

Think about crime 'opportunity blocking' at your home and while on travel. In automobile drivers' education, we are instructed to drive 12 seconds ahead, looking at the road in a distance and with our rear view mirror behind us, to keep ourselves a safe distance away from harm's way. The same is true with our own individual safety; be aware of your environment and surroundings, look ahead, think ahead, plan for safe travel and safe homes. If you live in a large metropolitan area, think about where you and your family would gather at a rendezvous location that is not your home? Do you have a safe house, a safe place, a refuge to gather if civil unrest overtakes your location?

As a rule, avoiding people, places, and situations that exude "negative energy" is a good rule to follow. During economic crises and periods of heightened crime opportunity, this is also an excellent rule to follow. Identify friends, associates, neighbors, and others living within your community who are serious juvenile delinquents or serious adult-aged habitual offenders and avoid them. Many individuals who are crime agents have other social or mental health problems that may be exacerbated by economic hardship, depression or substance abuse that may make them more unreliable, caustic, or dangerous to be around; avoid these people.

Be aware of your own children and their friends and intervene when necessary.

Plant a garden, tear up the lawn if necessary, but use the garden as a therapeutic opportunity to create work, learn discipline, and subsidize your monthly food bill. There are too few opportunities to teach good work habits to youth, and a home garden can create the necessary opportunity, as physical work is therapeutic and good. Work also tends to occupy the mind, thereby keeping those idle hands busy.

Determine if there are any crime hotspots in your neighborhood or workplace and avoid them. Further, consider if there are any crime "honey pots" (attractors) such as vacant housing, liquor stores, taverns, bars, clubs, laundromats, check-cashing centers, etc., and reduce your exposure to those areas of greater crime opportunity.

Beware of increased incidence of fraud known to occur during times of sharp economic crisis, related to relief aid, insurance, bankruptcy, diversion of aid, etc. Become familiar with the Internet-based fraud schemes identified in the appendices of this book, and avoid them.

Avoid contact, involvement, and participation with gangs of organized crime; these criminal organizations are likely to strengthen with the retreat of law enforcement spending, and considering safe passage around potential problems may be safer than confronting gangs and organizations at the individual level; though for governments, hitting gangs and organized crime hard and often is exactly what should be done.

Actively divert young male unemployed individuals most vulnerable to criminal involvement and steer them into lawful and meaningful employment opportunities in geographically remote areas.

Avoid "moral hazard," where economic incentive and get-gaining might encourage one to act unethically even though it is legally feasible; strive to keep a bright and clear line between what is right and what is wrong, reinforcing ethics through example, regulation, and training.

Educate and train family members and individuals about how to inoculate themselves from crime opportunity through implementing Situational Crime Prevention in places most vulnerable to crime.

Increase the effort needed to commit crime
  Target hardening
  Access control
  Deflecting offenders
  Controlling facilitators

Increasing the risk associated with crime
  Entry and exit screening
  Formal surveillance
  Surveillance by employees
  Natural surveillance

Reducing the rewards of crime
  Target removal
  Identifying property
  Reducing temptation
  Denying benefits

Removing excuses (and encouraging shaming)
  Rule setting for families and individuals
  Stimulating conscience
  Controlling dis-inhibitors to crime
  Facilitate compliance
  Promote victimization prevention education

Implement Crime Prevention Through Environmental Design (CPTED)
  Target hardening
  Access control
  Surveillance
  Image and maintenance
  Location specific activity support

Understand that restoration of meaningful employment is an important key to getting the train of society back on track again. Public officials should recognize that work has value unto itself. Support payments are important, but not the same as employment, and meaningful employment has increased positive psychological benefits. Let's put this nation to work in some great unifying effort, plan, and vision.

See the source materials on crime prevention information in the appendix for more information on what individuals can do to increase their safety and crime prevention preparedness, in their own homes and lifestyles.

8 | Epilogue

Up to this point, all of the observations provided by the author have been materially objective, referenced, cited, or otherwise grounded in a rationality that the world understands. In this section, the author strays from the objective grounded treatise, to speak to the readers as individuals as though we were close friends. The section provides specific counsel to the individuals seeking more than what is told today or available from our political leaders, industrial giants, and employers. What appears next is most probably what you would be told if you went to church to hear a sermon on these matters, or if the author were to speak to you as a friend on the matter of crime opportunity prevention in our current economic environment. I have added this section at the risk of losing objectivity, because part of the purpose of writing this book is giving a gift of self, a gift of something that helps you and your family navigate a softer landing at this critical and perilous time in history.

This economic crisis will widen and this deep recession will become an economic depression not seen since the Great Depression and perhaps worse in certain important respects. This second Great Depression too will rob many of their livelihoods and savings without warning, much as the December revelation of Bernie Madoff left thousands wanting, and has already caused loss of lives and has certainly led to loss of hope for multitudes. The author predicts that within one year from the seminal event of the Lehman Brothers collapse on September 15, 2008, it will become apparent that, in addition to the risk of economic depression, we now have significant crime opportunity risk in terms of heightened economic misery, insolvent governments with less money to spend on law enforcement services and adjudication, and lots of unemployed individuals with serious economic crises who are less concerned with trespass and hunting for food or game in the Sherwood forest, than in following the rule of law. In this environment, individuals and families are left largely to fend themselves as the ratio of law enforcement in our cities approximating 3-5 officers per 1000 can be overwhelmed by large movements and unrest. Crime will increase; indeed historians will label it a "crime wave" but what is important for the future is not that it will happen, but what we did to prevent it, or to inoculate our families from its heinous reach.

Crime is an event that requires several components. In the absence of these key components, crime cannot exist. Crime does not occur in a vacuum. Crime takes an offender, a victim, a place, a target of interest, a time, and laws or lack of laws or structure in order to occur. Crime occurs more frequently in densely populated areas, and in areas of greater heterogeneity (or disparity) of incomes. Crimes occur where there is an opportunity for crime – if you have nothing to steal, it won't be stolen. But there are old crimes that will remerge with fierceness during periods of economic calamity. During the Great Depression, and now again along the U.S.-Mexican border, corruption, kidnapping, extortion, drug trafficking, and murder are found to be on the rise. These crimes are fostered and committed by criminal gangs and organized crime outfits that may become more consolidated and organized during the economic crisis. This condition along the border is expected to continue until public officials and law enforcement eradicate internal corruption, and improve their response to meet the changing technological improvements enjoyed by the predators and traffickers of domestic terror along the border. There is little reason to believe that this type of crime milieu will not cross over the border and come into our country if we do not act to thwart it aggressively and responsively.

For the same reason that Willie Sutton, the famous bank robber, gave when asked why he robbed banks, "because that's where the money is", those living in affluent neighborhoods may find that they are more likely to be victimized because that is where criminals think the money is. With the current price of real gold higher than the price of fiat gold or paper gold (such as the GLD gold commodity ETF), there is more demand to possess gold personally and it would appear that some people are purchasing gold as a store of value. Where is your gold stored? At home? I would hope not. There is a reason why they call it 'Fort Knox' because what is encased in gold bars is so valuable and removable that they need to protect it with extreme physical security measures.

How many can afford the expense of making such improvements in their homes? One of the evidences of a crime wave is the increase in reported crimes, and the organization of communities to thwart crime. In Russia, where they have seen an almost 80% decrease in stock values, many have taken their money out of banks and taken it home, whether in gold or other currency. Not surprisingly, there has already been a reported increase in household burglaries and thefts of huge wealth from individuals withdrawing funds from banks and taking them home; some not even making it home with their treasure before organized crime hits them in transit and relieves them of their life's wealth through indescribable violence. The recent rise in the purchasing of handguns comes at a time when people are extremely anxious about their own protection, and when they are taking more valuables home with them. This is a huge risk, and be sure to divide your nest eggs to limit your downside risk of loss as modern pirates, gypsies, and marauders, unemployed and needy domestic helpers may visit one at home.

Besides the crimes that occur in the course of day-to-day life, there are particular types of crimes that increase during sharp crises related to recovery efforts including fraud related to recovery efforts, bankruptcy frauds, insurance frauds, recovery aid supply chain diversion theft, political corruption, and other crimes. There is also the potential of misuse of power, whether it is for a U.S. Senate seat, a prime contract, or the location of the approved site of the next new project.

Most people will choose to live lawful lives when given the opportunity to do so, but without the likelihood of lawful existence, most people will choose life over starvation; if it becomes a choice of right or wrong, hunger or food, they will choose to eat. Consequently, in times of crises like the one into which we are headed into now, it pays to be prudent, increase your own personal defense position, de-escalate your public perception as a store of wealth, and minimize your exposure or risk of kidnapping, extortion, or robbery. It is a fact that population density is closely related to crime likelihood, and moving farther out, or to a less populated area, can bring a more peaceful lifestyle for your family, if it comes to that. For those for whom moving is not an option, take care to increase the protection posture of your own homes through situational crime prevention measures including Crime Prevention Through Environmental Design (CPTED).

Throughout history, mankind has shown the precaution of protecting itself through building up fortresses, castles, moats, berms (mounds), barriers, and fences, to protect themselves. In the U.S., our greatest asset for protection has been our shores that provide a great body of water that must be passed before anyone can reach our shores. Obviously, with air travel, the value of the oceans as a protective barrier is minimal but the symbolic measure of placing a moat around our assets has not been completely discontinued. This should be done at home too, both physically and symbolically. Whether it is a gated community, a fenced yard, or a locked door, these measures create and define space. Defense in depth is a defensive strategy that takes into account geography and spreads risk along a continuum of measures to thwart intruder penetration and crime opportunity. Whether you live in the city, the suburbs, or in the country, there are ways to fortify your homes to reduce your risk likelihood. The more prominent a figure you are, the more opulent your life style is, the more you show your wealth, then the more you will need to pay for security in these troubled times.

Crime will increase for a period and like the economic recovery, we will fumble our way through the crime wave and develop new structures to combat crime, and we will be helped by an improving economy that returns many to lawful work from their participation in crime for their basic livelihood. During the Great Depression, it took four years for the crime wave to cause such misery that the public was moved to make crime fighting a primary objective. Hopefully we will not need to wait four years for our current leaders to focus on reducing crime opportunity. In such an environment, how do you keep yourself and your family safe? Unfortunately for some, joining the criminal gang holds more apparent safety than holding out or fleeing the gang. This is the sad reality in some of our nation's cities, where gangs hold a historical and generational life-grip on families and communities. But this need not be so; people can move their ground, fortify themselves with others of like mind and concern for their families. The old pioneers used to circle their wagons at night and place their livestock and families in the middle to protect them, and in a symbolic way, we need to find a way to do the same thing today.

Rudyard Kipling had a phrase, "the strength of the wolf is the pack," and the strength of a criminal is the power of number and strength of their peers. This same principle holds true for families and communities that draw unto themselves for combined strength against the forces that would do them harm. To be a lone wolf is not good. To be a holdout, the one that will not move when the flood is coming, is foolish. However, there is even a greater risk for those that live in the figurative plain of Jordan in the full view and grandeur of Sodom and Gomorrah thinking that you, like Lot in Genesis, can live near the action, but not suffer the consequences of your family being left alone like a lone wolf unprepared for sharp crises in a violent and strange world; such lack of foresight, listening, and planning can submit you and your family to great harm.

Knowing what I know now, having reviewed the literature, and having considered the current condition of the state of economy and the world, my counsel, if you are living in an area that cannot sustain itself in good times–and in this difficult time the economic and crime conditions are getting worse – is to move your ground, by any means possible to higher ground, as times will get worse before they get better. You can always come back, but if you do not protect what you have, you may risk everything. Do not stick your head in the sand like an ostrich and say, this will pass, because before it does pass, it may cause serious consequence to you and your family.

Early on in this financial crisis the author communicated with his close friends and family about his observations, intuition, and inspiration for what to observe, and how to respond proactively to this economic crisis. And it too will pass, but many of us will be psychologically scarred for life, just as were our grandparents or their parents who lived through the first Great Depression, and how we come out of this second Great Depression will have lasting impact on our own lives and the lives of our children and their children to the fourth generation. So, it is highly recommended to consider the advice I will set forth.

First, find your moral compass; be grounded. I believe that every person, regardless of race or religion, has been given a spiritual gift of intuition, an inner voice, a calming spirit that is a gift, and if you will listen to this voice, intuition, and promptings it can guide you to safer harbor – but only if you listen. Some call this inner voice conscience, intuition, reflection, or meditation. For me and my house, we call it a gift from God, and more specifically, the 'light of Christ,' but I am not concerned here with labels, but with the result and you may call it what you will. Each of us as human beings was born with an inner voice that tells us what is right and wrong, a moral compass you can say, and when we listen to that voice and act on it, our ability to do right for our own and our family's lives is likely to be more certain. Through prolonged failure to listen to this inner voice, one can actually drown it out so that one is no longer able to hear or be prompted by conscience and they lose their moral compass; you may know people who have lost their moral compass, beware of these individuals and stay clear for your own safety and well-being, particularly at the time of scarcity and economic depression, as they may have little resistance to get-gaining when opportunity presents itself.

Second, recognize and understand that there are many voices out there in the press, and among politicians and employers who have a vested interest in telling you untruths because if they told you or the whole world the truth, it could cause perhaps a worse condition, or a snowballing effect, where the changes they seek to prevent become worse because of their focus on it. During sharp economic crises, when a President Bush tells you "the fundamentals of the economy are sound" or when Warren Buffet, one of the richest men in the world, tells you "now is a good time to invest", or when an employer tells you that "our company is financially strong and you need not worry about this company or direction" – be worried. There is not an industry, market, or geography in the developed or undeveloped nations that has not been impacted by this great economic contraction.

Ask your accountants about their cadre of clients, and enquire if there is any client who is not impacted by this downturn, and they may tell you that all are impacted with the exception of education, health care, and funeral homes – and even in these three remaining markets, we find substitution effect: the act of switching down from private education to public education, from brand name drugs to generic drugs, from expensive funerals to the pine box or the incinerator. Everyone is impacted.

Third, you must act now to protect your family, your nest egg, your livelihood. The very purpose of this book is to tell you all that we are living through something like the Great Depression, with the only difference being that ours will be different somehow in our modern age. Economists, seeking always to be correct [and sadly I am no different], like to give bounded forecasts with frequent references to soft landing and hard landing scenarios. So here is the broad range of economic forecasts – if you exclude those pundits who have a vested interest in pumping up the market or selling you a product or keeping you frozen in your current investments—you will find that there is a bi-modal distribution of economic forecasts out there where one cluster (the soft landing) is forecasting some kind of turnaround in the economy evidencing itself in 2010 and gradually getting better over the next several years, hence the 2-4 year recovery scenario or soft landing. At the other end of the spectrum, there is a group of economists and futurists looking more darkly and forecasting a prolonged economic depression lasting between 8-12 years, perhaps more (this is the hard landing scenario). The most probable forecast lies somewhere between and will be influenced by what we do, how we as a nation and world respond, etc., and exogenous events we cannot control or easily predict.

It reality what matters ultimately is not whose economic forecast is right, but rather what you do about it in your planning. For example, if you choose to believe that the market is not as bad as everyone is saying and if you favor the soft-landing scenario and spend your precious resources (equity, savings, and future earnings through loans) as though in two to four years (or earlier) things will be better, and if it turns out that you were wrong and the economy is not better, you may run out of runway for your resources and crash before the end of the economic cycle and risk bankruptcy that will negatively keep you further economically depressed during the time when things should be turning around (as bankruptcy impacts you for 7-10 years in terms of future credit worthiness and economic possibility).

On the other hand, if you think that the hard landing scenario is more likely, and you change your ground, your spending, your outlook, and plan for a prolonged economic period of financial hardship, and you move to protect your nest egg, to reduce living expenses greatly, and focus on making your resources stretch to meet this longer forecast, and if it turns out that you were wrong – then you are twice blessed, as you will have capital, cash, and good credit to spend in the recovery when capital is scarce and opportunity to improve one's station is maximized.

Put simply, there are four possible outcomes of following the soft landing or hard landing economic forecasts (outlined below, and option B carries the greatest catastrophic risk if it occurs); of course there will be some who do nothing and their likely consequence will be worse than all others.

- Outcome A – believe in economic soft landing scenario of 2-4 years, adjust accordingly; soft landing occurs, all is well.

- Outcome B – believe in economic soft landing scenario of 2-4 years, adjust accordingly; soft landing fails and economy sustains prolonged contraction nearer the hard landing for several more years, and all is not well, you have spent your capital, risk bankruptcy, are prone to more grievous financial terms and economic misery because of running out of ammunition before the economic war ended.

- Outcome C – believe in economic hard landing scenario of 8-12 years, adjust accordingly; hard landing occurs, it is hurtful to all, but you manage better than most because you were prepared.

- Outcome D – believe in economic hard landing scenario of 8-12 years, adjust accordingly; soft landing occurs, it is great because you have resources plenty to re-invest in times of great opportunity, and all is well.

What is important here is that all forecasts show an end to the economic misery and predict that the economy will recover in time. The difference is the length of the recovery and the choices that we make during the interval. Having gone through this book, you should have seen that the author subscribes to the economic hard landing scenario and is adjusting accordingly. Happily, if the author is wrong, and he hopes he is, we will have a soft landing and all will be well sooner. However, this book is not about irrational hope, but about rational approaches to what is clearly a dire economic period in global history. Choose to subscribe to the hard landing scenario and make either option C or D whichever is acceptable to you, though again we can always hope that things turn around earlier.

Next, recognize that for most people, there will be no personal stimulus package of government spending or aid. You must create your own way. You must be proactive and use your own resources and intelligence to create your own personal stimulus package. The government stimulus package prepared by Congress in February 2009 was for roughly $900 billion dollars, or approximately 6% of our GDP. The spending package may be big in nominal terms but is small indeed compared to the broader market. It reflects just 6% of Gross Domestic Product, meaning that there is another 94% (that you and I create in our livelihoods). I personally am a supporter of Keynesian 'investment grade stimulus' targeted at hard problems that will take 10 or more years to solve. Sadly, the dubiously named stimulus package of February 2009 is mostly spending by consuming, and doesn't involve any significant investment; so, the long term benefits are equivalent to cutting down the apple orchard for fire wood, rather than planting more apple seeds for more apples in the future.

The Keynesian economic model makes the distinct difference between consumption and investment, and spending or consuming money on non-durable investments such as one-time aid that does not produce, but consumes, is in the long-run a waste of capital. We should be building roads, bridges, energy infrastructure, and solving huge scientifically challenging problems to employ hundreds of thousands in durable investments in our future – not spending scarce monies on keeping our standard of living above our means, or future means. We are robbing our children of the American dream by using the wood for their future homes, as our fireplace wood today; it is shameful!

Look at your own resources, look at your spending habits, and redefine what is essential and what is not. Many of our 'needs' are really wants and if we do not recognize this soon, we will have greater problems in the future. Make the hard decisions now and preserve resources for a future day. Get the daily consumption of items down. I recall that, on 9/19/08, four days after the Lehman Brothers collapse, an item that I had previously purchased on Costco online, a fantastic state-of-the-art large screen HDTV arrived at my home; it was beautiful, and sat in the box for a day while I watched the news, and quickly came to the realization that I cannot eat a new TV, and it went back to Costco. Thankfully, Costco accepted the purchase return with no penalty, but the time may come when all companies restrict or curb their return policies as the cost is too burdensome for them to bear as well. I used the HDTV return as an opportunity to signal to my family and children that we were coming into a new age. I explained to my children that this symbolic return of the large screen TV was reflective of the change in lifestyle that we would need to consider as we saved precious resources to make them stretch further. I also told them, just wait, in six months or so, I will be able to buy this same HDTV screen again for half the price; and I add now, if I wanted to, I could, but I still have not figured out how to roast the HDTV so that it tastes good.

Where is your capital? Is it in your mattress, the safety deposit box, in your pension fund or 401k, or in stocks, bonds, gold, or real estate? Figure out where your nest egg is, and also become aware of how to use it to prolong your personal and family well-being. Some of your assets may be illiquid – perhaps you own stock in a private company that has no accessible tradable street value, or you own a home that cannot sell in this market (at least at the price you want). There is also an order of battle for use of funds. For example, credit cards, home equity lines, and 401k funds all can generate cash for use, but they have different risks.

Credit cards are not cash. Credit cards are not a store of value. Credit cards should not be considered part of your emergency funding plan. The reader might ask why not? Credit cards are an extension of credit on good faith that you can repay the credit when used. There is a credit card bubble that shall soon burst and we may see many people walking away from credit cards through non-payment or bankruptcies, and the industry will contract in lending or credit availability to those seen more risky. American Express along with other credit card companies has been closely watching spending habits of customers and their peers across geographies. When individual spending habits of one household approximate those of others that have experienced negative consequences and non-payment or flight risk, the credit card companies have unilaterally contracted credit, limited lines, or discontinued credit, requiring repayment as soon as possible.

Consequently, if you have a credit card with a limit of $10,000 or $25,000 and you have only a $1000 balance, or no balance, do not think that this open credit will remain available for you in your time of greatest need. Credit is not cash. Cash is cash. And credit, though valuable, can be fleeting. My own advice is to have no credit card debt if you can live on cash; however, if you have credit card debt today, and your economic situation is at risk, I think in this environment it may be prudent to keep your cash in hand, service the credit card with minimum payments keeping it current so as not to incur penalties or penalty interest rates, and use your cash in a disciplined way to secure your ability to pay bills, or respond to emergencies. However, if you do not have the discipline to hold cash and not spend it, I suggest that you pay off your credit cards and hope that your good faith in paying credit down in a timely manner keeps the card open for you in your time of need; but this is a hope, and not a promise by the credit card companies. They are in the business of making money, not losing it, and if they think you are a flight or bankruptcy risk, or suddenly start using more credit than before, they may cut you off unexpectedly.

The author recommends that you start now and save a small amount of cash that is accessible in safety deposit box or other protected means sufficient for emergencies to get you through at least one-month of living expenses, and preferably three months. If you are able, the author suggests that you should secure up to one year of cash availability in bank deposits secured not at home, but in a bank that is FDIC-insured. Home equity lines are not cash and are similar to credit cards that can be reduced if your circumstances change significantly. If your home equity line is your emergency life line, then consider taking out funds from your home equity line and depositing it in a different bank bearing interest, and pay the small difference in interest between the two institutions as your risk premium for having the cash you need, accessible and available when you need it. Making life decisions with one year of cash in the bank is different from making life decisions with one week's cash in hand. Getting your family in a financial position to withstand longer-term economic shocks will give you greater confidence and peace of mind as short-term fluctuations, and today's news story, may not knock you off course of your financial strategy.

In this age of economic uncertainty, you must become more entrepreneurial and resourceful. You must become the best employee at your company so that you are the last one they would think of letting go. You should also be thinking of the next steps in case the unthinkable happens and you are let go. You will need to find economic opportunity wherever you go. Mothers will need to find new ways to help the financial economy of the home as financial security of the single provider home is disappearing for a season. There are many stay-at-home opportunities for parents working from home as 'home agents' providing services through the Internet on piece work paid by the call or problem they resolve. Accounting and bookkeeping are being performed more online. Concierge services are performed online. Research assistance, clerical work, shopping, and many other forms of work can be conducted online from your home and require no transportation. Beyond finding that second or third job, you might look in your garage or basement to find additional lost capital. Whether it is an eBay business selling obsolete or un-played-with toys, or wedding gifts you never use, or that 2nd or 3rd car, use these resources to help you simplify and turn into cash your latent assets around the home. Craigslist is also a wonderful resource for those items too heavy to ship, but beware: eBay and Craigslist sites are vulnerable to scam artists. Read through the advice given on how to spot and avoid Internet based frauds in the appendices of this book.

Some of you might be thinking of location or relocation. Where do you need to live in order to do the work that you do? The reality is that with the Internet and Southwest Airlines and their comparable counterparts, many people can live in much less expensive locations without having to live in an expensive location or continue an expensive lifestyle not in keeping with the times. In many markets, housing prices are cheaper than cars. Do you need to change locations to find more work? Do you need to change locations to lower your cost of living? If you have two homes, is there a location where you could live that would allow you to live comfortably with just one home? These are important questions that impact your consumption function and greatly determine your future ability to make it through these difficult times.

If crime patterns hold, there will be more crime occurring in the inner cities in high population density areas, and in areas of greatest population and economic heterogeneity. Yet you do not want to be a lone wolf at these times. Gather around people you love, trust, and who will protect you, and you can protect them. In a symbolic way, we need to do what the pioneers did to protect their families and their livestock. Just as there is increased vulnerability in high density population areas, there is also vulnerability in remote areas where little protection is available if you are confronted by a mob or gang looting stray places looking for easy targets. Do not think that Somali pirates are the only ones looting today.

Food is the new precious commodity; particularly, foods that can be stored with shelf life of five years or more. Every family should consider investing in their own foodstuffs to create a minimum three months' supply of food, and then as you can afford it, put aside a one-year supply of food including seeds for your own garden if feasible. Just as gasoline prices soared to unreasonable heights in the spring and summer of 2008, so also food prices can soar due to scarcity and food in the type or quantify that you are used to may not always be available for purchase. Disruptions of the food supply can happen for many economic reasons, but there are other potentialities that exist. Just because we are living through an economic depression does not mean that terrorism or other natural disaster cannot occur at the same time.

If we had an avian flu pandemic, or were to suffer a biological terrorism event, it is possible that for our own safety we may need to remain in our own homes for several weeks, and if we did not have sufficient food supplies or clean water, to venture outside into the public to get these items would place the courier at health or safety risk that they would not necessarily need to make if they had their own food supply. Some people, particularly the Mormons, have been preaching to their members for years to get a year's supply of food as a necessary precaution for life. Other individuals and emergency preparedness buffs have made similar preparations. The Amish and other agricultural communities will be favored in downturned economies as they can live simply. However, as most of our populations are concentrated in coastal communities in high density areas, where there are few gardens and even fewer gardeners, preparations for prolonged absence of food stuffs in an emergency may result in increased shortages, scarcity, and risk. Some respected economists and futurists are expecting the economic contraction to continue and food riots to be a possible result by 2012. Whether or not this occurs, being prepared will bring peace of mind and protect your family from unforeseen spikes in food prices.

There is widely held expectation among economists that the deflation that we are seeing in housing prices and commodity prices in 2008-2009 will end within a year or two, and that when the stimulus spending or recovery happens, then inflation will occur. Inflation may occur because of fast growth, but I think it is more likely to occur because of scarce supply. Companies cutting back on costs frequently cut employees, and with fewer employees you deliver fewer commodities. When the economy turns we may find a shortage of available commodities and this will impact inflation and purchasing power greatly. A balanced financial strategy for a household will include food storage between 3-12 months including preparations for a clean water supply whether by well water (with hand pump) or purification systems for treating other water sources.

The money from the stimulus package will be slow to hit the streets, taking 9-18 months in many instances, and the impact will likely be more targeted at select industries rather than trickle-down economics. In summary, the good feelings that may exist momentarily after the stimulus package hits the streets will wane in time, and by next fall, we may well see another leg down in the market. Further, even if we experience a leg up in this market, there is no reason to believe that President Obama or Congress may not torment us with a recovery crisis by raising taxes during a tenuous time of recovery, so that we suffer another Roosevelt recovery depression.

So my personal advice is this:

Think strategically of this economic downturn as lasting several years, not several months; the projection is for a soft landing in 3-4 years, or a hard landing 8-12 years – somewhere between lies the answer – but it is not likely to be next quarter, 4th quarter, or 2010. There will be a period of continued deflation for at least another year, followed perhaps by a period of inflation when the stimulus package actually starts to work in mid to late 2010 or beyond.

Change your spending (consumption and investment) habits now to accommodate another leg down in the stock market; bonds, once safe, may become devalued if interest rates rise; real estate has come down the fartherest, and may be a safer bet than other stores of value as currencies are likely to be devalued, and commodities are highly volatile. Be resourceful and think of alternative flows of money that you can earn, as diversity of income will be helpful. Figure out how to downsize your appetites from the "biggie-size" materialism we all enjoyed in the roaring 1990s and 2000s.

If you have debt going into this depression, it will likely be hardest on you. Economists forecast that the marginal cost of money will rise rapidly when the recovery starts to occur as the government seeks to forestall inflation, as when Volcker curbed inflation through raising interest rates in the early 1980s.

Figure out how to operate from cash, as you will get the best bargains and not risk untimely liquidations caused by credit runs. By my estimate, you will have about one year of cheap money (i.e., low interest rates and low inflation or deflation)– use it to change your ground, lower your debt, reposition – then when the stimulus package starts to work, the rates will be going back up as inflation becomes a greater threat.

Figure out how to live on less now – and put the savings away; personally, I am trying to figure out how to be debt free (including housing payments) within months.

Put together a readily accessible cash reserve equal for several months of operations – though this could be in a bank safety deposit box or FDIC insured savings account; if you do not have the savings, I think, as I detailed above, it is worth the risk of borrowing against your assets to put cash away, paying the small premium difference between the borrowing rate and savings interest rate.

Bankruptcy may become fashionable as a quick fix for some in dire circumstances, yet I highly discourage you from taking this path, as the other side of bankruptcy is 7-10 years of credit reporting, higher credit charges, and loss of integrity where your clients and creditors will ask you for cash, not accepting credit in the future. Bankruptcy should be avoided in nearly all instances, with the exception of catastrophic risk events, exceedingly large health care debt, or the disability of the bread winner. Bankruptcy is not needed to shed underwater mortgages – just give the keys and title back to the bank and walk away. However, do not tap your 401k if you think you may declare bankruptcy as these funds are beyond the reach of the bankruptcy court, and could be used by you to rebuild later when nobody else will give you credit.

In terms of 401(k) plans or roll-over IRA plans, you might also consider rolling over your stock, bond, and mutual fund-based 401k plans into self-directed real estate IRA accounts where you purchase and hold cash-flow producing real estate for the long-term. Real estate has been greatly deflated in home values through foreclosures in many areas and this could represent a fine retirement income; however, as with all investment decisions and advice in this book, consult with your own financial advisors before taking such actions.

Beware of gold – it may be a fool's bet – with all the bad news out there, gold should be $2k per ounce and it is not; Paul Volcker, President Obama's inside advisor, killed the gold bugs in the early 1980s when he moved to kill inflation – gold dropped from the 800s down to the 300s almost overnight. Beware the clarion call of popular ads selling gold. You cannot eat gold.

Protect your family from physical harm; this may relate to making yourselves less of a target, camouflaging assets, not showing opulence, or closing your garage door. In Florida, where they have been hard hit with foreclosures, trucks have been spotted frequently pulling up to houses and quickly driving away with appliances, trailers, boats, and other items that can be quickly sold. There is no reason that this could not happen anywhere when the economic misery gets bad enough that reasonable people become Robin Hoods to feed themselves and their families.

Get a copy of the free book, *Are You Ready? An In-depth Guide to Citizen Preparedness*, FEMA/DHS, available at **www.ready.gov**, or by calling 1-800-BE-READY.

Along the U.S.-Mexican border, spill-over violence of Mexican crime cartels have come into Arizona and other border states. Safeguard your families, fortify your homes and seek protection by collective support from others, and if you cannot protect yourself and your family, seek safer ground, travel in groups, seek collective protection from your friends and families. Home invasions, kidnappings, extortion, and robberies can occur anywhere, but are more frequent in rural isolated areas and heavily populated areas; ironically, the somewhat rural and suburban areas are less impacted than the extreme tails of the crime possibility grid.

Beware of terrorism. When our markets are down, our enemies like to strike us to kick the dog when it is down – hoping to add further misery and economic damage. Remember that the NASDAQ crash occurred in March 2000, and it was just 1.5 years later when terrorists attacked the World Trade Towers on September 11, 2001. These exogenous events can be the catalyst for another deep drop downwards, so merely planning for known events is not enough. We are in perilous times and we need to be prepared.

To sum up, we will not have another Great Depression exactly like the first Great Depression precisely because we have learned lessons from it; however, we will experience new challenges where on-the-fly experimentation will be the only available remedy, and not all solutions will work.

So at the end of the day, or this book, I hope that I am not telling you anything you probably don't already believe that you know, sense, or feel in your heart or gut, or that world leaders have not already told us. But what I am telling you is that you have been warned; I have given you my best thinking on the topic, having been prompted by much spiritual agitation and inspiration to focus on these issues at this time.

Although I have looked darkly at our current condition, I remain an optimist and believe that through addressing these problems head-on we are more likely to succeed in reducing the harm, violence, and misery of this economic contraction. The current economic crisis is somewhat of a lemon for us all – it is bitter, and not sweet. However, we can choose to view it as a lemon and wallow in self-pity, or we can get ourselves together and accept current trends and make some lemonade with the lemons handed over to us. We need not be unhappy in this downturn; however, we are not likely to find peace if we do not change our old patterns of excessive leverage and over-consumption. Change your thinking, change your ground, accept that life has forever changed since September 2008, and move on with a positive attitude even in this downturn. All cycles end; even the Great Depression ended.

Crime will increase for a time; indeed, historians will label it a "crime wave," but the future is not that it will happen, but rather, what we did to prevent it, or to inoculate our families from its heinous reach. May we all move to higher ground, to safer locations temporarily and symbolically, as we hold firmly to the hope of a brighter future that will surely come in time. In the meantime, may we make deliberate preparations and take steps that will preserve the economic wealth, health, safety, and security of our families as we live through this extraordinarily dark period of global economic history. May we become heroes to our own children and grandchildren so that at some future period, they will reflect on our lives as being purposive, proactive, peacemaking, resourceful, caring, and creative human beings that mustered through this dark economic period of life with a happy heart, with positive energy, and strong resolve to be good, and do good, and be good for something. During these hard economic times, we must not forget to be charitable and kind to others, and we would all do well to remember the sage words of my grandmother June, "money is only as good as the good that money can do." We must not lose faith in the good that people can do, and in the value that one person of integrity can have in persuading others to be honest also. In closing, may we live as those who made the world a better place–to this end, move with confidence, be safe, and find peace in this age of disruption.

Severin Sorensen, CPP
Gaithersburg, MD

9 Appendix

9.1 Crime Wave Focused Crime Control Strategy Policy Recommendations

Raise awareness of the economic situation and likely crime wave that is portended, and prepare now for the tsunami of crime opportunity. Call hearings, economic councils, criminal justice councils, and employment opportunity-creating working groups, to identify issues, and recommend policy actions.

Prepare an updated crime control plan. Consider within this plan the following strategy:

Strategy

Master planning for defense in depth strategy

Review of laws and focus and crimes of greatest impact to society

Review of criminal justice systems structure and performance

Focus on situational crime prevention at specific places

Think maneuver warfare, where crime 'opportunity blocking' is the objective

Understand that restoration of meaningful employment is an important key to getting the train of society back on track again; public officials should recognize that work has value unto itself; support payments are important, but not the same as employment, and meaningful employment has increased positive psychological benefits; let's put this nation to work in some great unifying effort, plan, and vision

Plan, and work to the plan; include within the plan…

Assessment
Coordination
Communication
Resource utilization

Evaluate what's working, and be quick to jettison that which is not working

Tactics

Target and incapacitate serious habitual offenders; extract serious habitual offenders from the general public and handle (manage) them in remote or controlled location(s).

Target crime hotspots and honey pots (attractors) and reduce crime opportunity

Target fraud related crimes that are known to increase during times of sharp economic crisis related to relief aid, insurance fraud, bankruptcy fraud, diversion of aid, etc.

Target the organized crime markets and take the money out of crime; tax the trade if possible, and remove crime opportunity from criminal organizations; decriminalize, regulate, and tax marijuana.

Actively divert young male unemployed individuals most vulnerable to criminal involvement and steer them into lawful and meaningful employment opportunities in geographically remote areas

Remove "moral hazard" as an economic incentive to commit crime, and strive to keep a bright and clear line between what is right, and what is wrong; reinforcing ethics through example, regulation, and training

Educate and train governments, businesses, communities, families, and individuals on how to inoculate themselves from crime opportunity through implementing Situational Crime Prevention in Places most vulnerable to crime

Increase the effort needed to commit crime
    Target Hardening
    Access Control
    Deflecting Offenders
    Controlling Facilitators

Increasing the risk associated with crime
    Entry and Exit Screening
    Formal Surveillance
    Surveillance by Employees
    Natural Surveillance

Reducing the rewards of crime
    Target Removal
    Identifying Property
    Reducing Temptation
    Denying Benefits

Removing excuses (and encouraging shaming)
    Rule setting
    Stimulating conscience
    Controlling dis-inhibitors to crime
    Facilitate compliance
    Promote victimization prevention education

Implement Crime Prevention Through Environmental Design (CPTED)
    Target hardening
    Access control
    Surveillance
    Image and maintenance
    Location specific activity support

Monitor performance and grow the technical body of research that examines and broadcasts Evidenced-based Crime Prevention Measures

Track what is working, and what is not working, and change courses when the evidence and circumstances warrant action. Think maneuver warfare, and keep criminals moving, changing methods, changing techniques, and discourage them to move on to softer targets.

9.2 Crime Wave Tracking and Risk Mitigation Resources on the Internet

www.crimewaves.com – official website of Economic Misery and Crime Waves, the Second Great Depression and the crime wave that followed, and what we can do about it

9.2.1 *Celebrate Safe Communities*

http://www.ncjrs.gov/celebrate_safe_communities/safebusinesses.html

Safe communities are the result of law enforcement working with residents as equal partners in preventing crime. In recognition of this principle, the Office of Justice Programs' Bureau of Justice Assistance (BJA), National Crime Prevention Council (NCPC), and National Sheriffs' Association (NSA) have joined together to Celebrate Safe Communities (CSC).

In coordination with these efforts to promote community safety, citizen crime prevention and volunteer efforts throughout the country during Celebrate Safe Communities Week, NCJRS presents this compilation of resources related to creating and maintaining safer communities.

9.2.2 *Safe Families, Homes and Self Protection*

http://www.ncjrs.gov/celebrate_safe_communities/neighborhoodsand communities.html
http://www.ncjrs.gov/celebrate_safe_communities/neighborhoodsand communities.html

Are You Being Stalked? Tips for Protection
Privacy Rights Clearinghouse, 2007
http://www.privacyrights.org/fs/fs14-stk.htm

Avoiding Investment Fraud
National Crime Prevention Council, No publication date indicated
http://www.ncpc.org/cms/cms-upload/ncpc/File/3671-Avoid%20Investment%20Fraud.pdf

Charitable Giving Done Wisely
National Crime Prevention Council, No publication date indicated
http://www.ncpc.org/cms/cms-upload/ncpc/File/charity%20fraud.pdf

Crime Prevention for People with Disabilities
National Crime Prevention Council, No publication date indicated
http://www.ncpc.org/cms/cms-upload/ncpc/files/disab.pdf

Don't Be Scammed!
National Crime Prevention Council, No publication date indicated
http://www.ncpc.org/ncpc_cms/Dont%20Be%20Scammed%20
Brochure.pdf

Home Security
National Crime Prevention Council, No publication date indicated
http://www.ncpc.org/cms/cms-upload/ncpc/files/homesec.pdf

Home Security Inspection Checklist
National Sheriff's Association, No publication date indicated
http://www.usaonwatch.org/pdfs/HomeSecurity.pdf

Identity Theft Prevention and Repair Kit
New Mexico Office of the Attorney General, 2007
http://nmag.gov/pdf/ID_Theft_LO_RES.pdf

Locking Your Home
National Crime Prevention Council, 2005
http://www.ncpc.org/resources/enhancement-assets/ncpc_cms/locking-
your-home-reva-1-pdf

Making Children, Families, and Communities Safer From Violence
National Crime Prevention Council, 1995
http://www.ncpc.org/cms/cms-upload/ncpc/File/communities_safer_
from_violence.pdf

A Parent's Guide to Internet Safety
Federal Bureau of Investigation, No publication date indicated
http://www.fbi.gov/publications/pguide/pguidee.htm

Preventing Burglaries - How to Protect your Home
National Sheriff's Association, No publication date indicated
http://www.usaonwatch.org/pdfs/HomeSecurityBooklet.pdf

Protect Yourself From Telephone Fraud
National Crime Prevention Council, No publication date indicated
http://www.ncpc.org/ncpc_cms/Protect%20Yourself%20From%20Teleph
one%20Brochure.pdf

Online Auction Fraud
National Crime Prevention Council, No publication date indicated
http://www.ncpc.org/cms/cms-upload/ncpc/files/aucfraud.pdf

Personal Property Identification Record
National Sheriff's Association, No publication date indicated
http://www.usaonwatch.org/pdfs/PersonalProperty.pdf

Personal Safety for Children: A Guide for Parents
Office of Juvenile Justice and Delinquency Prevention, 2002
http://www.ncjrs.gov/pdffiles1/ojjdp/psfceng.pdf

Project ChildSafe
Bureau of Justice Assistance, 2004
http://www.ncjrs.gov/pdffiles1/bja/204959.pdf

Safer Seniors
National Crime Prevention Council, No publication date indicated
http://www.ncpc.org/cms/cms-upload/ncpc/files/saferseniors.pdf

A Safety Checklist for Apartments
National Crime Prevention Council, No publication date indicated
http://www.ncpc.org/cms/cms-upload/ncpc/files/aptchk.pdf

Senior Citizens Against Crime
National Crime Prevention Council, No publication date indicated
http://www.ncpc.org/cms/cms-upload/ncpc/files/seniorsagainstcrime.pdf

Seniors and Telemarketing Fraud 101
National Crime Prevention Council, 2006
http://www.ncpc.org/publications/available-online/fraud/senfraud_rev4
.pdf

Use Common Sense to Spot a Con
National Crime Prevention Council, No publication date indicated
http://www.ncpc.org/cms/cms-upload/ncpc/files/spotcon.pdf

Vacation Checklist Brochure
National Sheriff's Association, No publication date indicated
http://www.usaonwatch.org/pdfs/VacationChecklist.pdf

"Urgent and Confidential" - the Nigerian Letter Scam
National Crime Prevention Council, No publication date indicated
http://www.ncpc.org/cms/cms-upload/ncpc/File/Nigerian%20Scam.pdf

Your Inside Look at Crime Prevention
National Crime Prevention Council, 2002
http://www.ncpc.org/cms/cms-upload/ncpc/files/inside_look.pdf

9.2.3 Safe Businesses

http://www.ncjrs.gov/celebrate_safe_communities/safebusinesses.html
http://www.ncjrs.gov/celebrate_safe_communities/safebusinesses.html

Burglary at Single-Family House Construction Sites
Office of Community Oriented Policing Services, 2006
http://www.cops.usdoj.gov/files/ric/Publications/e08064509.pdf

Business Alliance Program: Creating Business and Community Partnerships
Bureau of Justice Assistance, 1995
http://www.ncjrs.gov/pdffiles/busallnc.pdf

Business Watch Brochure
National Sheriff's Association, No publication date indicated
http://www.usaonwatch.org/pdfs/BWBrochure.pdf

Heavy Equipment is a Tempting Target for Thieves
National Insurance Crime Bureau, No publication date indicated
https://www.nicb.org/cps/rde/xbcr/nicb/Heavy_Equipment.pdf

Keeping Drug Activity Out of Rental Property: Establishing Landlord Training
Programs
Bureau of Justice Assistance, 2005
http://www.ncjrs.gov/pdffiles/landlord.pdf

Keeping Illegal Activity Out of Rental Property: A Police Guide for Establishing Landlord Training Programs
Bureau of Justice Assistance, 2000
http://www.ncjrs.gov/pdffiles1/bja/148656.pdf

Partnering with Businesses to Address Public Safety Problems
Office of Community Oriented Policing Services, 2006
http://www.cops.usdoj.gov/files/ric/CDROMs/POP1_60/Problem-Solving_Tools/PartneringwithBusinesses.pdf

Prevention at Work
National Crime Prevention Council, No publication date indicated
http://www.ncpc.org/cms/cms-upload/ncpc/files/workprep.pdf

Protect Your Motel from Drug Labs
Oregon Department of Human Services, 2005
http://oregon.gov/DHS/ph/druglab/docs/protectyourmotelwebversion.pdf

Protect Your Rental Property From Drug Labs
Oregon Department of Human Services, 2005
http://oregon.gov/DHS/ph/druglab/docs/protectyourpropertywebversion.pdf

Reducing Theft at Construction Sites: Lessons from a Problem-Oriented Project
Office of Community Oriented Policing Services, 2002
http://www.cops.usdoj.gov/files/ric/Publications/e12021822.pdf

Take Crime Prevention to Work
National Crime Prevention Council, No publication date indicated
http://www.ncpc.org/cms/cms-upload/ncpc/files/work2.pdf

United for a Stronger America: A Safe Workplace is Everybody's Business
National Crime Prevention Council, 2002
http://www.ncpc.org/cms/cms-upload/ncpc/files/partnership.pdf

United for a Stronger America: A Safe Workplace is Everybody's Business: Safety Tips
National Crime Prevention Council, 2002
http://www.ncpc.org/cms/cms-upload/ncpc/files/safewrk.pdf

Violence in the Workplace, 1993-99
Bureau of Justice Statistics, 2001
http://www.ojp.usdoj.gov/bjs/pub/pdf/vw99.pdf

Workplace Violence: Issues in Response
National Center for the Analysis of Violent Crime, 2003
http://www.fbi.gov/publications/violence.pdf

Workplace Violence Awareness and Prevention
Occupational Safety & Health Administration, No publication date indicated
http://www.osha.gov/workplace_violence/wrkplaceViolence.Table.html

SAFE SCHOOLS

http://www.ncjrs.gov/celebrate_safe_communities/safeschools.html
http://www.ncjrs.gov/celebrate_safe_communities/safeschools.html

A Blueprint for Safe Schools
Center for the Study and Prevention of Violence, 2001
http://www.colorado.edu/cspv/publications/factsheets/schoolviolence
/FS-SV15.html

Caregivers' Guide to School Safety and Security
National Crime Prevention Council, 2002
http://www.ncpc.org/cms/cms-upload/ncpc/files/BSS_CaregiversGuide_
Original.pdf

Combating Fear and Restoring Safety in Schools
Office of Juvenile Justice and Delinquency Prevention, 1998
http://www.ncjrs.gov/pdffiles/167888.pdf

Creating Safe Schools: A Comprehensive Approach
Office of Juvenile Justice and Delinquency Prevention, 2001
http://www.ncjrs.gov/html/ojjdp/jjjournal_2001_6/jj2.html

Early Warning, Timely Response: A Guide to Safe Schools
U.S. Department of Education, 1998
http://www.ncjrs.gov/pdffiles1/172854.pdf

Emergency "Go-kits"
U.S. Department of Education, Emergency Response and Crisis Management
Technical Assistance Center, Helpful Hints, Vol. 2, Issue 1, 2007
http://rems.ed.gov/views/documents/HH_GoKits.pdf

How Students Can Avoid School Victimization
Center for the Study and Prevention of Violence, 2001
http://www.colorado.edu/cspv/publications/factsheets/schoolviolence
/FS-SV14.html

Increasing School Safety Through Juvenile Accountability Programs
Office of Juvenile Justice and Delinquency Prevention, 2000
http://www.ncjrs.gov/pdffiles1/ojjdp/179283.pdf

Indicators of School Crime and Safety
Bureau of Justice Statistics, Annual Report
http://www.ojp.usdoj.gov/bjs/pubalp2.htm#indicators

Promoting Safety in Schools: International Experience and Action
Bureau of Justice Assistance, 2001
http://www.ncjrs.gov/pdffiles1/bja/186937.pdf

School-Based Partnerships: A Problem-Solving Strategy
Office of Community Oriented Policing Services, 2006
http://www.cops.usdoj.gov/files/ric/CDROMs/SchoolSafety/Related_
Resources/SchoolBasedPartnerships.pdf

School and Community Interventions To Prevent Serious and Violent
Offending
Office of Juvenile Justice and Delinquency Prevention, 1999
http://www.ncjrs.gov/pdffiles1/ojjdp/177624.pdf

School Health Guidelines to Prevent Unintentional Injuries and Violence
Centers for Disease Control and Prevention, 2001
http://www.cdc.gov/mmwr/PDF/rr/rr5022.pdf

School Safety and Security Toolkit: A Guide for Parents, Schools, and
Communities
National Crime Prevention Council, 2003
http://www.ncpc.org/cms/cms-upload/ncpc/files/BSSToolkit_Complete
.pdf

Secure Our Schools Initiative Fact Sheet
Office of Community Oriented Policing Services, 2008
http://www.cops.usdoj.gov/files/ric/Publications/e0906119.pdf

Stand Up and Start a School Crime Watch!
Office of Juvenile Justice and Delinquency Prevention, 1998
http://www.ncjrs.gov/pdffiles/94601.pdf

Tips for Working Together to Create Safer Schools
National Crime Prevention Council, No publication date indicated
http://www.ncpc.org/cms/cms-upload/ncpc/files/saferschools.pdf

Using Environmental Design to Prevent School Violence
Centers for Disease Control and Prevention, No publication date indicated
http://www.cdc.gov/ncipc/dvp/CPTED.htm

RELATED RESOURCES

Be Safe and Sound in School (B3S);
http://www.ncpc.org/programs/be-safe-and-sound-campaign

B3S is an initiative of the National Crime Prevention Council (NCPC);
http://www.ncpc.org/ conducted in collaboration with the Bureau of Justice
Assistance (BJA); http://www.ojp.usdoj.gov/BJA/. The B3S program seeks to
raise awareness of school safety and security issues and provide the tools and
resources needed to effectively address them.

Gang Resistance Education and Training (G.R.E.A.T.) Program;
http://www.great-online.org/

The G.R.E.A.T. Program, administered by the Bureau of Justice Assistance
(BJA), is a school-based, law enforcement officer-instructed classroom curriculum. The program's primary objective is prevention and is intended as an
immunization against delinquency, youth violence, and gang membership.
G.R.E.A.T. lessons focus on providing life skills to students to help them avoid
delinquent behavior and violence to solve problems.

9.3 Table of Abbreviations and Acronyms

ATM   Automated Teller Machine

BEAR   Bear Market used to connote downward trending market

BJS   Bureau of Justice Statistics

BULL   Bull Market used to connote upward trending market

CCC   Civilian Conservation Corps

CDO   Collateralized Debt Obligation (sometimes called CDOs)

CCTV   Closed Circuit Television

CPTED   Crime Prevention Through Environmental Design

FBI   Federal Bureau of Investigation

IMF   International Monetary Fund

NCJRS   National Criminal Justice Research Service

ROW   Rest Of World (nations other than the United States of America)

UCR   FBI Uniform Crime Report

WPA   Works Progress Administration

Economic Misery Index   = Unemployment Rate (U-3) + Interest Rate

Economic Misery Cocktail   = Unemployment Rate (U-6) i.e Total unemployed, plus all marginally attached workers, plus total employed part time for economic reasons, as a percent of the civilian labor force plus all marginally attached workers, being those persons characterized by the US Bureau of Labor Statistics.

Plus (+)

Loss of purchasing power (through inflation or deflation of consumer household income and assets impacting available consumer capital for purchasing including lost homeowner equity (from falling housing prices), lost household savings in retirement funds, 401k funds, college savings accounts through falling equity prices and speculation bubble bursts, and household credit contraction reducing purchasing power).

9.4 Bibliography

Arvanites, Thomas M. and Defina, Robert H., 2006. "Business Cycles and Street Crime." *Criminology*, Feb. 2006, 139-64.

Becker, Gary, S., 1968. "Crime and Punishment: An Economic Approach." In: Lee R. McPheters and William B. Strong, ed. *The Economics of Crime and Law Enforcement.* Article reprinted from *Journal of Political Economy*, March/April 1968, 169-217.

Bess, Michael, 2008. "Assessing the Impact of Home Foreclosures in Charlotte Neighborhoods, Charlotte-Mechlenburg Police Department, Charlotte, North Carolina." *Geography & Public Safety,* 1(3).

Bloch, Herbert A., 1949. "Economic Depression as a Factor in Rural Crime." *Journal of Crime, Law, Criminology and Political Science.* 40, 458-470.

Boardman, J., Grove, B., Perkins, R. and Shepherd, G. (2003), "Work and employment for people with psychiatric disabilities." *British Journal of Psychiatry*, 182, 467-468.

Box, S., 1987. *Recession, Crime and Punishment.* New York: Barnes and Noble.

Brantingham, Paul J. and Brantingham, Patricial L., 1991. *Environmental Criminology.* 2nd ed. Waveland Press.

Buffet, Warren, 2002. Annual Letter to Shareholders, Berkshire Hathaway p15.

Bushway, Shawn D. and Reuter, Peter, 2002. "Labor markets and crime risk factors." In: Lawrence W. Sherman , David P. Farrington, Brandon C. Welsh, and Doris Layton MacKenzie ed. *Evidence-Based Crime Prevention.* New York: Routledge, 167-197.

Canada, Department of Justice, 2008. *Organized Crime Control Strategies and their effectiveness,* "Assessing the Effectiveness of Organized Crime Control Strategies: A Review of the Literature." [online]. Available from: **http://www .justice.gc.ca/eng/pi/rs/rep-rap/2005/rr05_5/p8.html**

Carter, Susan, et. al., 2006. *Historical Statistics of the United States, Millennial Edition.* New York: Cambridge University Press, 2006.

Clarke, Ronald V., 1999. "Hot Products: Understanding, anticipating, and reducing demand for stolen goods." Police Research Series, Paper 112, The Home Office, UK.

Clotfelter, Charles T., 1976. "Urban crime and household protective measures." In: Ralph Andreano, and John J. Siegfried, 1980. *The Economics of Crime*. New York: John Wiley and Sons.

Cole, Harold L., and Ohanian, Lee E.,2004. "New Deal Policies and the Persistence of the Great Depression: A General Equilibrium Analysis." *Journal of Political Economy*, 112, 779-816.

Conly John A., 1971. *The New Deal's Response to Crime: The Politics of Law and Order*. Michigan State University, Thesis (Masters).

Cook, P. J. and Zarkin, G. A., 1985. "Crime and the Business Cycle," *Journal of Legal Studies*, 14, 115-28.

DeFronzo, James, 1983. "Economic Assistance to Impoverished Americans: Relationship to Incidence of Crime." *Criminology*, 21, 119-36.

Demerjian, Dave, 2008. Note to Next President: Modern-Day WPA Will Save the Economy. [online]. Wired Magazine Website, Wired.com, October 19, 2008.

Donohue, John J. III and Siegelman , Peter, 1998. "Allocating Resources among Prisons and Social Programs in the Battle Against Crime." *Journal of Legal Studies*, 27, 1-45.

Duncan, Gary, 2008. "Head of IMF Fears Unreset with Action on Economy," [online]. TimesOnline, 12/16/08. Available at **http://business.timesonline .co.uk/tol/business/economics/article5349277.ece**

Eck, John, 2002. "Preventing Crime at Places," In Lawrence W. Sherman, David P. Farrington, Bandon C. Welsh, and Doris Layton MacKenzie ed. *Evidence-Based Crime Prevention*. London and New York: Routledge.

Edmark, Karin, 2005. "Unemployment and Crime: Is There a Connection?" *Scandinavian Journal of Economics*, 107, 353-73.

Farrington, D., Gallagher, B., Morley, L., Ledger, R. and West, D., (1986). "Unemployment, School-leaving and Crime." *British Journal of Criminology*, 26, 335-56.

Felson, Marcus, and Clarke, Ronald V. 1998. "Opportunity Makes the Thief: practical theory for crime prevention," Police Research Series Paper 98, London: Home Office Policing and Reducing Crime Unit.

Field, Simon, 1992. "The Effect of Temperature on Crime." *British Journal of Criminology*, 32, 340-51.

_____,1999, "Trends in Crime Revisited." Home Office Research Study 195: London.

Finegan, T. Aldrich and Margo, Robert A., 1994. "Work Relief and the Labor Force Participation of Married Women in 1940." *Journal of Economic History*, 54, 64-84.

Fishback, Price V., Haines , Michael R. and Kantor, Shawn. "Births, Deaths, and New Deal Relief during the Great Depression." *Review of Economics and Statistics* (forthcoming).

Fishback, Price V., Horrace, William C., and Kantor, Shawn, 2005. "Did New Deal Grant Programs Stimulate Local Economies? A Study of Federal Grants and Retail Sales during the Great Depression." *Journal of Economic History*, 65, 36-71.

_____, 2006. "The Impact of New Deal Expenditures on Mobility during the Great Depression." *Explorations in Economic History*, 43, 179-222.

Fishback, Price and Thomasson, Melissa, 2006. "Social Welfare: 1929 to the Present." In Susan Carter, et. al. ed. *Historical Statistics of the United States, Millennial Edition*. New York: Cambridge University Press, 2006.

Fishman, Mark, 1978. "Crime Waves as Ideology." *Social Problems*, 25 (5).

Fleck, Robert K., 1999. "The Marginal Effect of New Deal Relief Work on County-Level Unemployment Statistics." *Journal of Economic History*, 59.

_____, 2001. "Population, Land, Economic Conditions, and the Allocation of New Deal Spending," *Explorations in Economic History*, 38, 296-304.

Freeman, Richard K., 1999. *The Economics of Crime*. LSE: Harvard University. Available at **http://webspace.qmul.ac.uk/fcornaglia/ economics%20od%20crime.pdf**

Gabor, Thomas, 1994. *Everybody Does It! Crime by the Public*. Toronto: University of Toronto Press.

Galbraith, John Kenneth, 1954. *The Great Crash*, 1929.

Goldstock, Ronald, et.al, 1990. *Corruption and Racketeering in the New York City Construction Industry: The Final Report of the New York State Organized Task Force.*

Grogger, Jeff, "Market Wages and Youth Crime." *Journal of Labor Economics*, 16 , 756-91.

Hannon, Lance, and DeFronzo, James, 1998. "The Truly Disadvantaged, Public Assistance, and Crime." *Social Problems*, 45, 383-92.

Harcourt, Geoffrey, 2008. "Economics: From Moral Sciences to Game Theory." In Peter Pagnamenta ed. *The University of Cambridge: An 800 year Portrait."* London: Millenium.

Hauser, Christine and Bakerm, Al, 2008. "Ailing U. S. Economy Brings Fears of a Crime Wave." *International Herald Tribune Newspaper*, October 10. Available at **http://www.iht.com/articles/2008/10/10/america/letter.php**

Helmer, William and Mattix, Rick, 1998. *Public Enemies: America's Criminal Past 1919 to 1940*. New York: Checkmark Books.

Howard, Donald S., 1943. *The WPA and Federal Relief Policy.* New York: Russell Sage Foundation.

Inter-University Consortium for Political and Social Research. *Historical, Demographic, Economic, and Social Data: The United States*, 1790-1970, file number 0003. The version has additions and corrections by Michael Haines, Department of Economics, Colgate University, Hamilton, NY.

_____. "Understanding Why Crime Fell in the 1990s: Four Factors that Explain the Decline and Six that Do Not." *Journal of Economic Perspectives*, 18, 163-90.

Jones, Sidney L, Letter, "Can Butterflies Become Caterpillars?" January 1, 2009, #3.

_____, Letter, "The End", November 29, 2008; #2

_____. Letter, "The US Economy: Prospects and Policies", October 28, 2008; #1.

Johnson, Ryan S., Kantor, Shawn Everett and Fishback, Price V., 2007. "Striking at the Roots of Crime: The Impact of Social Welfare Spending on Crime during the Great Depression". NBER Working Paper No. W12825. Available at SSRN: http://ssrn.com/abstract=956864

Kapuscinski, Cezary A., Braithwaite, John and Chapman, Bruce, 1998. "Unemployment and Crime: Towards Resolving the Paradox." *Journal of Quantitative Criminology*, 14 (3).

Kelleher, James B. "Buffett's 'Time Bomb' Goes Off on Wall Street." [online]. Reuters.com. Available at **http://www.reuters.com/article/newsOne/ idUSN1837154020080918**

Kleiman, Mark A. R., 1992. Against Excess: *Drug Policy for Results*. Basic Books.

Krauss, Melvyn B. and Lazear, Edward P., 1991. *Searching for Alternatives: Drug-Control Policy in the United States*. Stanford: Hoover Institution Press.

Kristof, D N, "Scholars Disagree on Connection Between Crime and Jobless." *Washington Post*, August 7, 1982, p.A8., republished in Box, Steven, Recession, *Crime and Punishment*. Barnes and Noble, 1987.

Kunz, H. J., 1976. *Economics of the Individual and Organized Crime*. Carl Heymanns Verland, 1976.

Lane, Roger, 1967. *Policing the City*: Boston 1822-1885. Cambridge University Press.

Leonardsen, Dag, 2006. Crime in Japan: "Paradise Lost?" *Journal of Scandinavian Studies in Criminology and Crime Prevention*, 7, 185-210.

Louis, Turthill, 2008. "Breaking New Windows – Examining the Subprime Mortgage Crises Using the Broken Windows Theory," in *Geography & Public Safety*, 1(3).

Machin, Stephen, and Meghir , Costas. "Crime and Economic Incentives." *Journal of Human Resources*, 39, 958-79.

Miller, Richard Lawrence, 1991. *The Case for Legalizing Drugs*. New York: Praeger.

Naylor, R.T., 2003. "Towards a General Theory of Profit-Driven Crimes." *British Journal of Criminology*, 43 (1) , 81 to 101.

Neustrom, M. and Norton, W. (1995) "Economic Dislocation and Property Crime." *Journal of Criminal Justice.* 23 (1), 29 – 39.

Pandiani, John A, 1982. "The Crime Control Corps: An Invisible New Deal Program." *British Journal of Sociology*, 33, 348-58.

Pyle, D. J. and Deadman, D. F., 1994. "Crime and the Business Cycle in Postwar Britain." *British Journal of Criminology*, 34 (3).

Radzinowicz,Leon and Wolfgang ed., 1977. *Crime and Justice: The Criminal in Society*, 2nd ed., Vol 1, New York: Basic Books Inc, 555-556.

Raphael, Stephen and Winter-Ebmer, Rudolf , 2001. "Identifying the Effect of Unemployment on Crime." *Journal of Law and Economics*, 44, 259-283.

Reed, Lawrence W., 2009. "A History Lesson for Obama: Great Myths of the Great Depression," The Peregrine Falcon Blog, February 10, 2009. Available at **http://theperegrin.com/2009/02/10/a-history-lesson-for-obama-great-myths-of-the-great-depression/**

Reuter, Peter H., MacCoun, Robert, Murphy, Patrick, Abrahamse, Allan and Simon, B., 1990. "Money From Crime: A Study of the Economics of Drug Dealing in Washington, D.C.", Rand Report, The Rand Corporation, Santa Monica, CA, 1990.

Roosevelt, Franklin D. "Address at the National Parole Conference," Washington, DC, April 17, 1939. Available at The American Presidency Project, **http://www.presidency.ucsb.edu.**

Rosen, Lawrence, 1995. "The Creation of the Uniform Crime Reports: The Role of Social Science." *Social Science History*, 19, 215-38.

Rosenfeld, Richard and Fornago, Robert, 2007, "Impact of Economic Conditions on Robbery and Property Crime: The Role of Consumer Sentiment." *Criminology*, 45 (4), 735 to 770.

Sacco, Vincent F., 2005. *When Crime Waves*. London: Sage Publications.

Scorcu, A. and Cellini, R., 1985. "Crime and the Business Cycle." *Journal of Legal Studies*, vol XIV.

Sherman, Lawrence W., Farrington, David P., Welsh, Brandon C. and Mackenzie, Doris Layton, 2002,. *Evidence-Based Crime Prevention*. New York: Routledge.

Sherman, Lawrence W., Gottfredson, Denise, MacKenzie, Doris, Eck, John, Reuter, Peter, and Bushway, Shawn, 1997. "PREVENTING CRIME: WHAT WORKS, WHAT DOESN'T, WHAT'S PROMISING, A REPORT TO THE UNITED STATES CONGRESS," Prepared for the National Institute of Justice, in collaboration with members of the Graduate Program, Department of Criminology and Criminal Justice (1997). [online]. Available from **http://www.ncjrs.gov/works/**

Sinclair, Andrew, 1962. *Prohibition: The Era of Excess.*

Sorensen, Severin L., 1998. "Empowering Capable Guardians in High Crime and Low Income Settings," *Security Journal,* 11, 29-35 (London: Elsevier Press, 1998).

_____, 1999. "Illegal Drug Selling and Place: Spatial Geography of Street-Level Drug, Or the 22 Immutable Laws of Illegal Drug Marketing," International Workshop on Drug Markets 1999. John Jay College of Criminal Justice, April 8-9, 1999. Available at **slsorensen@gmail.com**.

_____, 2008. Serial Weblog Posts. *Economic Misery and Crime Waves.* 2008-2009. **http://d2crimewave.blogspot.com/**.

Sorensen, Severin L, Hayes, John G., and Atlas, Randy, 2008. "Understanding CPTED and Situational Crime Prevention." In Randy Atlas, ed.. *21st Century Security and CPTED: Designing for Critical Infrastructure Protection and Crime Prevention.* CRC Press.

Sorensen, Severin L., Hayes, JG; Walsh EW, and Myhre M, 1997. *Crime Prevention Through Environmental Design (CPTED): Workbook,* (U.S. Department of Housing and Urban Development, Community Safety and Conservation Division; Washington, DC); updated 1998 and 2000.

Sung, Hung-En, 2004."State Failure, Economic Failure, and Predatory Organized Crime: A Comparative Analysis.", *Journal of Research in Crime and Delinquency,* 41 (2), 111 to 129.

Swaray, Raymond B. Bowles, Roger, and Pradiptyo, Rimawan, 2005. "Application of Economic Analysis to Criminal Justice Interventions: A Review of the Literature." *Criminal Justice Policy Review,* 16 (2), 141 to 163.

Tonry, Michael and Wilson, James Q. ed., 1990. *Drugs and Crime.* Chicago: University of Chicago Press.

Toffler, Alvin, 1970. *Future Shock.* Random House.

United Nations Social Defense Research Institute, 1974. "Economic Crises and Crime: Interim Report and Materials," UNSDRI, Publication no. 9, Rome, Italy.

U.S. Bureau of Census, 1975. *Historical Statistics of the United States: Colonial Times to 1970.* Washington, DC: Government Printing Office.

U. S. Bureau of Economic Analysis, 1989. *State Personal Income: 1929-1987.* Washington, DC: Government Printing Office.

U.S. Bureau of Labor Statistics. "Unemployment data by race, gender, and age for period 1954-2009." [online]. Available at **http://data.bls.gov/PDQ/servlet/SurveyOutputServlet.**

U. S. Bureau of Labor Statistics. "The Employment Situation." January 2009.

U.S. Department of Commerce, Bureau of Foreign and Domestic Commerce. *Consumer Market Data Handbook, 1936.* Washington, DC: Government Printing Office.

U.S. Department of Commerce, Bureau of Foreign and Domestic Commerce. *Consumer Market Data Handbook, 1939.* Washington, DC: Government Printing Office.

U.S. Department of Labor, Children's Bureau, 1937. Trends in Different Types of Public and Private Relief in Urban Areas, 1929-35. Publication No. 237, Washington, DC: Government Printing Office.

U.S. Federal Bureau of Investigation, *Uniform Crime Reports.* Washington, DC: Government Printing Office, various years.

U.S. National Resources Planning Board, 1942. Security, Work, and Relief Policies. Washington, DC: Government Printing Office.

U.S. Federal Security Agency, Social Security Board, 1942. Public and Private Aid in 116 Urban Areas, 1929-38, with Supplement for 1939 and 1940. Public Assistance Report No. 3, Washington, DC: Government Printing Office.

Wallis, John Joseph, 1989. "Employment in the Great Depression: New Data and Hypotheses." *Explorations in Economic History,* 26, 45-72.

Wallis, John Joseph and Benjamin , Daniel K., 1981. , "Public Relief and Private Employment in the Great Depression." *Journal of Economic History,* 41, 97-102.

Wallis, John Joseph, Fishback , Price and Kantor, Shawn, 2006. "Politics, Relief, and Reform: Roosevelt's Efforts to Control Corruption and Manipulation during the New Deal." In Edward Glaeser and Claudia Goldin ed. *Corruption and Reform*. Chicago: University of Chicago Press, 343-72.

Washington, Gary, 2009. "US Intelligence Chief Calls Economic Crisis a Security Threat," Voice of America, 2/12/2009. Available at **http://www.voanews.com/english/2009-02-12-voa58.cfm.**

Wector, Dixon, 1948. *The Age of Great Depression 1929-1941*. London: Macmillan Company.

Welsh, Brandon C. and Farrington, David P., 2002. "What works, what doesn't, what's promising, and future directions." In Lawrence W. Sherman, David P. Farrington, Welsh, and Doris Layton MacKenzie ed. *Evidence-Based Crime Prevention*. London and New York: Routledge.

Wilson, J.Q. and Kelling, G.L., 1982. "Broken Windows: The Police and Neighborhood Safety." *Atlantic Monthly*, 249. See also, **http://www.theatlantic .com/doc/198203/broken-windows**

Weatherburn, Don, 1992. "Economic Adversity and Crime: Trends and Issues in Crime and Criminal Justice.," *Australian Institute of Criminology*, 40.

Witte, A D, and Long S K, 1982. "Some Thoughts Concerning the Effects of Recession and the Level of Illegal Activity." *Unemployment and Crime Joint Hearings*, 198-219.

Witte, Ann Dryden and Witt, Robert, 2001. "What We Spend and What We Get: Public and Private Provision of Crime Prevention and Criminal Justice." *Fiscal Studies*, 22, 1-40.

Woods, G. D., 1978. "Unemployment and Crime—A General Perspective." *Proceedings: Unemployment and Crime*. Institute of Criminology, No. 36, University of Sidney, Australia.

Wright, Kevin N., 1981. *Crime and Criminal Justice in a Declining Economy*. Cambridge, MA: Gunn & Hain, Publishers.

Zhang, Junsen, 1997. "The Effect of Welfare Programs on Criminal Behavior: A Theoretical and Empirical Analysis." *Economic Inquiry*, 35, 120-37.

10 | Internet Crime Prevention Tips

Internet crime schemes that steal millions of dollars each year from victims continue to plague the online public. The following are preventative measures that will assist you in being well-informed prior to entering into transactions over the Internet :

AUCTION FRAUD

- Before you bid, contact the seller with any questions you have.
- Review the seller's feedback.
- Be cautious when dealing with individuals outside of your own country.
- Ensure you understand refund, return, and warranty policies.
- Determine the shipping charges before you buy.
- Be wary if the seller only accepts wire transfers or cash.
- If an escrow service is used, ensure it is legitimate.
- Consider insuring your item.
- Be cautious of unsolicited offers.

COUNTERFEIT CASHIER'S CHECK

- Inspect the cashier's check.

- Ensure the amount of the check matches in figures and words.

- Check to ensure that the account number is not shiny in appearance.

- Be watchful that the drawer's signature is not traced.

- Official checks are generally perforated on at least one side.

- Inspect the check for additions, deletions, or other alterations.

- Contact the financial institution on which the check was drawn to ensure legitimacy.

- Obtain the bank's telephone number from a reliable source, not from the check itself.

- Be cautious when dealing with individuals outside of your own country.

CREDIT CARD FRAUD

- Ensure a site is secure and reputable before providing your credit card number online.

- Don't trust a site just because it claims to be secure.

- If purchasing merchandise, ensure it is from a reputable source.

- Promptly reconcile credit card statements to avoid unauthorized charges.

- Do your research to ensure the legitimacy of the individual or company.

- Beware of providing credit card information when requested through unsolicited emails.

DEBT ELIMINATION

- Know who you are doing business with — do your research.

- Obtain the name, address, and telephone number of the individual or company.

- Research the individual or company to ensure they are authentic.

- Contact the Better Business Bureau to determine the legitimacy of the company.

- Be cautious when dealing with individuals outside of your own country.

- Ensure you understand all terms and conditions of any agreement.

- Be wary of businesses that operate from P.O. boxes or mail drops.

- Ask for names of other customers of the individual or company and contact them.

- If it sounds too good to be true, it probably is.

DHL/UPS

- Beware of individuals using the DHL or UPS logo in any email communication.

- Be suspicious when payment is requested by money transfer before the goods are delivered.

- Remember that DHL and UPS do not generally get involved in directly collecting payment from customers.

- Fees associated with DHL or UPS transactions are only for shipping costs and never for other costs associated with online transactions.

- Contact DHL or UPS to confirm the authenticity of email communications received.

EMPLOYMENT/BUSINESS OPPORTUNITIES

- Be wary of inflated claims of product effectiveness.

- Be cautious of exaggerated claims of possible earnings or profits.

- Beware when money is required up front for instructions or products.

- Be leery when the job posting claims "no experience necessary."

- Do not give your social security number when first interacting with your prospective employer.

- Be cautious when dealing with individuals outside of your own country.

- Be wary when replying to unsolicited emails for work-at-home employment.
- Research the company to ensure it is authentic.
- Contact the Better Business Bureau to determine the legitimacy of the company.

ESCROW SERVICES FRAUD

- Always type in the website address yourself rather than clicking on a link provided.
- A legitimate website will be unique and will not duplicate the work of other companies.
- Be cautious when a site requests payment to an "agent" instead of a corporate entity.
- Be leery of escrow sites that only accept wire transfers or e-currency.
- Be watchful of spelling errors, grammar problems, or inconsistent information.
- Beware of sites that have escrow fees that are unreasonably low.

IDENTITY THEFT

- Ensure websites are secure prior to submitting your credit card number.
- Do your homework to ensure that the business or website is legitimate.
- Attempt to obtain a physical address, rather than a P.O. box or maildrop.
- Never throw away credit card or bank statements in usable form.
- Be aware of missed bills which could indicate your account has been taken over.
- Be cautious of scams requiring you to provide your personal information.
- Never give your credit card number over the phone unless you make the call.

- Monitor your credit statements monthly for any fraudulent activity.
- Report unauthorized transactions to your bank or credit card company as soon as possible.
- Review a copy of your credit report at least once a year.

INTERNET EXTORTION

- Security needs to be multi-layered so that numerous obstacles will be in the way of the intruder.
- Ensure security is installed at every possible entry point.
- Identify all machines connected to the Internet and assess the defense that's engaged.
- Identify whether your servers are utilizing any ports that have been known to represent insecurities.
- Ensure you are utilizing the most up-to-date patches for your software.

INVESTMENT FRAUD

- If the "opportunity" appears too good to be true, it probably is.
- Beware of promises to make fast profits.
- Do not invest in anything unless you understand the deal.
- Don't assume a company is legitimate based on the "appearance" of the website.
- Be leery when responding to investment offers received through unsolicited email.
- Be wary of investments that offer high returns at little or no risk.
- Independently verify the terms of any investment that you intend to make.
- Research the parties involved and the nature of the investment.
- Be cautious when dealing with individuals outside of your own country.
- Contact the Better Business Bureau to determine the legitimacy of the company.

LOTTERIES

- If the lottery winnings appear too good to be true, they probably are.

- Be cautious when dealing with individuals outside of your own country.

- Be leery if you do not remember entering a lottery or contest.

- Be cautious if you receive a telephone call stating you are the winner in a lottery.

- Beware of lotteries that charge a fee prior to delivery of your prize.

- Be wary of demands to send additional money to be eligible for future winnings.

- It is a violation of federal law to play a foreign lottery via mail or phone.

NIGERIAN LETTER OR "419"

- If the "opportunity" appears too good to be true, it probably is.

- Do not reply to emails asking for personal banking information.

- Be wary of individuals representing themselves as foreign government officials.

- Be cautious when dealing with individuals outside of your own country.

- Beware when asked to assist in placing large sums of money in overseas bank accounts.

- Do not believe the promise of large sums of money for your cooperation.

- Guard your account information carefully.

- Be cautious when additional fees are requested to further the transaction.

PHISHING/SPOOFING

- Be suspicious of any unsolicited email requesting personal information.

- Avoid filling out forms in email messages that ask for personal information.

- Always compare the link in the email to the link that you are actually directed to.

- Log on to the official website, instead of "linking" to it from an unsolicited email.

- Contact the actual business that supposedly sent the email to verify if the email is genuine.

PONZI/PYRAMID

- If the "opportunity" appears too good to be true, it probably is.

- Beware of promises to make fast profits.

- Exercise diligence in selecting investments.

- Be vigilant in researching with whom you choose to invest.

- Make sure you fully understand the investment prior to investing.

- Be wary when you are required to bring in subsequent investors.

- Verify the legitimacy of any investment independently.

- Beware of references given by the promoter.

RESHIPPING

- Be cautious if you are asked to ship packages to an "overseas home office."

- Be cautious when dealing with individuals outside of your own country.

- Be leery if the individual states that his country will not allow direct business shipments from the United States.

- Be wary if the "ship to" address is yours but the name on the package is not.

- Never provide your personal information to strangers in a chat room.

- Don't accept packages that you didn't order.

- If you receive packages that you didn't order, either refuse them upon delivery or contact the company where the package is from.

SPAM

- Don't open spam. Delete it unread.

- Never respond to spam as this will confirm to the sender that it is a "live" email address.

- Have a primary and secondary email address – one for people you know and one for all other purposes.

- Avoid giving out your email address unless you know how it will be used.

- Never purchase anything advertised through an unsolicited email.

THIRD PARTY RECEIVER OF FUNDS

- Do not agree to accept and wire payments for auctions that you did not post.

- Be leery if the individual states that his country makes receiving these types of funds difficult.

- Be cautious when the job posting states, "no experience necessary."

- Be cautious when dealing with individuals outside of your own country.

11 | End Notes

[1] Euripides writes that "the gods visit the sins of the fathers upon the children" (Phrixus, undated fragment 970) and that "when good men die their goodness does not perish…As for the bad, All that was theirs dies and is buried with them." (Temeniadae, undated fragment 734). Other authors have echoed these same themes: Horace (23 B.C.) says that the children, though guiltless, must suffer for the sins of the father; Shakespeare (1596) wrote that the sins of the father are to be laid upon the children; and Hawthorne (1851) wrote that wrongdoing of one generation lives into successive ones. The Old Testament records the parable of sour grapes and the children's teeth set on edge several times: Exodus 20:25 (Moses), and then later prophets Jeremiah 31:29 and Ezekiel 18:2. More on the topic is found at Yael Danieli, *Multigenerational Legacies of Trauma* (1998), Published by Springer.

[2] NPR, 'Experts - Bad Economic Don't Lead To Crime Waves,' November 21, 2008, **http://www.npr.org/templates/story/story.php?storyId=97234406**.

[3] As quoted in Kristof, D.N., "Scholars disagree on connection between crime and jobless," Washington Post, August 7, 1982, p.A8., as published in Steven Box, *Recession, Crime and Punishment*, Barnes and Noble, 1987.

[4] Home Office Research Study, 195, Trends in Crime Revisited, NCJRS 182135

[5] Sidney L. Jones, earned his MBA and Ph.D. in Economics from Stanford University (1956-60), had subsequent positions in academia, and most notably the following public policy experiences during periods of sharp economic contractions: 1969-71 Senior Economist and Special Assistant to the Chairman, Council of Economic Advisers; 1972-73 Minister-Counselor for Economic Affairs, U.S. Mission to NATO, Brussels, Belgium; 1973-74 Assistant Secretary for Economic Affairs, Department of Treasury 1974-75; Deputy Assistant to the President and Deputy to the Counsellor for Economic Policy, The White House; 1975-77 Counselor to the Secretary and Assistant Secretary for Economic Policy, Department of the Treasury; 1978 Assistant to the Board of Governors, Federal Reserve System; 1983-85 Under Secretary for Economic Affairs, Department of Commerce; and 1989-93 Assistant Secretary for Economic Policy, Department of the Treasury. More information on Jones writings at **http://www.ford.utexas.edu/library/guides/Finding%20Aids/Jones,%20Sidney%20-%20Papers.htm**

[6] From the Bureau of Labor Statistics, "employers took 2,769 mass layoff actions in February that resulted in the separation of 295,477 workers…Thirteen of the 19 major industry sectors reported program highs in terms of average weekly initial claimants for the month of February--mining; construction; manufacturing; wholesale trade; retail trade; transportation and warehousing; finance and insurance; real estate and rental and leasing; professional and technical services; management of companies and enterprises; educational services; accommodation and food services; and other services, except public administration." See: **http://www.bls.gov/news.release/mmls.nr0.htm**

[7] Sidney L. Jones, Letter, "Can butterflies become caterpillars?", January 1, 2009, #3.

[8] Ronald V. Clarke, Hot Products: Understanding, anticipating, and reducing demand for stolen goods, Police Research Series, Paper 112, The Home Office, UK., 1999.

[9] The Employment Situation, Bureau of Labor Statistics, January 2009, **http://www.bls.gov/news.release/empsit.nr0.htm**

[10] Definition of avarice, courtesy, **wordnet.princeton.edu/perl/webwn**.

[11] Isaac Asimov, quote on Great Depression, (Russian born American science-fiction Writer and Biochemist. 1920-1992), **http://thinkexist.com/quotes/with/keyword/great_depression/**

[12] *New York Times*, October 14, 1929; as reported online at http://www.iraq-war.ru/article/120692

[13] News dispatch from Washington, January 1930; as reported online at http://www.iraq-war.ru/article/120692

[14] Guest Post: The Great Depression, as I remember , Fortune.com; http://postcards.blogs.fortune.cnn.com/2008/11/20/guest-post-the-great-depression-as-i-remember/?source=yahoo_quote

[15] Quote attributed to Elder Boyd K. Packer, President of the Quorum of Twelve Apostles, Church of Jesus Christ of Latter-Day Saints, in a talk delivered on 10/12/08 in a Sacrament meeting at the Forest Bend Drive Chapel, Salt Lake City, Utah.

[16] William Helmer (1998), *Public Enemies: America's Criminal Past*, 1919-1940, p. xii

[17] See, "El Secuestro en Mexico" ("Kidnapping in Mexico"), by Jose A. Ortega, who is also the president of Mexico's Citizens' Council for Public Security and Penal Justice.; http://m3report.wordpress.com/2009/01/15/mexico-homocide-and-kidnapping-statistics-for-2008-are-staggering/; http://www.freerepublic.com/focus/f-bloggers/2166442/posts

[18] The world must never forget that Hitler's rise to power was facilitated by conditions of extreme economic misery, and a people wanting change for change's sake. The table below shows the party results of Hitler's rise in the political system in Germany. Note the dates and years of influence and one can readily see that Hitler's meteoric rise was facilitated by the Great Depression and the absence of social insurance, and a people looking to be led by someone they thought would lead them out of misery. How sad the world history is of the treachery of Hitler's regime and a people fooled by the veil of his Socialist front, that led to a Fascist totalitarian regime that exterminated with impunity so many Jewish people with cold hearted inhumanity.

Nazi Party Election Results				
Date	Votes	Percentage	Seats in Reichstag	Background
May 1924	1,918,300	6.5	32	Hitler in prison
December 1924	907,300	3.0	14	Hitler is released from prison
May 1928	810,100	2.6	12	
September 1930	6,409,600	18.3	107	After the financial crisis
July 1932	13,745,800	37.4	230	After Hitler was candidate for presidency
November 1932	11,737,000	33.1	196	
March 1933	17,277,000	43.9	288	During Hitler's term as Chancellor of Germany

Source of Table, Wiki, Hitler's rise to power (2009).

[19] Geoffrey Harcourt, "Economics: From Moral Sciences to Game Theory", *The University of Cambridge: An 800 year portrait*, Peter Pagnamenta, ed, 3rd Millenium Publishing, London, 2008, P.168.

[20] Definition of Economics given by the online encyclopedia Wiki - **http://en.wikipedia.org/wiki/Economics**.

[21] G.D. Woods, "Unemployment and Crime – A General Perspective," Proceedings: Unemployment and Crime, Institute of Criminology, No. 36, University of Sidney, Austrailia, 1978.

[22] The misery index is an economic indicator created by the economist Arthur Okun. It is found by adding the unemployment rate to the inflation rate. It is assumed that both a higher rate of unemployment and a worsening of inflation create economic and social costs for a country. **http://en.wikipedia.org/wiki/Misery_index_(economics)**.

[23] **http://www.miseryindex.us/**

[24] Who Is Counted As Unemployed, US Bureau of Labor Statistics; **http://www.bls.gov/cps/faq.htm#Ques5**

[25] International Labor Organization. **http://www.ilo.org/global/What_we_do/ Statistics/topics/Underemployment/guidelines/lang--en/index.htm**

Resolution concerning the measurement of underemployment and inadequate employment situations - [pdf 26 KB] was adopted by the 16th International Conference of Labour Statisticians in 1998. The Resolution concerning the measurement of Underemployment and Situations of Inadequate Employment provides guidelines on two types of underemployment: *time related underemployment*, which is due to insufficient hours of work, and *inadequate employment situations*, which are due to other limitations in the labor market which limit the capacities and well being of workers. A person can be simultaneously in these two forms of underemployment.

TIME-RELATED UNDEREMPLOYMENT

Persons in *time-related underemployment* are those who during the short reference period, were willing to work additional hours, were available to do so, and had worked less hours than a selected number of hours. This definition is circumscribed to a short reference period, which must be the same that is used to measure employment and unemployment (usually one week).

- The **willingness to work additional hours** is the main criterion and identifies persons who, independently of the number of hours already worked during the reference week in all their jobs, express a desire or preference to work more hours.

- The **availability to work additional hours** identifies those persons who are ready to work additional hours within a subsequent period, if they had the opportunity to do so, from those that are not available.

- The criterion of having **worked less than a threshold relating to working time** excludes those workers who want to work additional hours and are available to do so, but who already work a "sufficient" number of hours and therefore, for policy reasons, are considered to have reached their full employment level. This criterion is necessary when a country wants to link the time-related underemployed population with employment policies, to determine who are those who worked less hours than what is considered as full-time work.

INADEQUATE EMPLOYMENT SITUATIONS

Persons are in an *inadequate employment situations* when, during the reference period, they wanted to change their current work situation for reasons that limit their capacities and well-being and were available to do so. A worker may want to replace on their current paid or self-employment jobs for another, transform their activities and/or the way in which they are carried out ; or the two options simultaneously.

- The **willingness to change** their current work situation distinguishes persons whose full employment level from the point of view of productivity and work quality, as assessed by workers themselves, is above their current level of productivity, and who want to change their current work situation. This criterion is equivalent to the willingness to work additional hours in the definition of time-related underemployment and is similar to the active job search in the unemployment definition. As with time-related underemployment, it is important to separately identify those workers who actively looked to change their current work situation.

- The **reasons** identify persons in inadequate employment situation, on the basis of the workers' assessment of their own work situation regarding the potential that they have to increase their productivity and quality of work. Three response categories are separately recognized:

  - The inadequate or insufficient use of workers' occupational skills: this reason gives way to the identification of persons in skill-related inadequate employment

  - The inadequate income in the current job(s): this reasons gives way to persons in income-related inadequate employment

  - Excessive hours of work: this reason gives way to persons in inadequate employment related to excessive hours

[26] Cezary A. Kapuscinski, John Braithwaite and Bruce Chapman, "Unemployment and Crime: Toward Resolving the Paradox," *Journal of Quantitative Criminology*, Springer Netherlands, v14, No. 3, September 1998.

[27] Freeman (1999).

[28] Richard B. Freeman, *The Economics of Crime*, 1999, Harvard University and NBER Center For Economic Performance, LSE, **http://webspace.qmul.ac.uk /fcornaglia/economics%20od%20crime.pdf**.

[29] D.J. Pyle and D.F. Deadman, "Crime and the Business Cycle in Post-War Britain," *British Journal of Criminology*, Vol. 34, No. 3, Summer 1994.

[30] Christine Hauser and Al Bakerm, "Ailing U.S. economy brings fears of a crime wave," *International Herald Tribune Newspaper*, October 10, 2008 http://www.iht.com/articles/2008/10/10/america/letter.php.

[31] World Health Organization (WHO), "Promoting Health in the Human Environment," Australian Social Welfare, Vol.6, Sept 1975; as reported in Milton Luger, "Dilenquency and Unemployment," Proceedings of the Institute of Criminology, Unviersity of Sydney, Australia, No.36, 1978.

[32] http://www.coldwellbankeratlanta.com/search/FMLS-SF-DetailDisplay. cfm?fmlsnumber=3849027.

[33] Stephen Raphael and Rudolf Winter-Ebmer, "Identifying the Effect of Unemployment on Crime." *The Journal of Law and Economics*, vol 44, (April 2001), University of Chicago.

[34] P J Cook and G A Zarkin (1985), "Crime and the Business Cycle," *Journal of Legal Studies,* 14: 115-28, reference cited is on p. 126.

[35] Dag Leonardsen, "Crime in Japan: Paradise Lost?" *Journal of Scandinavian Studies in Criminology and Crime Prevention*, Routledge Press, Vol.7, pp 185-210, (2006).

[36] IBID, p. 199-200.

[37] Peter H. Reuter, Robert MacCoun, Patrick Murphy, Allan Abrahamse, and B. Simon, "Money From Crime : A Study of the Economics of Drug Dealing in Washington, D.C.", Rand Report, The Rand Corporation ,Santa Monica, CA 1990.

Positive Relationship	Time Series	Cross-Sectional
Yes	Box and Hale, 1985 Brenner, 1978 Cook and Zarkin, 1985 Ehrlich, 1975 Fleisher, 1963 Glaser and Rice, 1959 Land and Felson, 1976 Leveson, 1976 Philips,et.al., 1972 Philips, 1981 Singell, 1967 Votey, 1979 Wolpin, 1978	Allison, 1972 Bechdolt, 1975 Block, 1979 Booth,et.al., 1977 Brown,et.al., 1972 Carroll and Jackson, 1983 Chapman, 1976 Cohen and Land, 1984 Danziger, 1976 DeFronzo, 1983 Hakim, 1982 (a re-analysis of Carr-Hill and Stern, 1979) Hemley and McPeters, 1974 Hoch, 1974 Kvalseth, 1977 Pyle, 1982 Sampson,et.al, 1981 Schmid, 1960 Sjoquist, 1973 Zedlewski, 1983
No	Danziger and Wheller, 1975 Danser and Laub, 1981 Fox, 1978 Orsagh, 1981 Vandaele, 1978	Avio and Clark, 1976 Bartel, 1979 Danziger and Wheeler, 1975 Forst, 1976 Gylys, 1970 Pogue, 1975 Schuessler and Slatin, 1964 Singell, 1967 Spector, 1975 Stevens and Willis, 1979 Swimmer, 1974 Wadycki and Balkin, 1979 Williams and Drake, 1980

Sources: Data in table updated from table created by Steven Box (1987), Recession, Crime and Punishment, table 3.1

[41] Farrington, D., Gallagher, B, Morley, L, Ledger, R, and West D, (1986), "Unemployment, School-leaving and Crime," *British Journal of Criminology*, 26: 335-56.

[42] H J Kunz, *Economics of the Individual and Organized Crime*, Carl Heymanns Verland, Germany, 1976.

[43] Mark Fishman, "Crime Waves as Ideology," *Social Problems*, Vol 25, no.5, June 1978.

[41] Ibid.

[42] Christine Hauser and Al Bakerm, "Ailing U.S. economy brings fears of a crime wave," *International Herald Tribune Newspaper*, October 10, 2008: **http://www.iht.com/articles/2008/10/10/america/letter.php**

[43] Simon Field, "the Effect of Temperature on Crime," *British Journal of Criminology*, Vol. 32, Summer 1992.

[44] TABLE 1

THE THREE DS OF RECESSION: A BRIEF HISTORY

- Duration
- Depth
- Diffusion

Months	% Change in Real GNP	Maximum	% of Industries w/ Declining Employment	Maximum
Three Depressions				
Jan. 1920- July 1921	18	n.a.	11.9	97
Aug. 1929- Mar. 1933	43	-32.6	24.9	100
May 1937- June 1938	13	-18.2	20.0	97
Six Sharp Recessions				
May 1923- July 1924	14	-4.1	5.5	94
Nov. 1948- Oct. 194	11	-1.5	7.9	90
July 1953- May 1954	10	-3.2	6.1	87
Aug. 1957- Apr. 1958	8	-3.3	7.5	88

Months	% Change in Real GNP	Maximum	% of Industries w/ Declining Employment	Maximum
Nov. 1973-Mar. 1975	16	-4.9	9.0	88
July 1981-Nov. 1982	16	-2.6	10.8	72
Five Mild Recessions				
Oct. 1926-Nov. 1927	13	-2.0	4.4	71
Apr. 1960-Feb. 1961	10	-1.2	7.1	80
Dec. 1969-Nov. 1970	11	-1.0	6.1	80
Jan. 1980-July 1980	6	-2.5	7.8	63
July 1990-March 1991	8	-1.2	6.9	73
Averages				
1920-1938 (5)	20	-14.2	13.3	92
1948-1991 (9)	11	-2.4	7.7	80

Source: Based on table A-2 in G. H. Moore, Business Cycles, Inflation and Forecasting, 2nd ed., 1983. Note that the brief and mild recession of 1945 is omitted here.

[46] Geoffrey Moore, Recessions (2009); **http://www.econlib.org/library/Enc1/Recessions.html**

[47] The NBER does not define a recession in terms of two consecutive quarters of decline in real GDP. Rather, a recession is a significant decline in economic activity spread across the economy, lasting more than a few months, normally visible in real GDP, real income, employment, industrial production, and wholesale-retail sales. For more information, see the latest announcement from the NBER's Business Cycle Dating Committee, dated 12/01/08. **http://www. nber.org/cycles.html**; Contractions (recessions) start at the peak of a business cycle and end at the trough.

[49] Source: US Bureau of Labor Statistics; "Unemployment data by race, gender, and age for period 1954-2009;" **http://data.bls.gov/PDQ/servlet/Survey OutputServlet**

Series Id:	LNS14000003
Seasonal Adjusted Series title:	(Seas) Unemployment Rate - White
Labor force status:	Unemployment rate
Type of data:	Percent
Age:	16 years and over
Race:	White

Year	Jan	Feb	Mar	Apr	May	Jun	Jul	Aug	Sep	Oct	Nov	Dec	Annual
1954	4.5	4.9	5.0	5.5	5.3	5.0	5.3	5.6	5.9	5.1	4.7	4.1	
1955	4.5	4.1	4.0	4.3	3.8	3.7	3.6	3.6	3.6	3.7	3.6	3.7	
1956	3.5	3.6	3.7	3.6	3.8	3.7	3.8	3.4	3.5	3.4	3.8	3.8	
1957	3.8	3.6	3.4	3.5	3.6	3.7	3.7	3.7	3.9	4.0	4.6	4.7	
1958	5.2	5.7	5.9	6.7	6.7	6.6	6.8	6.7	6.4	6.0	5.5	5.5	
1959	5.3	5.2	4.9	4.7	4.5	4.4	4.5	4.6	4.9	5.0	5.3	4.7	
1960	4.6	4.3	4.8	4.6	4.6	4.8	4.9	5.1	5.1	5.5	5.5	5.9	
1961	5.9	6.2	6.2	6.2	6.3	6.2	6.3	5.9	5.9	5.7	5.4	5.3	
1962	5.1	4.8	4.8	4.7	4.8	4.8	4.8	5.0	5.0	4.8	5.0	4.8	
1963	5.0	5.3	5.0	5.1	5.2	4.9	5.1	4.8	4.8	4.8	5.0	5.0	
1964	5.0	4.9	4.9	4.8	4.5	4.7	4.3	4.4	4.5	4.6	4.3	4.5	
1965	4.3	4.5	4.3	4.4	4.2	4.2	3.9	4.0	3.8	3.8	3.7	3.6	
1966	3.5	3.4	3.4	3.3	3.5	3.4	3.3	3.3	3.2	3.3	3.2	3.3	
1967	3.4	3.3	3.3	3.4	3.3	3.5	3.3	3.4	3.3	3.5	3.5	3.4	
1968	3.3	3.4	3.2	3.1	3.1	3.4	3.2	3.2	3.1	3.0	3.0	3.0	
1969	3.0	3.0	3.0	3.0	3.0	3.1	3.2	3.1	3.4	3.4	3.2	3.3	
1970	3.6	3.8	4.0	4.1	4.4	4.5	4.6	4.7	5.0	5.2	5.4	5.6	
1971	5.5	5.3	5.5	5.4	5.4	5.5	5.5	5.6	5.4	5.4	5.6	5.4	
1972	5.2	5.1	5.2	5.3	5.1	5.1	5.1	5.1	5.0	5.1	4.7	4.6	
1973	4.5	4.5	4.4	4.5	4.3	4.3	4.2	4.3	4.3	4.1	4.3	4.4	
1974	4.6	4.6	4.5	4.5	4.6	4.8	4.9	5.0	5.4	5.4	6.0	6.4	
1975	7.4	7.4	7.8	8.0	8.4	8.1	8.0	7.7	7.7	7.7	7.6	7.4	
1976	7.2	6.9	6.9	6.9	6.7	6.9	7.1	7.1	7.0	7.0	7.1	7.0	

Year	Jan	Feb	Mar	Apr	May	Jun	Jul	Aug	Sep	Oct	Nov	Dec	Annual
1977	6.8	6.9	6.7	6.4	6.3	6.4	6.0	6.0	6.0	5.9	5.8	5.5	
1978	5.5	5.5	5.4	5.3	5.2	5.0	5.3	5.1	5.2	5.0	5.0	5.2	
1979	5.1	5.1	5.1	5.0	4.8	4.9	4.9	5.3	5.2	5.2	5.2	5.2	
1980	5.5	5.5	5.6	6.1	6.6	6.7	6.9	9.9	6.6	6.6	6.5	6.3	
1981	6.7	6.6	6.5	6.4	6.6	6.5	6.3	6.3	6.6	6.9	7.3	7.5	
1982	7.6	7.8	8.0	8.3	8.2	8.5	8.7	8.7	9.0	9.2	9.6	9.7	
1983	9.1	9.3	9.1	8.9	8.8	8.7	8.2	8.2	8.0	7.7	7.4	7.1	
1984	6.9	6.8	6.7	6.7	6.4	6.2	6.3	6.4	6.4	6.3	6.2	6.3	
1985	6.3	6.2	6.2	6.3	6.2	6.5	6.4	6.2	6.1	6.1	5.9	6.0	
1986	5.7	6.3	6.2	6.1	6.2	6.2	6.1	5.9	6.0	6.0	6.0	5.8	
1987	5.7	5.7	5.7	5.4	5.4	5.4	5.2	5.1	5.1	5.2	5.0	4.9	
1988	5.0	4.9	4.8	4.6	4.7	4.6	4.7	4.8	4.8	4.7	4.6	4.6	
1989	4.6	4.3	4.2	4.5	4.4	4.5	4.5	4.5	4.5	4.5	4.6	4.6	
1990	4.6	4.6	4.5	4.7	4.6	4.5	4.7	4.9	5.0	5.1	5.3	5.4	
1991	5.6	5.8	6.0	5.9	6.1	6.2	6.2	6.2	6.2	6.2	6.3	6.5	
1992	6.4	6.5	6.5	6.5	6.6	6.9	6.7	6.7	6.7	6.5	6.5	6.5	
1993	6.3	6.2	6.1	6.1	6.2	6.2	6.1	6.0	5.9	6.2	5.7	5.8	
1994	5.7	5.7	5.7	5.6	5.2	5.3	5.3	5.2	5.1	5.0	4.8	4.8	
1995	4.8	4.7	4.7	5.0	5.0	4.9	4.9	4.9	4.9	4.9	5.0	4.9	
1996	4.9	4.8	4.8	4.8	4.9	4.6	4.7	4.4	4.5	4.5	4.6	4.6	
1997	4.5	4.5	4.4	4.3	4.1	4.2	4.2	4.2	4.2	4.1	3.9	3.9	
1998	4.0	3.9	4.0	3.7	3.8	3.9	3.8	3.9	3.9	3.9	3.8	3.8	
1999	3.8	3.8	3.6	3.8	3.7	3.8	3.7	3.7	3.6	3.5	3.5	3.5	
2000	3.4	3.6	3.5	3.4	3.5	3.4	3.5	3.6	3.5	3.4	3.5	3.5	
2001	3.6	3.7	3.7	3.9	3.8	4.0	4.0	4.3	4.3	4.7	4.9	5.1	
2002	5.1	5.0	5.0	5.2	5.1	5.1	5.2	5.1	5.1	5.1	5.1	5.1	
2003	5.2	5.1	5.1	5.3	5.4	5.5	5.4	5.4	5.3	5.1	5.2	5.0	
2004	5.0	4.9	5.1	5.0	4.9	5.0	4.7	4.7	4.6	4.6	4.6	4.5	
2005	4.5	4.6	4.5	4.4	4.4	4.3	4.3	4.2	4.4	4.4	4.3	4.2	
2006	4.1	4.1	4.0	4.1	4.1	4.1	4.1	4.1	3.9	3.9	3.9	3.9	
2007	4.1	4.0	3.8	4.0	3.9	4.1	4.2	4.2	4.2	4.2	4.2	4.4	
2008	4.4	4.4	4.5	4.4	4.9	5.0	5.2	5.5	5.5	6.0	6.2	6.6	
2009	6.9												

Source: US Bureau of Labor Statistics; http://data.bls.gov/PDQ/servlet/SurveyOutputServlet; Unemployment data by race, gender, and age for period 1954-2009

[50] R.V. Clark and M. Felson, (1993), "Introduction: Criminology, Routine Activity, and Rational Choice, in *Routine Activity and Rational Choice.*

[51] Roger Lane, Policing the City: Boston 1822-1885, published by Cambridge University Press, 1967.

[52] Andrew Sinclair, Prohibition: The Era of Excess (1962).

[53] John Kenneth Galbraith, The Great Crash, 1929, (1954).

[54] Lawrence W. Reed, "A History Lesson for Obama: Great Myths of the Great Depression," The Peregrin Falcon Blog, February 10, 2009. **http://theperegrin.com/2009/02/10/a-history-lesson-for-obama-great-myths-of-the-great-depression/**

[55] "Chicago Votes In Terror," Columbus Evening Dispatch, April 10, 1928, page 1; as reprinted in Helmer, William, with Rick Mattix, Public Enemies: America's criminal past, 1919-1940; section heading, Chicago's Pineapple Primary, p. 106.

[56] Blog: Was Rod Blagojevich, Pay-to-Play and Corruption the Exception or Rule of Chicago and Illinois Politics?, February 2, 2009, **http://www.suntimes.com/news/blogentries/index.html?bbPostId=BAa1CjsNhtIKB7cYqDYD6kNoB8ZTj0mx9qIWB82RDaGPFHQB&bbParentWidgetId=B8k88rWwXopuz5STgLeVwBLu**

[57] A good treatment of the St. Valentine's Day Massacre is contained in Helmer, William, with Rick Mattix, Public Enemies: America's Criminal Past, 1919-1940; p. 118-123.

[58] See Dixon Wector, The Age of Great Depression 1929-1941, Macmillan Company, 1948.

[59] New York Times, July 1, 1933, 1:7, a noted criminologist said that individuals and techniques that made millions selling illicit booze would be transferred to drugs, kidnapping, and bank robberies, as reported in Harry Barnes, "The real source of our crime problem," in <u>American City</u>, 48:62, S'33; as reported in John Conely (1971).

[60] FDR: Public Papers, vol III, p 494.

[61] Mark Twain, Autobiography (1924).

[62] (http://www.npr.org/templates/story/story.php?storyId=97234406#comme ntBlock)

[63] Wector (1948), IBID.

[64] Wector (1948), IBID.

[65] For more extensive coverage on the WPA see Dave Demerjian, Note to Next President: Modern-Day WPA Will Save the Economy; Wired Magazine Website, Wired.com, October 19, 2008.

[66] Johnson, Ryan S., Kantor, Shawn Everett and Fishback, Price V.,Striking at the Roots of Crime: The Impact of Social Welfare Spending on Crime During the Great Depression(January 2007). NBER Working Paper No. W12825. Available at SSRN: http://ssrn.com/abstract=956864

[67] Franklin D. Roosevelt, "Address at the National Parole Conference," Washing-ton, DC, April 17, 1939. Accessible at The American Presidency Project, http:// www.presidency.ucsb.edu., as cited in Kanton, Fishback, and Price (2007).

[68] Per capita relief spending represents a population-weighted average for 114 cities. Relief per capita is the total of all direct relief, work relief and private relief funds. Direct relief includes direct relief under the FERA, by state and local gov-ernments, and categorical assistance for dependent children, old-age assistance, and aid to the blind. Prior to 1935, the categorical assistance categories refer to funds provided by state and local governments through mothers' pensions, old-age pensions, and state aid to the blind. Work relief includes payments to workers on state and local government, FERA, CWA, and WPA projects. Private relief is the value of relief funds from private and public sources administered by private agencies. Average annual relief benefits were calculated as the ratio of total relief expenditures per number of households on relief. The data source reported the information monthly and we summed across months for the annual estimate. The 1940 data were only reported through June, so we doubled the amount reported to derive the annual estimate. We do not have information on the federal share of relief prior to 1932, but it was probably similar to 1932's value. The federal share of relief information includes the cost of administering the programs. The 1932 federal figure includes $3.7 million in federal workers' compensation payments. The state and local expenditures include workers' com-pensation, general relief, old-age assistance, aid to dependent children, aid to the blind, and state shares of unemployment compensation, WPA, CWA, and the National Youth Administration.

Sources: Relief spending data are reported in Baird (1942) and Winslow (1937). Population data are from Haines and ICPSR (2005). Linear interpolation was used for years between 1930 and 1940 censuses. For federal share of relief spending, see U.S. National Resources Planning Board (1942, 292, 598-603). Average relief expenditures per household were calculated from data on households receiving relief and total expenditures on relief in U.S. National Resources Planning Board (1942, 557-61). Average annual manufacturing earnings are from U.S. Bureau of the Census Bureau (1975, 166). Unemployment rates for the entire United States are calculated from Series Ba470, Ba474, and Ba477 on pp. 2-82 and 2-83 in Carter, et. al., 2006. Federal emergency relief workers were included as unemployed in this calculation. Source: Kanton, Fishback, and Price (2007).

[69] Conely (1971), p21.

[70] Photo Source Library of Congress, as appearing in **http://www.mlive.com/ kalamabrew/index.ssf/2008/12/prohibition_overturned.html**

[71] John A. Conley, The New Deal's Response to Crime: The Politics of Law and Order, Masters Thesis, Michigan State University, 1971, p.3.

[72] Herbert A. Bloch, Economic Depression as a Factor in Rural Crime, Journal of Crime, Law, Criminology and Political Science, vol 40, 1949, pp. 458-470.

[73] N.Y. Times, June 23, 1932, and May 16, 1934. Sec also E. D. Sullivan, K Snatch Racket (N. Y*, 1932). The decade's most famous abduction, that of Charles Augustus Lindbergh, jr., first-born of the aviator, on March 1, 1932, was, however, perpetrated by an amateur. The frantic search, appeals to the underworld, discovery of the child's body, arrest of the murderer in 1934 through tracing of the gold certificates that the extorted, his trial and electrocution in 1936, evoked mass emotions of an intensity scarcely seen before morbidness, vulgar curiosity, national anxiety, neighborly grief and sympathy. S. B. Whippic, Tlw Trial of JBrano Richard Hauptmann (N. Y., 1937); see also, Wector (1948).

[74] See Wiki, CrimeLibrary.com **http://www.crimelibrary.com/notorious_ murders/famous/lindbergh/trial_6.html**

[75] James B. Kelleher, "Buffett's "time bomb" goes off on Wall Street", Reuters. com, **http://www.reuters.com/article/newsOne/idUSN1837154020080918**

[76] Warren Buffet, 2002 Annual Letter to Shareholders, Berkshire Hathaway p15, **http://www.berkshirehathaway.com/letters/2002pdf.pdf**

[77] Quote by Gerald Celente of Trends Research Institute The Gold Defaut, October 30, 2008. **http://news.goldseek.com/GoldenJackass/1225389600.php**

[78] Quote attributed to the Hunt brothers in their economic quest to create wealth.

[79] Bess, Michael, October 2008, "Assessing the Impact of Home Foreclosures in Charlotte Neighborhoods, Charlotte-Mechlenburg Police Department, Charlotte, North Carolina.; in Geography & Public Safety, Volume 1, Issue 3, October 2008.

[80] Tuthill, Louis, *Breaking New Windows – Examing the Subprime Mortgage Crises Using the Broken Windows Theory*, National Institute of Justice, in Geography & Public Safety, Volume 1, Issue 3, October 2008.

[81] **http://d2crimewave.blogspot.com/2009/02/un-drug-czar-says-financial-crises.html**

[82] Hans von Hentig, Crime: Causes and Conditions, New York, 1947, pp. 14-28, and pp. 223-225., as cited in Herbert A. Bloch, Economic Depression as a Factor in Rural Crime, Journal of Crime, Law, Criminology and Political Science, vol 40, 1949, pp. 458-470.

[83] Loon Radzinowicz, "Economic Pressures," in Leon Radzinowicz and Marvin E. Wolfgang (eds), Crime and Justice: The Criminal in Society, 2nd ed., Vol 1, (New York: Basic Books Inc, 1977), pp 555-556.; as reported in Kevin N. Wright, Crime and Criminal Justice in a Declining Economy, (Cambridge, MA: Oelgeschlager, Gunn & Hain, Publishers, 1981).

[84] Boardman, J., Grove, B., Perkins, R. & Shepherd, G. (2003) Work and employment for people with psychiatric disabilities. British Journal of Psychiatry. 182: 467-468; as reported in, Peter Kinderman, More work less therapy, blog, **http://www.psychminded.co.uk/news/news2004/oct04/kindermancolumn.htm**.

[85] UN 1974 Economic Crises and Crime Workshop participants included: P Allewijin, G. Alprin, F. Archibugi, P.L. Blac, A. Blumstein, H. Brenner, B.S. Brown, G. Cassidy, M. Chean, C. Dias, H. Edelhertz, J. Eyler, F. Ferrarotti, J.F. Glastra Van Loon, W. Grinker, R. Hueting, E. Jensen, G. Kaiser, F.H. McClintock, T. Morris, S. Rottenberg, and M Shikita.

[86] "Economic Crises and Crime: Interim Report and Materials, UNSDRI, United Nations Social Defense Research Institute, Rome, Italy, Publication no. 9, September 1974.

[87] IBID, p.16-17

[88] Some of the best work in street-level narcotics market awareness conducted in the 1990s was performed under the supervision of the author by a few of Ronald V. Clarke's doctoral candidates trained in Situational Crime Prevention that completed their criminal justice research for the Ph.D. degree while working for the author at Sparta Consulting Corporation, Bethesda, MD; most notably, Marina Myhre, a Ph.D. candidate from Rutgers University conducted street interviews in Washington, D.C. with illegal drug dealers and garnered some salient and valuable insights from their practices that informed our CPTED curriculum and technical approach to crime in public housing; and Nancy LaVigne, who went on to become the Director of NIJ, Crime Mapping Research Center. Other significant researchers who participated in crime studies at Sparta included Dr. John G. Hayes, VP Consulting; Ellen M. Walsh, VP Operations; and Matthew Perkins, MA, Senior Research Associate, and Lt. Col. Andrew Walker, MBA who kept us in line, on task, and on time.

[89] Sorensen, Severin (1999), Illegal Drug Selling and Place: Spatial Geography of Street-Level Drug, Or the 22 Immutable Laws of Illegal Drug Marketing, International Workshop on Drug Markets 1999

[90] John Jay College of Criminal Justice, April 8-9, 1999; presentation available to law enforcement personnel and bonafide criminal justice professionals on request to **slsorensen@gmail.com.**

[91] Ronald V. Clarke, Hot Products: Understanding, anticipating, and reducing demand for stolen goods, Police Research Series, Paper 112, The Home Office, UK., 1999.

[92] John Eck, (1997) "Preventing Crime at Places," Chapter 7, PREVENTING CRIME: WHAT WORKS, WHAT DOESN'T, WHAT'S PROMISING, A REPORT TO THE UNITED STATES CONGRESS, Prepared for the National Institute of Justice, by Lawrence W. Sherman, Denise Gottfredson, Doris MacKenzie, John Eck, Peter Reuter, and Shawn Bushway, in collaboration with members of the Graduate Program, Department of Criminology and Criminal Justice University of Maryland.; **http://www.ncjrs.gov/works/chapter7.htm**

[92] John Eck, "Preventing crime at places, " Chapter 7, in Evidence-Based Crime Prevention, Eds. Lawrence W. Sherman, David P. Farrington, Bandon C. Welsh, and Doris Layton MacKenzie, (London and New York: Routledge, 2002).

[93] John Eck, (1997) IBID.

[94] Sixteen Techniques of Situational Crime Prevention in Public Housing (Adapted from Severin L. Sorensen and Ronald V. Clarke, "Situational Crime Prevention and High Density, Low Income Housing," 5th International Seminar on Environmental Criminology and Crime Analysis (University of Tokyo: Tokyo, July 1996).

[95] Brandon C. Welsh and David P. Farrington (2002), "What works, what dosent, whats promising, and future directions," in Chapter 10, Evidence-Based Crime Prevention, Eds. Lawrence W. Sherman, David P. Farrington, Bandon C. Welsh, and Doris Layton MacKenzie, (London and New York: Routledge, 2002).

[96] http://www.einstein-quotes.com/content/view/23/37/

[97] http://www.charleslindbergh.com/history/paris.asp

[98] On the Orbitz travel site on 2/16/09, offered are airline tickets on Air France, which operates 4 regularly scheduled daily non-stop flights from New York (JFK) to Paris, France (CDG), departing between 4:55pm and 11:00pm, and one additional non-stop flight regularly scheduled to depart at 9:00pm and arrive at 10:15am, everyday except Monday. The average travel time from New York, NY to Paris, France is 7 hours and 16 minutes; http://www.orbitz.com/flight-info/AF/AF-JFK-CDG.html

[99] http://www.fas.org/irp/offdocs/iccs/iccsi.html

[100] Gary Washington, "US Intelligence Chief Calls Economic Crisis a Security Threat," Voice of America, 2/12/2009; http://www.voanews.com/english/2009-02-12-voa58.cfm

[101] Crisis brings threat of crime wave to China, AFP Shenzen, http://www.google.com/hostednews/afp/article/ALeqM5iB6ItKi3H7Lwxlf7-1mOL-53A96g

[102] Radio talk show host - http://www.prisonplanet.com/growing-list-of-officials-and-experts-warn-of-depression-induced-violence.html

[103] WTO chief warns of looming political unrest, 2/07/09, Berlin, Germany, http://news.yahoo.com/s/afp/20090207/bs_afp/financeeconomygermany-tradewto_20090207141558

[104] Gary Duncan, Economics Editor, TimesOnline, "Head of IMF Fears Unreset with action on Economy, 12/16/08. http://business.timesonline.co.uk/tol/business/economics/article5349277.ece

[105] Sci-Tech Encyclopedia: Retaining Wall, from http://www.answers.com/topic/retaining-wall. A generic structure that is employed to restrain a vertical-faced or near-vertical-faced mass of earth. The earth behind the wall may be either the natural embankment or the backfill material placed adjacent to the retaining wall. Retaining walls must resist the lateral pressure of the earth, which tends to cause the structure to slide or overturn. Retaining walls are often used in the marine environment, where they separate the retained soil from the water. Gravity walls (known as seawalls) can be constructed where strong wave and current forces are exerted on the wall. Bulkheads are more commonly found in sheltered areas such as harbors and navigation channels. *See also* Harbors.

[106] Tsunamis and tidal waves, and their parallel to crime waves. Just as sea walls are not singularly responsible for holding back the tide, but must be used as part of a greater defense in depth strategy, combating crime tidal wives is no different. There is no silver bullet or singular strategy that will hold back the crime wave. Illustrated in a news article below is this story, dealing specifically with sea walls and stones.

[107] James Q. Wilson and George L. Kelling, "Broken Windows," *The Atlantic Monthly*, March 1982. Other

WILL CRIME RATES RISE WITH THE FAILING ECONOMY?

http://www.perpetuityresearch.com/news.html#economy

The Home Security Secretary, Jacqui Smith, is warning that violent crime could grow by nearly a fifth based on increases seen during the last recession. But the academic evidence suggests that won't be the only crime type that's set to rise; fraud, forgery, burglary, robbery, theft, and arson have all been linked to recession and unemployment.[1]

The relationship between the economy, unemployment and crime is a well researched but complicated topic. Some argue that it's easy to blame rising crime rates on economic adversity when in fact economic factors provide only part of the explanation.[2] This is of course true but, although the underlying causes may be complex, on the whole, there is clear evidence to suggest that the downturn will mean an increase in crime alongside rising unemployment.

So what does this mean for you? It's clear that at a time when budgets are being reduced, cutting back on crime reduction and security is not an easy option since that could result in rising costs of crime. Instead, it's a good time to review your existing spending and processes to identify any opportunities to improve efficiency and work smarter to cut costs, achieving greater value for money.

Perpetuity has been working with local authorities and the private sector to maximize the value for money achieved through spending on crime reduction and security. If you need assistance in exploring how you can make the most out of your current investments – contact **prci@perpetuitygroup.com**

---

[1] Cook, P. and Zarkin, G. (1985) Crime and the Business Cycle in Journal of Legal Studies, vol XIV January 1985; Neustrom, M. and Norton, W. (1995) Economic Dislocation and Property Crime in Journal of Criminal Justice, Vol 23, No1, pp29 - 39

[2] Scorcu, A. and Cellini, R. (1998) Economic Activity and Crime in the Long Run: An Empirical Investigation on Aggregate Data from Italy, 1951 – 1994 in International Review of Law and Economics 18:279-292

---

[108] FBI Internet Crime Complaint Center, Internet Fraud Protection Tips, 2009. **http://www.ic3.gov/preventiontips.aspx**

Index

About the Author

Severin L. Sorensen, CPP, M. Phil., is President and CEO of Sikyur LLC (**www.sikyur.com**), a security management consulting company that advises Chief Security Officers (CSO), C-level executives, and boards of directors. Mr. Sorensen leads the security management consulting practice. Practice areas include security assessments and master planning, security systems assessment and design/build projects, security industry expert witness and advisory services related to mergers and acquisitions, and technical assistance and training in Crime Prevention Through Environmental Design (CPTED) and Situational Crime Prevention.

Sorensen is active within the security industry and is the immediate Past Chairman of the Physical Security Council, and of the ASIS Physical Security Council, representing ASIS International and around 35,000 security professionals worldwide (**www.asisonline.org**). He is the current Academic Program Advisor for ASIS Asset Protection Course I, for ASIS International. He is also one of five members of the ASIS Political Action Committee; Chairman of the Security Guard Management Workshop (2009); and Past Chairman of ASIS Video Surveillance Workshop (2005 and 2008).

Sorensen is an entrepreneurial business executive with 20 years senior-level executive management experience in the physical security sector. He routinely advises thought leaders in the security industry on emerging trends in security, advanced video surveillance, outdoor perimeter protection technologies, and Crime Prevention Through Environmental Design and Situational Crime Prevention. Besides authoring *Economic Misery and Crime Waves* (2009), Sorensen is the lead author of "CPTED and Situational Crime Prevention," which figures as Chapter 6 in 21st *Century Security and CPTED* (2008), edited by Randy Atlas, In addition to these he has several Internet blogs and published works.

Prior to founding Sikyur.com, Sorensen was VP, Business and Applications Development, for Westec Interactive Security Inc. (**www.westecnow.com**), the largest remote video monitoring company in the US, a position he obtained upon the sale of his former consulting and monitoring firm to Westec in July 2005. From 1994 to July 2005, Sorensen was the founder, President and CEO of Sparta Consulting Corporation that took up security consulting, security systems integration, and remote video monitoring solutions. While at Sparta, Sorensen held additional responsibilities that included being Program Manager of HUD's Crime Prevention Through Environmental Design (CPTED) initiative from 1994 to 2002. Sorensen has designed wide-area surveillance systems and remote video monitoring applications for New York City Police Department, Los Angeles, Atlanta, and many other police offices, housing management firms, and municipalities.

Prior to Sparta, Mr. Sorensen served in the first Bush White House (1992-93) as a Special Assistant to the President and Regional Liaison, Bureau of State and Local Affairs, Office of National Drug Control Policy (ONDCP). Throughout his career, Sorensen has provided consultation to the US Government, state and local governments, commercial industry, Organization of American States, International Monetary Fund, the World Bank, and other international bodies, on security matters. Sorensen is board certified in security as a Certified Protection Professional (CPP), the accreditation of ASIS International (1997). Mr. Sorensen has acquired the M. Phil. degree in Economics ("International Political Economy") from King's College, Cambridge University, England (1988), and B.S. degrees with honors in Economics and Political Science from the University of Utah (1986).

Severin L. Sorensen, CPP, M. Phil.
President and CEO
Sikyur LLC
P.O. Box 3310, Gaithersburg, MD 20885
(202) 258-7300 tel; (240) 597-8877 fax
sev@sikyur.com